C. Emily Dibb

IVORY, APES AND PEACOCKS

BY THE SAME AUTHOR

The Bite
Spotted Soldiers

Ivory, Apes and Peacocks

by
C. EMILY DIBB

Illustrated by Hannes Meintjes

Bulawayo
BOOKS OF ZIMBABWE
1981

BOOKS OF ZIMBABWE PUBLISHING CO. (PVT.) LTD.
P.O. Box 1994, Bulawayo.

Publishers of new Zimbabwean literary
works and Rhodesiana reprints.

First Published 1981
©C. Emily Dibb
©Illustrations: Hannes Meintjes

Hardback edition: ISBN 0 86920 240 5
Softback edition: ISBN 0 86920 241 3

Photoset in Times by
BOOKSET (PVT.) LTD., BULAWAYO
Printed by
BOOKPRINT (PVT.) LTD., BULAWAYO
Bound by
MARDON PRINTERS (PVT.) LTD., BULAWAYO

To my Parents.

Once in three years came the navy of Tharshish,
bringing gold, and silver, ivory, and apes,
and peacocks.

I KINGS, 22

Quinquireme of Nineveh from distant Ophir
Rowing home to haven in sunny Palestine,
With a cargo of ivory,
And apes and peacocks,
Sandalwood, cedarwood, and sweet white wine.

Cargoes — John Masefield

Acknowledgements

I owe a great debt of gratitude to all who assisted me in the preparation of this book. My thanks go to those who advised me on numerous technical matters, and particularly to the many kind people who gave me accounts of their own experiences. Their generosity and helpfulness have made it possible to preserve these stories, which might otherwise have been lost for ever.

Publishers' Note

The country known in the past as Southern Rhodesia or Rhodesia is now Zimbabwe. In this book the author has used the name which applied at the time of the events described.

Contents

CHAPTER   PAGE

1   THE ENCHANTED LAND   1

2   SNAKES IN THE GRASS   7

3   GREAT SNAKES   21

4   A FEAST OF FLOWERS   35

5   A TREEFUL OF OWLS   44

6   WHEELS   54

7   LION COUNTRY!   61

8   IN THE PRESENCE OF THE KING   75

9   SUICIDE MONTH   93

10   WINESKIN CLOUDS   113

11   BUSH BABIES   132

12   MAKULU & COMPANY   159

13   PIGS IN PARADISE   184

14   PYTHONS AND PEACOCKS   198

15   GENTLY SMILING JAWS   224

16   CROCODILE TEARS   258

1

The Enchanted Land

IT IS ALWAYS difficult to know where to begin a story. Should I grope back into the dim mists of the past, or should I commence with the events of today and work backwards, like a detective in a murder mystery? Whichever way one approaches the problem, the past intrudes on the present — the bones beneath the flesh, influencing its form and nature. I believe that after all I shall have to begin with Grandpa, because he started it all.

My grandfather was minister of the Presbyterian Church in Bulawayo. The small manse attached to the church was very cramped for a family of six children, and so in 1912 my grandparents purchased some forty acres of virgin bush in the district called Matsheumhlope, and here on the top of a granite kopje they built a great rambling stone house. It was named Kaya Pezulu, house on a hill. There were three boys and three girls in the family. My mother was Elizabeth, the eldest. She was followed by my aunt Emily, and the twins Cornelius and Jim. Then came Julian, and finally Jane. When the children grew up, some of them married and built their homes nearby. In those days architects and municipal regulations were practically unheard of, and most of the family dwellings included one or two bizarre features. The building materials were stone and thatch, as they were locally available. Indeed, granite and grass were the fundamental fabrics of our lives, and even today I feel uneasy in a house built of such poor stuff as brick.

My two brothers and I grew up in a loosely connected family compound, within hailing distance of our cousins and grandparents. We were closest to Julian's three children, both in the proximity of our houses, and in identities of interest and age. Of the six of us, John my brother was the eldest, and the rest of us in descending order of age were Ewen, Charles — my second brother — Caroline, myself and Tom. Childhood memories are closely tied to the people we see every day, and so it is that almost all of my early recollections are plaited into events that took place in the company of my brothers and my cousins. They constituted my world. I was unaware of having an individual identity, for together we formed a corporate body with six heads, twelve legs, sixty fingers and an incalculable capacity for mischief.

The district of Matabeleland in which we lived was a paradise for children, being kopje country, a region of broken hills and granite outcrops, laced by seasonal streams. Between the kopjes grew fields of yellow assegai grass that gleamed and rippled under the caressing hand of the wind like the fur of a beast. The grass stood six or seven feet tall so that a footpath through it was enclosed in a golden canyon with the wind hissing eerily between the dry stalks. In one of these fields the twin uncles Jim and Niels had ploughed up a fantastic assortment of old Iron Age weapons and implements that now decorated the long front verandah of Grandmother's house. There were a number of spear heads, rather rusted, and several curiously contrived hoe blades — the first heart-shaped, another in a crescent and a third like an executioner's axe. Mother always wore round her wrist a gold anklet that had been discovered in the same way, and was thought to have belonged to one of the wives of the former king, Lobengula.

Those were magical days, and little wonder for we lived in a land of magic. The very trees were enchanted, sacred even — especially the old rock-fig. No man could touch it with an axe for fear of offending the spirits. In the dazzle and heat of midday the old fig furnished an oasis of welcome shade. Its gaunt white branches spread out protectively over the crown of the kopje, while its roots like petrified pythons, writhed and plunged deep into the earth, forcing apart great rocks in their desperate search for water. A gang of road workers had dug into one of the roots a hundred yards away, to expose a living rope as thick as a man's arm, and flowing with the fig's sticky white milk.

There were magic rocks too, magic birds, magic streams and magic mountains whose slopes had to be burned by fire before the rains would come. Although in public we children used to scoff at these African superstitions, in my heart I used to believe in them fervently. One could *feel* the magic in the air, a tangible presence like the dust and the sunshine. One could smell it in the kopjes, particularly in the bone-dry rock shelters where the little yellow bushmen had left their paintings. In one of these, whose entrance was choked by the prickly stems of a donkeyberry bush, we had found a scattering of perfect, little, quartz arrowheads, some ostrich eggshell beads and a few broken shards of pottery. Ewen even turned up a human femur, green and gruesome. Little wonder that in those days Caroline and I were preoccupied with spells and the casting of assorted enchantments on our friends and foes. How else could we hope to compete with the sorcery and witchcraft that coiled and wreathed about us like invisible vapour?

Of all the buildings in the family complex, our house was structurally the most unusual. It was not really a 'house' at all in the strictest sense of the word, being a loosely related cluster of thatched rondavels that nestled on top of a kopje and spilled down its side, with the kitchen, dining-room and workshop on the level land below. The bathroom and P.K. (as the W.C. is called in this part of Africa) were also separate buildings, and each part of the house communicated with the others by an intricate system of gravel paths and steep flights of stone steps. It bore a resemblance to the Acropolis at Great Zimbabwe, with its unexpected terraces, cliffs and secret stairways. It must have been desperately inconvenient for Mother in many ways, especially if any member of the family were ill. Astonished guests who visited us for the first time invariably exclaimed: "But what do you do when it rains?"
"We get wet," was the simple reply.
But then, getting wet in that climate was no more than a trifling

inconvenience. One soon dried off. The dust was the greater nuisance, for every room had an outside door, and the dust was swept out daily in great piles at the end of the broom.

I slept alone in my rondavel in a state of splendid isolation, and relished the solitude, so much so that in later years I found it extremely difficult to adapt to sleeping in a conventional house — people talking, the distant mutter of a wireless, clinks and clatters from the kitchen and all the ordinary homely sounds that are a part of a normal household, were foreign and strange. When I went to bed in my rondavel, my door and windows stood open to the night and the only sounds were the rustle and giggle of geckos in the thatch, the creaking of the old fig's branches and the soft whimper of a bat's wings as it flitted round my room hunting for moths and mosquitoes.

Alone in the dark, I had my fair share of childhood terrors, but burglars and bogymen, devils and goblins were not among them. Only the few yards of veld round the house were kept clear of the tall grass or cultivated at all. Beyond the backyard and the mealie patch was the bush that teemed with spiders, scorpions, centipedes and a host of less poisonous insects of every conceivable shape and size. And of course while I knew there were no lions close by, I none the less used to lie in my bed and think about them, one perhaps that had been driven off from its pride and compelled by necessity to become a man-eater . . . these things were known to happen, and who was there to hear me, supposing I *did* call out for help? There were snakes, too. They were no myth; snakes were around all the year through and no one made any bones about them — they were killers.

In the face of these bed-time fears, it was necessary to prepare a charm to keep them at bay. If the bush had its magic, why then so did I, and it was by the uttering of a particularly powerful incantation that I was able to keep the snakes out of my rondavel at night. The moment I was tucked into my bed and the light was switched out, I imagined them beginning their stealthy advance, slithering out from under rocks, pouring themselves down from the trees and slipping swiftly and silently towards my rondavel. My magic spell was infallible, however. As soon as the room was plunged into darkness, I closed my eyes and

began: "Our Father which art in Heaven . . ."
The snakes quickened their pace so as to reach me before the
final damning phrase would bar them from my room·for the
night. ". . . and lead us not into temptation," I hurried on, for
they were right at the door now, some of them preparing to
wriggle up the legs of the bed, *but deliver us from evil"* — the
master phrase, the key words whose power would stop the
snakes in their tracks and force them to return dejectedly to their
lairs.

It was tempting on occasions to blurt out the magic words at
once, quickly, without all the preamble: "Deliver us from evil!"
But this wouldn't work, I knew, and the spell only operated if the
whole prayer were recited in the correct order. Neither would it
do to gabble it with indecent haste, and accordingly the ending
too carried its weight, and I would fall asleep immediately after
"the power and the glory, for ever and ever, amen," secure in the
knowledge that for another night I was safe from the dangers of
the dark.

All good things come to an end. When I was nine the bottom fell out of my world. First John, and then Charles went away to boarding-school at Plumtree. Then, to compound my loss, Julian and his family moved to Salisbury. Bad enough to lose my brothers, but to be deprived of my cousins as well was a cataclysm. Try as I would, neither my magic spells nor my prayers were able to turn the tide of events, and my disillusionment with the supernatural was profound.

My life that had been filled to the brim with colour, adventure and intrigue, shrank and shrivelled to nothing. Each day yawned before me, as hollow and echoing as an empty pumpkin shell. In a desperate search for companionship I turned first to our cats, and striking in them a rich vein of humour and camaraderie, I began to enlarge my circle of animal friends and acquaintances. One discovery led to another, and soon I found myself in an ever-widening ring of enchantment. From the toktokkie beetle to the tortoise, from the hornbill to the hawk, no creature was too small, too hostile, too shy to escape my overtures of friendship.

In this regard my experiences were far from unique, for the delight of an animal's company has brought to many a lonely existence in Africa a living treasure of excitement and laughter.

2

Snakes in the Grass

ONE OF THE FIRST things I observed about the animal kingdom was that it bore a striking resemblance to the world of men. The animals too have their good guys and bad guys, their dunderheads and their clowns, their heroes and their cowards, and it was vitally necessary to distinguish between them, because a false judgement could cost you your life.

The button-spider for example, with her clutch of eggs like miniature golf balls, is as deadly as a capsule of cyanide, and if snakes loomed over-large in my imagination, it was no doubt because they *were* extremely dangerous. In our family it was customary to pooh-pooh the hardships of life in the bush, and it was frowned on to grumble about insignificant discomforts caused by the heat and the dirt and the flies and the mosquitoes. Snakes, however, were another matter and the presence of a snake was always regarded with grave concern.

Not all the snakes were poisonous, of course. The constrictors, like the brown house snake and the python, were actually beneficial to have around for they kept down the number of rodents, but several of the other species were sufficiently venomous to kill a bullock in a matter of minutes.

The cats were devils with snakes. Until we got one of our own, I had always supposed that Siamese cats were nothing more than pampered pansies, the affected fops of the feline world who would graciously allow one to tempt them with a morsel of Strasbourg pâté. It was a revelation to see Siamese cats in the bush. They proved to be as primitive, as predatory, as cunning, as voluptuously dusty and disreputable as any wild beast. Once hooked on Siamese cats, naturally we found ourselves addicts, unable to contemplate life without them. Far from being civilised sophisticates, they loved nothing more than to roll in a patch of hot sand and then stalk off into the bundu, covered with dust and specks of stick and dead leaf. They were formidable hunters, with one endearing peculiarity — if their quarry were just out of reach, they used to sit and bleat at it, yammering involuntarily with quivering jaw and twitching whiskers, in a very agony of frustration. It was quite remarkable to observe the Siamese's camouflage in the veld. Their cream-and-chocolate fur harmonised perfectly with dead grass and rocks, and Choc-choc our old tom could lie almost invisibly anywhere he chose. The only aspect of life in the tropics that troubled them was the dazzle of the sun on the bare earth, and on those hot, dry, electric days before the rains when the very air was blinding white, the cats would slouch round the yard with eyes narrowed down to slits against the glare.

Perhaps our most memorable cat was a female Siamese called Jezebel who lived to the splendid old age of fifteen. She was of the squat and chunky build, with a short tail and temper, very pale blue eyes and a harsh croaking voice. Not a beauty, but a little tigress when it came to hunting snakes. Her consuming passion in life was to capture them alive and then play with them, the favourite old game of a piece of wriggling string, but enacted in earnest with the real thing — a game indeed of life and death. I wonder what ancient Oriental instinct taught her the intricate manœuvres, the lightning leaps and twists to avoid the lashing head. One could see that she loved every minute of it, now springing vertically into the air with exaggerated alarm, now coyly patting the snake's tail with extended paw, her ears pricked forward in dainty amusement. I dreaded these encounters for as far as I was concerned, the sun shone out of Jezebel's eyes, and I was in daily terror that she would be killed by one of her 'toys'.

On one occasion Jezebel's snake-hunting was inadvertently the cause of great alarm to a distant neighbour, a curious

fellow of a somewhat nervous disposition who in former years
had taught at Plumtree School. Now, whether his experiences
there had broken his nerve, or whether he had always been
imaginatively inclined, we could not decide. The fact remained
that he was forever blowing up the most humdrum episode into
an International Incident in which he enacted the leading role of
the Aggrieved Party. It used to take all Mother's charm and
diplomacy to keep on cordial terms with the old boy, because he
continually fancied that he was being 'got at'. Just before dusk
one evening Mother, Father and I were sitting outside enjoying a
cup of coffee with Jezebel, like a sacred idol, sitting erect on the
verandah wall, her tail curled round her toes and a far-away look
in her eyes. In the restful silence we all heard the soft slither and
rustle from the stone flags near the front door. In a trice, Jezebel
had sprung down from the wall and begun to bounce round the
head of a huge, yellow cobra that was making its leisurely way
past the house. The snake spread its hood and struck out at her,
but Jez shot into the air and continued to dart in at it, trying to get
at the back of its head. Father hurried indoors for the shot-gun
while I tried to capture Jezebel and Mother kept an eye on the
snake to see where it went. Father returned, feeding a big
scarlet cartridge into the breech, just as the snake commenced to
pour itself down a hole. It was unfortunately no longer possible
to dispatch it with a single head-shot, so Father put several into
its body. Perhaps one shot *might* have been enough, but he
didn't wish to prolong the snake's suffering and it seemed better
at the time to be quite certain that it was truly dead.

Jezebel sulked for the rest of the evening, but her displeasure was nothing to the hysteria which the sound of gunfire had
aroused in our neighbour. The following morning there appeared
before our astonished eyes the spectacle of this strange individual stalking warily through our garden, his rifle aimed before
him commando-style, his hat pulled down firmly over his eyes,
his every move illustrative of the keenest degree of vigilance and
nervous expectation. He was pathetically crestfallen when
Mother stepped outside and bade him a cheery good morning,
and he explained in the tones of deepest disappointment that he
had heard 'heavy firing' from our house the previous night, and

fearing that we had all been murdered in our beds, he had come over at considerable personal risk to make an on-the-spot investigation. The sight of the corpse of the enormous cobra did little to mollify his injured dignity, and relations between us were strained for quite some weeks!

Wretched cat, she must have made the life of our factotum, Bernard, a continual nightmare! He would appear with a look of profound disgust on his features, to announce: "Jezebel she has snake in sitting-room."

Then the fun would begin. Mother, Bernard and I armed with sticks and brooms would be endeavouring to get the snake *out* from its place of refuge — under the sofa, or twined round the legs of a coffee table, or coiled up behind the cushions of a chair — and Jezebel would be equally determined to poke the snake back *in*. Not infrequently our combined efforts only succeeded in losing the snake altogether, and we'd then have the dubious pleasure of knowing that a snake of some description was lurking *somewhere* in the house.

When Jezebel had been hunting, it was her custom to carry her trophy in from the bush, holding her head high and uttering deep muffled yeowls to attract our attention. No doors or windows were ever closed at night, and the cats used to come in and go out as they pleased. One night Father was woken by the sound of Jezebel approaching with her 'hunting call', and presently there was a predictable scuttle and thump under his bed. Quite evidently she had brought some creature inside and was preparing to play with it for the rest of the night. Jezebel really used to let herself go on these occasions, snorting and coughing in mock indignation, or springing about from one piece of furniture to another in a wild carnival of self-congratulation. Irritated at being woken up, and unable to get back to sleep while the cat disported herself in this way, Father switched on the light, determined to put a stop to her high jinks. To his annoyance he observed that she had brought in a slim, grey snake which was doing its best to get in among the bed-clothes. Grumpy and half asleep, Father sprang out of bed, picked up the snake and threw it out of the window. Only then did he wake up to the realisation of what an insane thing he had done, and of course after that the last vestiges of sleep were banished for the rest of the night! The following morning both Jezebel and Father were in poor humour, scowling at one another from opposite ends of the bed.

One August afternoon Jezebel met her match. I was reading in the garden, when I heard her calling from a considerable distance. Her cry was quite unlike her usual hunting song. It sounded muffled and broken, and instead of approaching steadily, it appeared to come and go in a peculiar fashion. Feeling vaguely uneasy, I set off to find her, alternately calling her name and listening for her reply. Her voice led me to a part of the veld that was made up of large loose slabs of rock and tussocks of coarse grass. From a distance I could see her blundering about among the stones in a most eccentric fashion, walking into things, falling down, getting up again, swaying on her feet, and on and off producing that horrible bubbling cry. I ran then, shouting to her, and she turned towards my voice. Poor little cat! Her whole face was covered in froth, she was foaming at the mouth, her eyes were opaque and streaming with a thick, yellow juice, and her throat so swollen that she was choking with every breath.

When I picked her up, she changed her cry, trying to talk in her eloquent Siamese way, a series of complaining grunts interspersed with an awkward hiccupping purr. Every now and then she'd break out with a loud "Wa-a-ow!" her voice charged with the drama and peril of her predicament. I carried her back to the house, talking soothingly to her all the way, but I was in an agony of anxiety. No one else was at home at the time, and I didn't know what to do for her. As she nearly always slept in my room, however, I sensed that this would be her most familiar place of refuge. She crawled gratefully under the bed, and there she stayed washing her face, coughing, rubbing at her eyes and periodically producing a hollow howl. When Mother came home, she concluded that Jezebel had had a brush with a spitting cobra, and suggested we wash out the cat's eyes with milk. The poison of the spitting cobra can cause permanent blindness, and we were very worried about her for several days, for she remained under the bed looking dismal and refusing all food.

However, perhaps the milk helped, or maybe she was tough enough to withstand the venom, for within a week she had completely recovered.

Of all the snakes, the mambas were regarded with the severest dread. Their reputation for attacking without provocation was perhaps ill deserved, but their other qualities were alarming enough. In the first place, the mamba is a very large snake, occasionally measuring as much as twelve feet. Added to this, it is conspicuously agile, slithering about in the trees and over the ground with terrifying speed. The potency of its bite and the abundance of venom is enough to command respect from

one and all. The mamba's is a fast-acting neurotoxic venom that paralyses the respiratory and cardiac muscles. On one occasion Father had a disagreeable encounter with a black mamba. He was walking briskly through a field of long grass, and was quite unaware of the snake's presence until it had fastened on to his leg. By sheer chance he happened to be wearing a pair of grey flannels. The snake had latched on to a fold of the cloth just below the knee, injecting into the fabric so much venom that the fluid ran down the trouser leg. Before Father could say 'dammit' the snake had released its hold and shot away into the grass, but from that day onwards Father never wore shorts when he was in the veld.

Snakes were very much a part of everyone's lives in those days, and many stories were told to round-eyed audiences of awestruck children. The gripping thing about these yarns was that for the most part they were true. Indeed, all too often the children themselves were on hand to witness their parents' exploits in dealing with serpents of one kind and another.

Ronald Napier who came to the country in the very early days was known as something of a daredevil, a reputation which he justly earned in the eyes of his little daughter, then aged seven or eight. The family had spent the night at the small country hotel at Umvuma. The following morning, the housekeeper went in to clear one of the bedrooms, and stooped down to gather into her arms a pile of sheets that had been stripped off the bed. As she did so a great snake rose up towards her out of the tumbled folds of linen. She had a fleeting impression of its shifting coils looping and gathering together before she fled outside shrieking, slamming the door behind her. Despite all her entreaties, none of the staff could be persuaded to go in and deal with so large a monster. Attracted by the hubbub, Ronald Napier offered to see what he could do. Arming himself with a rake, he entered the room and shut himself inside with the creature, while his anxious family waited outside, listening with mounting alarm to the bangs and thuds and crashes as he pranced about, now on the bed, now on the floor, now leaping over a chair. His adversary turned out to be a very large black mamba, and it rapidly became plain that it was more than a match for Napier and his rake. Like Kipling's shipwrecked mariner, however, he was a man of infinite resource and sagacity! He managed to seize up a blanket from the bed and slinging this across one shoulder and arm as a shield, he once more engaged battle with the snake, much like an old Roman gladiator with his net and trident. To his family's unspeakable relief, Napier finally emerged victorious with the mamba draped round his neck.

In our part of the country the most common inflictor of bites was the Egyptian cobra. They were fond of kopje country and used to haunt farmsteads where they hoped to find rodents and other small items of food. Cobra venom is deadly, a severe bite resulting in blood-stained vomiting, paralysis and cardiac failure. Cobras were generally considered to be less of a problem during the winter months than in the hot weather, for they tended to return to their burrows to hibernate. With the onset of spring, Father frequently used to admonish us to be on our guard against snakes: "They'll be coming out to bask in the sun, so watch where you're putting your feet!"

Quite often after the first warm days there will be a sudden cold snap — *guti* we call it — when a thin, cold drizzle driven by a fierce wind will blow up from the Limpopo valley. Oliver Goldsmith, a close friend of ours, was at home on his small-holding in the Matopo Hills one cold Sunday when the *guti* was blowing hard. After lunch he went to his room to have a snooze, snuggled up in a warm rug. When he awoke an hour or so later, he felt a mysterious weight on his arm. Still half asleep, he tossed back the blanket to see what it could be, and found a big cobra coiled round and round his arm, hugging him for warmth. In his first reaction of alarm and revulsion, he half rose up in bed and flung out his arm to try to dislodge the snake. The cobra, however, dismayed at this discourteous treatment, struck out and bit Goldsmith on his upper lip.

Now a snakebite anywhere on the head is very grave news indeed, because there is nothing that can be done to slow down the spread of the venom to the vital organs. The only other member of the family at home that day was his fifteen-year-old daughter, Lorna, who had recently started learning how to handle the utility truck. Casting aside any scruples she might have had about the highway code, Lorna got her father into the truck and drove like fury for Bulawayo, thirty miles away. The breakneck dash to the hospital saved his life, and we all agreed that he was a lucky man.

Although so many of our snakes were dangerous, I still hated to see them killed, especially when they had done us no actual harm. We never really saw 'in one piece' the biggest cobra that visited our home. Just below the kopje was the dam. In the summer, its thick earth wall held back a good stretch of water which dried up each winter. The wall itself was planted with tough, thick kikuyu grass whose sinuous roots helped to bind the soil together. The dam wall was the home of great numbers of crabs and frogs. Father frowned on their presence, partly because they burrowed in the wall and caused leaks, and partly because they attracted snakes. One morning he was cutting the kikuyu grass on top of the dam wall, using a motorised scythe. All at once the blades of the mower threw into the air a number of pieces of yellow hosepipe, each about a foot long. Puzzled, Father switched off the machine. The 'hosepipe' turned out to be an unfortunate snake. Poor thing, when we put all the bits together they measured over six feet, very large for a cobra.

When my brothers were at Plumtree it was the accepted thing for the boys to keep unusual pets, and the back premises of each house always had their fair share of tame eagles, hawks, bush-babies, snakes and other oddities. We used to go down to Plumtree about once every six weeks to visit the boys, and on these occasions it was *de rigueur* to admire the current pet. Several times I compelled myself to submit to having someone's tame snake wind its way up my arm and round my neck, but I must confess that I did this more out of a sense of bravado than with any feelings of real enjoyment!

A strange thing happened to Charles when he was in his final year at Plumtree. He was walking up to the School Hall to write the second last of his Public Examinations when he observed a snake speeding across the gravel path ahead of him. It looked like a herald snake, a relatively harmless variety much favoured by the boys. Charles laid hold of the creature intending to pop it into his shirt. It transpired however that it was not a herald, a fact instantly communicated to him by the painful nature of its bite. He reluctantly decided to abandon it, and continued on his way while the snake's venom started to take effect. He emerged from the Hall with the full range of toxic symptoms — nausea, headache, dizziness, severe pain at the bite itself and cramps in all his limbs. He didn't mention it to any of the masters for fear they would prevent him from writing his last paper! To this day we don't know what kind of snake it was that bit him, but it would be of some academic interest because on the results of those exams Charles went on to win a much-coveted scholarship!

Among the Africans a pet snake is considered a powerful item of household equipment, and various tribes hold to the belief that a few friendly snakes in a village are desirable on account of their deterrent properties, helping to fend off thieves and evil spirits. Dr. Dudley Lawrence told me about his boyhood experiences of this very situation. In the early days of the century his father purchased a farm near Norton, where they grew tobacco and reared poultry. One morning the family were startled to hear Mrs. Lawrence scream from the fowl-run where she had gone to collect eggs. Knowing that only a snake could make his wife scream like that, Mr. Lawrence seized the shotgun and ran out to the fowl-run, arriving there at the same moment as the African poultry-man. It was a cobra, sure enough, coiled up in one of the nesting boxes, and Mrs. Lawrence had happened upon it when she put her hand in to gather the eggs. The poultry-man begged Mr. Lawrence not to shoot the snake, explaining that he wanted it to take back to his house. Mr. Lawrence who knew about and disapproved of this practice of keeping snakes in the compound, wouldn't hear of it, though he felt a twinge of regret at the poultry-man's obvious disappointment.

His decision was vindicated some days later, however, when the poultry-man's brother reported sick. He was one of Mr. Lawrence's best tobacco graders and a most useful man on the farm. He arrived at the grading sheds in very poor shape indeed, supported on his feet by members of his family, and haemorrhaging profusely from all over his body. When Mr. Lawrence asked them how long ago the snake had bitten him, they adamantly denied that a snake had had anything to do with it, although the bite itself was all too hideously conspicuous. They immediately rushed him in to hospital in Salisbury, but it was too late and the poor fellow died the following day.

A snake with a particularly sinister type of venom is the

boomslang, an arboreal species that preys on birds and chameleons. Its venom fangs are at the back of the mouth so that when attacking it does not strike-and-recoil like a cobra, but hangs on and chews. Its poison is a decoagulant of the blood and although the bite itself is less painful that that, say, of the puff-adder, and although the symptoms take longer to develop, it is extremely serious. After some hours the boomslang's victim commences to bleed from any small cuts or abrasions. Later, blood appears in the saliva and urine, followed by extensive subcutaneous bleeding that resembles massive bruising all over the body. We all entertain a very healthy respect for the boomslang.

Mother's only experience with them was rather unusual and came as a result of a modest shopping expedition. She had purchased a stem of green bananas which she left to ripen on a table on the back verandah outside the kitchen door. Some days later on going to see whether any of the bananas were ripe, she observed a cluster of little eggs sticking together among the fruit. They were soft and leathery, the colour of parchment and each about the size of a peanut. Taking them for lizard eggs, mother loosened them from the bananas, meaning to show them to us. However, the little eggs separated with a jerk, rolled off the table and broke on the floor. Immediately a swarm of tiny boomslangs emerged, the same pale colour as their shells. They were less than an inch long with disproportionately large heads, so that each one resembled a comma. Before Mother had recovered from her surprise, the little creatures had wriggled away and vanished!

Not long ago we had a boomslang in the bamboo clump near our cook's house. It first made its presence known in a somewhat dramatic manner. Cook's wife Susan had been sitting sewing under the arching shade of the bamboos when all at once there was a violent rustling in the leaves above her head and a chameleon plopped on to the ground right beside her, followed immediately by a brilliant-green snake. The first we knew of this was Susan's screams, from the nature and intensity of which we concluded that she was being attacked. Cook, the children and I dropped whatever we were doing and rushed to her rescue armed with a variety of weapons — a broom, a kitchen knife, a

brick — whatever came first to hand. My son Tom was first on the scene, arriving in time to witness the boomslang slithering back into the bamboos. Susan had taken refuge in her house and, concluding that it had been the snake that had frightened her, Tom called out: "It's all right Susan, the snake has gone!"
Susan's eye appeared at the door of her house.
"The snake was nothing, Tom," she said in a trembling voice, "It was chasing a *chameleon*, and oh!" here she stopped to shudder, "the chameleon had *no tail*!"
While Susan peered out fearfully, we hunted for the luckless chameleon, finally locating it hiding in a bed of marigolds. I lifted it out gently and examined it. Sure enough, it had no tail, but this was an old injury for the stump was completely healed over. The chameleon's tail is prehensile, serving as a fifth limb to assist it to climb, so the loss must have been grievous indeed. More serious than this, however, were three pronounced punctures in the chameleon's side and shoulder, where the snake's fangs had penetrated the skin. A small thread of blood was issuing from each and the lower bite had already swollen to the size and shape of a marble. I indicated these to Susan, but she only shuddered the more and hid her face against her shoulder. To the African the chameleon is the object of the greatest loathing and dread, and it was giving her the horrors to see me handling the reptile. About the boomslang she was totally unconcerned, and when we offered to drive it out of the bamboo she protested: "No, don't chase it," she said, "it will do no harm."
We released the chameleon in a gardenia bush near the front door, though it seemed doubtful if it would survive. An hour later it had completely disappeared, so we never learned the end of its story.

It has been estimated that three-quarters of the serious snakebites from our part of the world are inflicted by the puff-adder. Among the more disagreeable properties of its venom is the fact that it commonly results in mortification and sloughing of the flesh in a huge area around the bite itself. A severe puff-adder bite is enough to kill a cow. The puff-adder is a short, thick, sluggish snake rather like a gaudy golf stocking with its harlequin design in tones of honey, cream and caramel. Unlike most other reptiles which deposit their eggs in a secret place to hatch on their own, the female puff-adder carries her eggs inside her body until they are almost ready to hatch. In this way she is able to see to it that they are kept in the most favourable position — full sunlight. This accounts for the puff-adder's notorious habit of lying basking in a pathway, and for their reluctance to move out of the way. Added to this, their warning puff is so soft that it is quite easily lost among the other gentle noises of the veld — the whisper of the wind in the long grass, or the rustle of leaves in the trees.

When I was a teenager in Bulawayo I had a narrow escape from one of these sleepy devils. It happened one hot October morning when I was showing a friend over a Stone Age site near Hope Fountain Mission. The dry hill-slope was literally covered with enormous stone tools. It excited the imagination to picture those primitive men so many thousands of years ago squatting there in the sun and knocking out their axes and cleavers from the hard, red ironstone. All around us the bush was alive with termites. They responded to every step we took by setting off a rattling fusillade amongst the dead leaves, a kind of bush telegraph to alert their neighbours of our presence. By stamping repeatedly on the ground, we succeeded in stirring the entire district into a state of mass hysteria, till the bush resounded to their dry rataplan, like roll upon roll on a tiny kettle-drum. The two of us were heartlessly teasing the termites in this way without regard to where we were stamping, and heaven knows what made me look down . . . not two feet away was a beautiful gold-and-brown puff-adder lying quite still, watching us with her jewelled eyes! I felt sick with fright, and both of us were a lot more careful with our feet for the rest of the morning!

3

Great Snakes!

QUITE APART from the numerous stories of snakes in African folklore, there has grown up a body of herpetological mythology which is more recent in origin. Whenever conversation works its way round to snakes, sooner or later someone will come out with a regional variant of the story of the little girl, the cup of milk and the cobra. Despite the most penetrating researches, I have not yet been able to interview anyone who has first-hand experience of this phenomenon. It always resolves itself into "a story my grandmother told me", or "my neighbour in Gwanda had a friend whose child . . .". Mind you, it's a good yarn if told with the right circumstantial details! The story as I first heard it relates how a little girl of three used to take away her cup of milk to share with a 'friend'. As her older brothers and sisters were away at school, it was assumed that the child had invented a friend to brighten up the long, lonely mornings. Frequently the little girl invited her mother to come and meet the friend, but suspecting that it was fictitious, the woman fobbed her off with one excuse or another. Finally the child's entreaties prevailed upon a kind-hearted guest who followed her down the garden and in behind a huge bush of yellow jasmine (remembering the circumstantial details!). There the child sat down and called "Snakey! Snakey!" and presently out slithered an enormous grey cobra which made straight for the cup of milk. It was not permitted to drink it all, however. The child snatched the milk away with a stern rebuke.

"No, Snakey! Don't be greedy. My turn."

And so the little ceremony proceeded, with a drink for the snake and a drink for the child, until the whole cup of milk was finished. Thereupon the snake returned to its hole under the jasmine.

It is an appealing story in its way and encourages credibility in that there are many well-authenticated cases of children who *have* played with poisonous snakes and not been harmed by them. One of these concerns George Elcombe's nephew, then a little toddler of two. One afternoon he disappeared from the farmhouse. A search was mounted and the child was discovered in the fowl-run, inside one of the enclosed hen-coops where he could be heard talking and chuckling away. Relieved that he was safe, his mother stooped to call him out, but her relief was short-lived. Her little boy was sitting cross-legged on the straw with a great cobra reared up in front of him. As the snake drew itself up to its full height, the child struck it on the back of its head with a tiny twig.

"Lie down!" he commanded, and the snake, knocked flat, lay down. Next minute, however, while the child laughed and wriggled delightedly, the snake rose up once more.

"Lie down!" the little boy ordered again, and once more tapped the cobra on the hood. Heaven knows how long this wonderful game had been going on. It says a lot for the mother's presence of mind that she was able to coax the child away without alarming him or the cobra.

Of all the fabulous and fantastic snake legends which I have encountered, the most amazing comes — not unexpectedly, perhaps —from a fisherman. Not long ago I was endeavouring to extract a good fishing story from a man whose exploits as an angler are not only extravagant but completely authentic. Unfortunately from my point of view, he is a very modest fisherman and I couldn't persuade him to talk about any of his more memorable experiences, although with considerable reluctance he agreed to relate what happened to 'another fellow'. It appeared that the man had spent the greater part of the day angling for trout in one of the dams near Inyanga. Little success had attended his efforts and he was comforting himself from time to time with a nip of brandy from his hip-flask. Shortly before the sun set, he cast his principles aside and resolved to bait up his line with a frog. Searching up and down the bank for a frog's hole, he came across a snake carrying off a frog in its mouth. He caught the snake behind the head, but could not persuade it to let go of the frog. Finally in desperation he dribbled a little brandy into the snake's mouth. Immediately the snake spat out the frog, the man released the snake and commenced to bait up his line. Presently he felt something cold touching his leg, and glancing down there he found the same snake again, with another frog in its mouth!

Not very surprisingly, I found at the conclusion of this story that one of my legs was considerably longer than the other!

A much-quoted adage was, "remember, a dead snake can kill". As children we accorded to this the usual degree of disrespect. Dr. Dudley Lawrence, Rhodesia's first veterinarian, established the veracity of this particular old wives' tale, however. One day a woman brought to his laboratory a dead snake which had been killed early in the morning. At about two in the afternoon Dr. Lawrence opened its mouth and attempted to extract a little of the venom. It was by then very thick and sticky, but at last he persuaded a drop to emerge from one of the fangs. He diluted this single drop with water and injected it into two rats which were dead within minutes.

We children cheerfully called any snake with a stripy

design of green and yellow a 'grass-snake'. Indeed our ignorance about snakes was matched only by our ghoulish fascination with them. At that stage we fondly believed that "a dead snake can kill" was a lot of old rubbish, and consequently whenever a snake was killed there was fierce competition between ourselves and the servants for ownership of the corpse — we used to use it to terrify our friends and acquaintances, and they to make 'muti'. (Among the Matabele, snake fat was highly prized as a remedy for arthritis.) Frequently we would strike a compromise — we would have the use of the snake for the first hour or two, and thereafter it was theirs to dispose of as they wished. Caroline and I made the interesting discovery that if we blew on a dead snake the cool air made its muscles contract so that it wriggled in a delightfully lifelike manner. It was excellent entertainment to exhibit the snake in a cardboard box and then blow on it to the terror of our unsuspecting victim!

There is a cruel streak in children which for some curious reason makes it particularly good fun to torment the timid and the susceptible. I recall with shame how we tortured one of our neighbours, a gentle, pleasant woman who had a pathological fear of snakes. It was not that we had anything against her, in fact rather to the contrary, we all *liked* Mrs. R., but there was simply something irresistible in the idea of frightening her out of her wits.

One golden spring morning during the school holidays when Ewen, Caroline and Tom were down from Salisbury, and John and Charles were home from school, the six of us set off to prowl round the neighbourhood, as had been our custom in the past. It was exhilarating to be together again and I dare say that this added a zest to the occasion. The cherry on the top of our joy was a dead snake, freshly killed, which Julian's gardener had presented to the children on the occasion of their return. We consulted among ourselves as to how this trophy could best be put to use. One of us hit on the diabolical idea of introducing it somehow into Mrs. R.'s house, and then hiding nearby to enjoy the show. Naturally this splendid idea won the approval of the entire party. Accordingly Tom and I were detailed to make a recce. It was considered that we as the youngest members of the group would get into the least trouble if we were caught, a philosophy that was not infallible as we learned to our cost on a later occasion. On this day, however, the gods favoured our venture, and we returned breathless to report that we should select the master bedroom as the target area. Not only was Mrs. R. busy tidying it up and bustling in and out, but there were numerous old magazines lying around the room under which we could conceal the injured portion of the snake's spine, where the gardener had hammered it with a rock. The whole manœuvre was ridiculously simple. The french windows of the bedroom stood invitingly wide, and it was the work of a moment to rush the snake into the room, partially conceal it under a magazine and dart out again, while Mrs. R. clattered about in another part of the house.

So often when one has set a trap for a person, they will selfishly refrain from falling into it. With irritating obstinacy they dawdle about, performing other irrelevant tasks and refuse to direct their steps along the Path of Doom. One waits and waits with mounting impatience, and finally out of sheer boredom one is compelled to abandon the project. Not so on this occasion, however. Mrs. R.'s reaction was gratifyingly quick and exceeded our wildest expectations. I can truthfully say that I have never, before or since, seen anyone so completely terror-struck.

From our hiding-place among a cluster of rocks, we heard her brisk light footsteps approaching the bedroom, and we held our breath, our eyes popping excitedly. The next moment there came shriek after shriek and Mrs. R. burst through the french windows, both hands in her hair, her head flung back, eyes rolling, mouth open. Presently she lost her breath and staggered about as if mad or injured. In fact, so alarming was her appearance that we all rose to our feet despite ourselves and stood in a row gaping with admiration at her splendid performance. All at once she caught sight of us. Choking and holding a hand to her chest, she came tottering forward.

"Ewen!" she gasped, rolling her eyes towards the house, "Oh Ewen, I'm so glad you're here! There's a - a - a -" she gave a great whooping intake of breath, "- a *snake* in my bedroom!"

"Is there?" Ewen's surprise was well simulated. "Right then, leave it to me," he went on in stern tones. Seizing up a hockey stick that leaned against the wall of the house, he strode into the bedroom with a masterful air, the rest of us following at a discreet distance and trying to look suitably nervous. While Mrs. R. stood outside clasping and unclasping her hands and crying out, "Oh dear, oh do be careful!" Ewen whacked the snake all over the injured portion of its spine, and emerged triumphantly with the serpent dangling from the crook of the hockey stick. Mrs. R. was pathetically grateful, thanked Ewen with tears in her eyes and invited us all round to the kitchen for an orange drink. We returned home glowing with the satisfaction that comes on the heels of a highly successful campaign.

Some twenty years later Ewen was more or less hoist with his own petard. One of his children had been given a rubber snake for Christmas, a hideously lifelike abomination which the children put to great purpose by hiding it in unexpected places about the house and garden. Returning home after dark one night, Ewen found this brute lying on the front doorstep, no doubt ready to startle him as he entered the house. "Blasted children and their rubber snakes," he grumbled to himself, for the creature had as a matter of fact, given him a considerable shock. He stooped to pick it up, whereupon the 'rubber' snake struck upwards at his hand. Closer inspection showed that it was a night adder, very much alive!

While its bite is, relatively speaking, less serious than some, the night adder accounts for the preponderance of snake-bites that occur inside people's houses. They have a fondness for coming into a building just after dusk to soak up the last warmth of the day. They are short and sluggish like the puff-adder, but can put on an impressive display of aggressiveness if cornered. My sister-in-law Anne once put her foot into a shoe that contained a night adder. Fortunately her reflexes were quicker than the snake's!

Ame Robb told me the story of how she was actually bitten by a night adder when she was a little girl of ten. This occurred back in the 1920s when the treatment for snakebites was of a rough-and-ready order. The Robbs lived on an isolated farm on the Zambezi escarpment, with the nearest village forty miles away along a narrow, twisting bush-road.

"We were having our evening meal," she told me, "when my father said: 'Ame, I saw you repairing your bicycle with my tools. Did you put them away when you finished?' I said: 'Yes, Dad', although I had no idea what I had done with them. I thought to myself, as soon as we have finished dinner, I'll go and look for them."

Probably afraid of betraying herself, Ame didn't take a light with her when she went out on to the back verandah where the tools were normally kept. She started trying to locate them in the dark. "I was feeling about on the shelves when something bit my heel, and I knew immediately that it was a snake. I ran into the kitchen and fetched the hurricane lamp and sure enough, there in front of the shelves was this little yellow devil about a foot-and-a-half long, curled up, with its tongue darting in and out, in and out. I flew into the house, colliding with my mother who was just coming out. 'Mum, Mum!' I cried, 'A snake has bitten me!'

"Mrs. Robb was a Scot with all the cool nerve that a tough life in the wilds demanded of her. She merely replied sternly: 'Away with ye, away with ye! Ye're always calling wolf, wolf!' "

It was with considerable difficulty that Ame persuaded her family to come out and see the snake for themselves. At last all of them were clustered round the adder, puzzling over what kind of snake it was, when a little piccanin grasping a small curved axe pushed his way through the ring of spectators. He bent forward and chopped the snake in half with a disgusted grunt, as much as to say, 'What's all the fuss about?'

Not that much fuss had been made of the little girl, who was still badly frightened. "Everyone had a look at the two little, black bites on my heel, but no one seemed very impressed by them. Mother and Father concluded that the fangs hadn't penetrated the thick skin of my heel, for we never wore shoes on the farm and my feet were like the black piccanin's. I was simply told to take myself off to bed. Well, as a child, I was less hurt by the snake than by my parents' apparent lack of concern. Finally at about ten o'clock that night, I decided: 'To heck with this, I'm not going to die. I might as well go to sleep.' " Ame concluded her story with the remark: "I often wonder what they would have done if a big poisonous one had bitten me, miles from the nearest doctor; and we didn't have snake serum in those days . . ."

It is curious how a normally level-headed person is provoked into rash and thoughtless actions by the presence of a snake. A few years ago the police were summoned to investigate a case of murder and arson in the Matopos. At first glance it appeared that the victim, a storekeeper, had been the subject of a brutal attack, after which the miscreants had rounded off their felony by tossing explosives into his blazing store. The police-man in charge of the case was a cautious fellow, and a number of singular features led him to search further for the cause of the fire. While sifting through the smoking rubble, he had come upon pieces of a rifle and assorted lengths of a large cobra, both quite close to the body of the storekeeper. When all the evidence was in, the picture that emerged was both tragic and unusual. The storekeeper, it seemed, had opened his shop and surprised a cobra inside it. In his haste to shoot the snake, he had not given enough thought to the contents of his store. The bullet ricocheted and whined off behind the counter where it detonated a whole

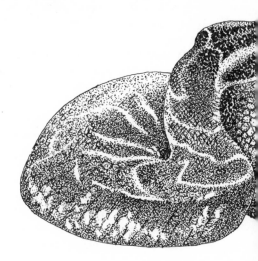

case of dynamite. In the colossal explosion that followed, both the snake and the storekeeper were blown to bits and the store was burned to the ground.

In a similar chain of misadventures, a puff-adder was indirectly the cause of the Elcombes' cook being bitten by a Great Dane. One quiet afternoon when all the family were out and Mrs. Elcombe was alone in the farmhouse, she took the opportunity of getting some letters written. The living-room was pleasantly warm, with great squares of sunlight falling through the windows on to the rugs and the polished floor. It was restful and still, the only sounds were the soft scratching of Mrs. Elcombe's pen, and from the kitchen the distant tinkle of a teaspoon on china, where the maid was preparing to bring a tray of tea. A few minutes later there came from the door of the living-room a piercing scream of 'Nyoka!' (snake!). The entire tea-tray crashed to the floor and the maid fled from the house, shrieking as if fifty devils were after her.

Startled to her feet by this inexplicable commotion, Mrs. Elcombe found her exit from the living-room cut off by a fat puff-adder. The snake, too, had been disturbed by the precipitate arrival of the tea things. It had been lying basking in one of the

squares of sunlight close to the door, but now raised its head and began to huff indignantly at Mrs. Elcombe.

Some people are afflicted with an unreasoning aversion to cats or cockroaches, spiders or scorpions. For Mrs. Elcombe, the quintessence of horror was represented by a snake — any kind of snake. The very sight of one paralysed her with dread, and now she stood rooted to the spot, knowing that she would be unable to get out of the living-room until help arrived.

In the meantime, all the available help had taken to their heels in the opposite direction. So infectious was the maid's terror that the rest of the household staff, together with the gardener and the dairyman, joined impulsively in the rout. And now the dogs, who had been dozing on the verandah, became caught up in the excitement, and were galvanised into action by Mrs. Elcombe's cries for help. There is something irresistibly attractive to a dog when it sees people making a bolt for it. Barking furiously, the Great Dane and the other dogs hurled themselves after the fleeing scullions. The roars of alarm from the stout cook who was in the rear only spurred the dogs on to redouble their efforts, and Mrs. Elcombe watched despairingly from her prison in the living-room while the whole pack of them vanished down the road in a cloud of dust.

By the time Mr. Elcombe arrived from another part of the farm the cook's trousers were in need of repairs, and there was enough tension in the air to start World War III. Mr. Elcombe had his time cut out to restore order and pacify his staff, his dogs and his wife!

There is something indefinably eerie about a snake that haunts a particular house or room, and I have often sympathised with the ancient Egyptians for revering the snake as a sacred emblem, a familiar spirit that inhabits the temple of its own choosing. There was just a touch of the supernatural in Mrs. Bain's parlour, as they used to call the living-room in those days. Salisbury, at the turn of the century, was not an easy place for a mother of nine, and Mrs. Bain had her hands full to keep the household running on oiled wheels. I suspect that every woman cherishes something as a symbol of tranquillity or beauty — a painting perhaps, or a treasured piece of china. For Mrs. Bain it was violets. Indeed, in the heat and dust of a pioneering town it was quite an accomplishment to have a bed of violets at all, and she always kept a little bowl of them on the corner of the piano in the parlour. It used to madden her to come into the room and find the flowers drooping.

"Here you are, *nine* of you," she used to say, "and no one who'll take the trouble to fill up my violet bowl with water!"

The eldest daughter, who was sixteen or seventeen at the time, was very musical. In the evenings she used to close the door of the parlour and play the piano alone to herself in the gloaming. Occasionally after one of these sessions she would emerge looking puzzled and uneasy to say that she was sure that the room was haunted. She used to get the feeling that someone or something was in the room with her, and once she burst out more than usually agitated, claiming that she had distinctly felt something stirring her long skirt as it hung round the piano stool. No one paid much attention to her stories, for she was imaginatively inclined, and at an age when a girl likes to tint her everyday life with glowing colours.

One hot afternoon Mrs. Bain retired to the parlour herself, and locked the door feeling as many mothers have before and since, that if she didn't get away from it all for five minutes, something was going to snap. She lay down on the sofa, put up her feet, closed her eyes and tried to relax. After a few moments she heard a rustle from the direction of the piano. Reluctantly she opened her eyes, to see the head of a snake peeping over the piano top. Too surprised to move, she lay absolutely still while a long and very beautiful green snake eased itself up on to the lid. It looked like polished jade and it had bright, golden eyes. With graceful aplomb the snake slid confidently along the piano till it came to the bowl of violets. Here it lifted its head, nosed its way between the leaves and flowers, and presently Mrs. Bain heard the soft sound of the snake drinking. So at last the mystery of the water in the violets was explained!

It strikes me as unjust, somehow, that snakes are forever being represented as the villains of the animal world. They, too, have their fair share of hardship and are preyed on mercilessly by other creatures. Nor are they immune to parasites — there is a particular species of tick that feeds on snakes and snakes alone. My brother-in-law, Lloyd, once watched a snake being killed by a flock of hens. It had entered the fowl-run presumably to steal eggs or chicks, but was spotted by one of the bright-eyed ladies who cackled out a warning to her sisters, and in no time at all the snake was surrounded by a circle of murderous hens. No matter how desperately the snake whirled and struck out, there was always one hen behind it, ready to stab it with her beak. After each strike a snake has a moment of helplessness while it gathers its coils together once more, and the hens were quick to seize this advantage. They finally succeeded in pecking it to death.

I had a white leghorn called Pollen who once ate a snake whole. During the day the hens had the free range of the garden, where they were very useful in pecking up snails and army-worms and other pests. All at once Pollen came tearing round the side of the house, wings outspread, neck extended, and from her beak there dangled some eighteen inches of writhing snake. The next moment the rest of the hens came flapping into view, a desperate band of pirates some eight or ten strong, each of them bent upon stealing Pollen's prize. In and out of the orchard they ran, through the flower-beds, back past the kitchen, under the washing-line, round the house again, Pollen still in the lead, the snake wriggling valiantly. Determined to eat her snake at all costs, Pollen resorted to desperate measures. With a last despairing burst of speed she flapped up on to the roof of the garage and there by a series of frantic backward jerks of her head, she swallowed the whole snake, still very much alive! From her vantage place she peered down at the others with a decidedly smug air, but I shudder to think what it must have felt like with the snake writhing and twisting away inside her crop!

Clearly a snake holds few terrors for a hen. No doubt their plumage serves as a suit of armour. It is interesting to see how the tall secretary-bird will use his outspread wings as a decoy, when battling with a snake. He'll tempt the reptile to strike at the proffered wing, then jump in with lightning speed and pin the snake to the ground with his long talons. We humans are a lot more vulnerable, especially when we are crouched down on the ground and so meet the snake on its own level. At the age of fifteen Barbara Clinskel was deticking her dog on the verandah of the house, dropping the ticks into a tin of paraffin. The dog's restlessness made her glance over her shoulder and there, only a few feet away, was a cobra, approaching her with hood extended threateningly, its tongue flicking in and out. Both she and the dog sprang out of harm's way, but the experience left her with a nervous twitch that persisted for years afterwards.

In similar circumstances I once had an eyeball-to-eyeball encounter with a banded cobra. We had stopped for a picnic lunch on the banks of the Umvumvumvu River. All the indigenous trees were in blossom, and I wandered off on my own to enjoy their wonderful variety. Presently I knelt down to admire a huge crimson flower which had dropped out of a sausage tree and now lay on the ground like a floppy jester's cap. A very small whisper made me glance up. Inches from my face was the wide-open mouth of a cobra, a glistening pinky yellow, and from it came the tiny exhalation of breath — "Huh, huh, huh." At the same moment my eye was caught by the movement of coil upon shining coil gathering together among the leaves where I was kneeling. The snake was swelling out her hood indignantly and making every possible gesture to inform me that I was intruding on her privacy. I didn't linger to argue my case but rolled sideways and backwards and scrambled on to my feet again, very shaken indeed. She'd had ample time to strike me if she'd been that way inclined, but her good manners earned my undying gratitude. With profound respect, I tiptoed away and left her in peace!

As a final comment on the power of the snake over our imagination, I must relate one of my father-in-law's favourite stories. The old boy was very fond of his quail shooting, as much for the veld itself as for the sport. His favourite companions were an immensely fat, cheerful man called Tings, and Tings's black dog Kettles. On this occasion they were camped in kopje country, impressive natural castles of granite that held the heat of the sun long after day was past. Between the boulders were treacherous thickets of nettles and wag-'n-bietjie thorn. It was good snake country, and to make matters worse they'd seen several in the course of their first afternoon's shoot. Evening was drawing on when Tings decided that he required to make a brief sortie into the bush on his own. He had got so far as to remove his trousers and was crouching down when he felt something cold touch the skin of his behind. Tings shot from cover like a rocketing pheasant, yelling blue murder! The old boy ran up to see what was the matter, only to find what Tings had taken for a snake was nothing more than Kettles's cold nose!

4
A Feast of Flowers

FROM MY PILLOW I could see the last of the setting moon, deep yellow and misshapen, lying awkwardly in the western sky. It was nearly dawn. Drowsily I was aware of the first notes of the Kurrichane thrush, a shrill spike of sound probing the day. "Pee-peeoo!" he repeated insistently. He flew down from the branches of the fig and presently I heard his furtive rustle and scratch among the dead leaves behind my room. He was turning them over one at a time, flicking them aside like a conjurer to disclose the unsuspecting grub beneath.

Soon the bulbuls chimed in. Toppies we called them. They are the clowns of the bush, cheeky, garrulous, quarrelsome, fiercely loyal to their own kind and the first to proclaim to the world at large the presence of a snake or an owl. Smaller than a thrush, the bulbul is distinguished by his saucy, black crest and a comical, little tuft of sulphur yellow beneath the tail.

"Prick prick prick prick," they were singing in tones of rising excitement.

"Prick-prick, prick-prick prick the —." They paused and several of them giggled in twittering, tittering idiocy like children attempting to tell a naughty joke. Then at last one of them plucked up the courage to bawl out the whole phrase: "Prick-prick-prick-the-CREEPER-do!"

"Creeper-do! Creeper-do!" the rest agreed enthusiastically, whereupon the whole flock collapsed into showers of shimmering notes of mirth.

It was SPRING! And what need was there for fairy-tales when the most subtle magic in the world was unfolding all around me? Spring in Matabeleland was a triumph not so much over the cold as over the drought, a joyful gesture of defiance at the harshness of the environment. For seven months there had been no rain, indeed scarcely a single cloud had flecked the empty, blue bowl of the sky. Scorched by the sun and bitten by frost, the veld had shrunk into itself, a sombre symphony of greys and browns. Grey rocks, grey trees, grey leaves in deep, crackling drifts beneath the boulders, and over them all a film of grey dust. The dry, dead grass in the vlei was golden-brown, the bare earth of the yard a blinding brilliance in the sun, baked biscuit-dry. Grey and brown, ash and dust, the colours of death stretching unbroken to the horizon. Even the dam, where the last green growth had clung, was now a barren expanse of cracked chocolate-coloured mud, stone-hard, fissured and broken into crazy pavings whose edges curled up like old shoes, popping and snapping under my bare feet.

And yet it was spring! At first it is no more than a change in the air, an easing of the restless wind that has blown steadily from the south-east, month after month. Every tree, every field of grass in the whole of Matabeleland leans away from the wind. You can fix your compass bearing from them — north-west, north-west they point, following the wind like electrified hairs yearning after the comb.

And then, one morning, there is a stillness. The wind loses its purpose, eddies here and there in aimless dust-devils, lifting the dead leaves and laying them softly down again. There is a mistiness in the sky, a deepening sense of secret expectation, a trembling in the air, a pulsating beat like the approach of a distant engine, heard but not seen.

In those first breathless days it felt as if the doves embodied the essence of spring. Their liquid calls throbbed all through the afternoons, and in the evenings they congregated in flocks of twenty or thirty, jostling one another at the lip of the bird-bath, a hollow boulder whose crown we kept filled with water. The laughing-doves were small and immaculate, with dainty, pink feet and cinnamon-spotted breasts. *They* knew it was spring, for already the males were courting, humping up their backs and bobbing their heads, pursuing their prospective brides at a trot over the hot ground. The turtle-doves were heavier and darker, more pompous and dignified, with a distinctive, black ring behind their necks. Very occasionally we'd have a visit from the 'water-bottle bird', the emerald-spotted wood dove, whose bubbling call descended in a soft, stammering cadence like water glugging out of a narrow-mouthed flask. We used to say she was chanting: "Some birds lay one egg, but I lay TWO. Two, two, two-two-two."

There is an easing of the wind, an imperceptible thickening of the air and then abruptly, as if startled from the bowels of the earth by a subterranean explosion, the veld is ablaze with flowers. Not the gentle crocus or the snowdrop, but a riot of brilliant, primitive colours whose clangour beats against the very heavens! Harsh, vital, violent, the Matabele spring is a war-dance of victory in the teeth of overwhelming odds.

Jubilantly, the corky-barked erythrinas lead the revels. Early in August their gnarled and thorny branches produce at their tips mysterious, little bundles of rust-coloured fur. These swell rapidly to burst into barbed spikes of dazzling scarlet, each petal shaped like an Iroquois canoe and hiding at its base a drop of bitter-sweet nectar. We called them lucky-bean trees because of their curious seeds shaped like a sugar-bean, pillar-box red, with an ebony dot at the hilum, giving each seed the appearance of an angry, bloodshot eye with its black pupil at the centre.

The erythrinas are followed in quick succession by the wild cassias and the mukwas, sporting soft clusters of intricate chrome-yellow cups. Then the rain-trees erupt, with drooping bunches of lavender blooms like giant wistaria that almost obscure their dusty, green foliage. They are called rain-trees because of the tiny beetles that excrete drops of foam while feeding off the juicy stems of the flowers.

In the spring the humble dombeyas come into their own. For eleven months of the year they are insignificant, thin, scraggy trees whose tough bark resembles sticks of grey Edinburgh rock, but in August their spindly branches are bowed down under masses of cream and pink blossom whose sugary scent fills the air and draws bees from miles around. On a still afternoon we could *hear* the dombeyas humming and throbbing with insect life. After two weeks the petals turn brown and papery, and rustle stiffly together like a million miniature crinolines.

Down in the vlei behind the dam wall there grew two wild gardenias. Spiny and inhospitable, they stood close together like Tweedledum and Tweedledee. I was always a little in awe of the gardenias for their branches were spangled with dense traps of spiders' webs, and they had an air of sinister isolation that did not encourage familiarity. But even they celebrated spring in their own grim way, producing a frugal crop of enormous wax-white saucers with colossal petals. Their heavy scent flooded the nights like the ghostly fragrance of some evil spectre.

On every rubbish heap, in every ditch the snake-apples were in flower, crude purple stars like those of an outsize egg-plant, whose cousin indeed they are, though their fruits are deadly poisonous. In stony places a species of combretum crept stealthily along the ground, suddenly exploding with startling puffs of flame, their firecracker flowers rapidly developing into large winged pods of a shiny blood-red.

Most striking were the flamboyant trees whose flattened umbrellas of fern-like foliage began to foam with crimson flowers. Each bud was a masterpiece. Shaped like a leathery green grape, it slowly opened, splitting down five regular grooves to reveal an inner lining that was stained scarlet, matching the crumpled petals still folded in its heart. Each night the two flamboyants near my rondavel were invaded by armies of savage scarab beetles who fought desperate battles with one another over the feast of flowers. The trees buzzed and clicked to the noisy warfare of these armour-plated warriors and in the morning the ground beneath the trees would be cayenne-peppered with chewed fragments of the crimson petals.

The richest varieties of colour were provided by the bougainvillaeas. They sprawled over garden walls, swarmed eagerly up poles and trellises and raced across roofs to tumble down in dazzling cascades of brilliance. They ranged from a deep hypnotic purple through wine, ruby, rose and coral to the most delicate peach and amethyst. My favourite was the one that spilled down the edge of the kopje behind my rondavel. When young and soft, its furry spathes had a rich, rusty glow, then as they expanded and matured, they bleached from copper to a dry pinky-gold. This wonderful bush would contain a dozen different shades all at once, a feast of colour against the drab greys and browns of the veld.

Spring was unquestionably the time of year for birds. Every river and spruit was bone-dry, so that our bird-bath was the only water for miles around. Father rigged up a pencil-thin copper pipe with a minute tap at its end that released a steady drip-drip on to the bird rock, day in and day out. Father loved his birds, and we were forbidden under pain of the severest penalties to rob a nest or molest a bird in any way. There was one bird, however, whose mischievous habits used to drive him almost to distraction, and Father was forever calling down on it monstrous curses coupled with threats of extermination — threats, needless to say, which he never carried out. The villain in question was the go-away bird.

The go-away bird gets its name from its call, a strident, sneering exclamation that sounds remarkably like some languid dandy dismissing an unwelcome mendicant: "Go! Go 'way!" They are large, pale-grey birds with long tails and spectacular crests which they use to great purpose when displaying surprise and indignation. They lived off the sweet, round fruits of the wild fig, and what they could steal from our guava and mulberry trees. Their nest was in a dense clump of thorn trees below the kopje, near a deep gravel pit, a part of the plot that we seldom visited. Here they used to lie in ambush, awaiting their opportunity to drive Father mad.

It was Father's custom to come home for lunch each day, a hasty and informal meal, after which he would retire to his rondavel for forty winks. Where many of us suffer from a feeling of heaviness that lingers on for hours if we doze in the afternoon, Father had a cat-like ability to drop asleep for five or ten minutes and awake like a giant refreshed. However, he *did* ask for

relative silence during the few minutes that it took him to fall asleep, and we children knew to keep well away.

The go-away birds had no such scruples. The instant they saw Father toiling up the kopje for his afternoon snooze, they would lurch out of their thorn thicket and come labouring through the air towards the fig-tree. They were desperately ungainly in flight, giving the impression that each floundering wing-beat was their last. They would crash heavily into the leaves uttering soft hiccupping chuckles of delighted anticipation. Once in the tree, these clumsy clowns of the air transformed into a troupe of daring and skilful acrobats. They could run along the branches with the speed of a chicken tearing across the backyard. In addition they were incredibly nimble, leaping vigorously from twig to twig with remarkable poise and agility.

Having taken up their stations in the top of the tree, for a while they would peer down through the branches in perfect silence, raising and lowering their crests excitedly. Father in the meantime, oblivious of the impending doom, would tramp up the last flight of stone steps and disappear into his rondavel. Then carefully, stealthily, the go-aways would begin their descent, hopping down through the tree until they were all perched in the lower branches just outside the bedroom window. Presently one of them would begin.

"Haw," he'd say, opening the bowling. This introductory remark would be greeted by a soft, approving chorus of chucks from the others.

"We-e-h," another would add, a drawling, condescending observation that always drew a heated "Haw-weh. Haw, haw, haw-WEH!" from the rest, and Father would appear at the door, scowling darkly.

"Push off!" he'd roar, throwing up his arms in an angry gesture calculated to send them packing.

Shooting up their crests in amazement, the go-aways would scramble back into the topmost branches, and from there peer down at Father with extravagant cranings of their necks and indignant flickings of their tails, uttering hoarse grunts and burps of defiance. Father would retreat into his rondavel, muttering, and silence would reign for a while. Presently, however, the whole absurd performance would start again.

Every once in a while Father's tolerance would be pushed too far, and driven half-mad by their teasing, he would send them about their business with a well-aimed pebble. Coughing with wrath, they'd flounder back to their thorn thicket, to scold from a safe distance.

While we are on the subject of birds, I feel compelled to take up the cause of a particular little fellow who is almost universally reviled and persecuted. This is the fiscal shrike, usually known as the butcher bird or jackie hangman on account of his sanguinary feeding habits. The jackie has conspicuous black-and-white plumage and a loud grating call which he will utter from some prominent look-out — a telephone pole or a bald twig on the top of a tree. From this vantage-point the butcher bird surveys his territory, head bent downwards in an attitude of fierce attention. Spying his prey — a mouse or a locust — he'll whirr down to the ground and then fly off with it to his 'larder', which may be a thorn bush or a stretch of barbed-wire fence. There he will impale his victim on one of the spikes, and leave it until it is quite dry and hard. Our rough-skinned lemon tree is a favourite pantry for the butcher birds. On one occasion I counted on the thorns one chameleon, two frogs, a lizard, three grasshoppers and the wing of a sparrow. We may piously deprecate jackie hangman's grocery list, but is it in truth any more gruesome than our own? Various people claim that their gardens are devoid of birds because of the jackies. In these cases, I always tend to suspect that a pellet gun is the likelier culprit. We have butcher birds in the garden year in and year out, and there is never any shortage of other species.

5

A Treeful of Owls

OF ALL THE BIRDS with whom I became friendly, the owls were my favourite. Perhaps I was drawn to them because there is something inescapably feline in an owl's appearance — the round, intelligent, forward-looking eyes, their direct stare, their whiskers and pricked ears. Then there was the added attraction of their supposedly supernatural qualities, which enhanced them in my estimation. When I was nine the Sadlers Wells Company came to Bulawayo for the Rhodes Centenary Exhibition, and put on a memorable performance of *Swan Lake*. Naturally I was entranced by the Prince, the swans and the cygnets, but I had never seen a real swan, let alone a prince, and they were alien creatures from the realms of fantasy. Far more real, far more bewitching in my eyes was the owl, the evil magician who came gliding out of the shadows on great, dark wings, driving the swans before him.

It is not only in Western mythology that owls have been associated with demons and enchantment. In Matabeleland, and indeed throughout most of Africa, the owl is regarded with dread — a sinister creature of the night who sits on graves and soaks up the spirits of the departed. Zizi, they call him, and among some tribes such is their abhorrence of the owl that if one of the birds perches on the roof of a hut, the following day the building must be burned to the ground. In South Africa the barn owl is referred to as the *doodvoël* or deathbird, an allusion to the superstition that if a barn-owl screams from the roof-top there

will be a death in the household.

We were on particularly good terms with a resident family of spotted eagle owls. These birds inhabited the kopje at Kaya Pezulu when my grandparents first occupied the land in 1910. It is now seventy years later and the family of owls are still in residence. I often wonder for how many hundreds of years they had been there prior to our arrival. They are the second largest owl in Africa, standing as high as a man's knee. Their aspect is ferocious, with their huge, staring, golden eyes, enormous ear-tufts and short, cruel beaks, but their most dangerous weapons, as I learned to my cost, are their talons which are needle-sharp, very powerful and long enough to transfix a rat.

The eagle owls are most beautifully marked, slightly paler on their bellies than on their backs, but speckled boldly all over in a geometric pattern of cinnamon, amber and bronze like an intricate cashmere shawl. During the day the owls roosted among the branches of Grandmother's silver oak trees, huddled close to the main trunk. In that dappled light they were almost invisible, sitting there quite motionless with eyes closed, their plumage blending perfectly into the coarse, speckled bark of the old trees. If one of us walked by underneath, they would sleepily open one great, yellow eye and stare fixedly until we moved on. If the dogs were with us, that was another matter. Both eyes would fly open, and they'd snap their beaks and utter a weird, whistling screech.

Towards evening they were habitually mobbed by the smaller birds. I never could understand why the birds paid them no attention during the day when the owls were in fact most 'owlish'. Yet, as soon as dusk began to fall, they would congregate in their dozens around each owl — toppies and thrushes, babblers, drongos and weavers, all screaming and dive-bombing the poor owls in the most offensive manner. For a while the owl would pay no attention, hunched moodily on its branch. Little by little, however, as the mobbing of the birds reached fever-pitch, the owl would begin to sit up and stretch, left leg and left wing, and then right leg and right wing, ducking its head and cracking its beak at the boldest birds who dared to dive-bomb too close. Presently the owls would begin to look about and hiss to one another, shrill staccato utterances like the abrupt tearing of a sheet of paper. The smaller birds reacted to this as if their very worst expectations had been realised. Shrieking hysterically, they would tumble out of the silver oaks and scatter like leaves before the wind. In the ensuing silence, one heard the crickets softly tuning up under the sun-warm rocks, and then the owls would begin to call.

"HOO, hu," one would demand in a loud husky voice.

"Hu, *whoop*, hu," another replied quietly.

"Hoo," softly concluded a third, and then as if something had been agreed between them, they would sail out of their trees on great, silent wings and float away into the dusk for the night's hunting.

The eagle owls had a number of favourite perches which they used as look-out posts, places of security where they could eat their dinners undisturbed. One was the very top of the flagstaff on Big Rock, the highest point of the kopje, another was the electricity pole in the middle of our dam, and a third was the cone-shaped, copper cowling over the apex of my rondavel roof. Almost every night I would hear the soft click and screech of their talons gripping the metal, followed by the usual question and answer of the owls calling to one another. They would keep up a desultory conversation throughout the night, their restful remarks succeeded before dawn by the whimpering "Whee, whip-wip-wee" of the nightjar. In the morning I would find a scatter of fresh owl pellets outside my door, fascinating, little bundles containing such treasures as a mouse's skull or a mole's teeth, curved and yellow, neatly wrapped in a coating of matted fur.

Overlooking the field which had formerly been the abode of one of Lobengula's wives, was a sheer granite precipice some thirty feet high which we called the Little Precipice. About half way up this there was a long wide ledge which could not be reached from below, though it was just possible to get down to it from above. Caroline and I used it as a secret retreat and we would sit there, our legs dangling over the edge, hidden away from the rest of the world with the field of grass blowing and bending far below. At one end of this ledge a small duiker-berry bush had obtained a precarious hold on the rock, and under it each spring Mrs. Owl placed her eggs. They were almost completely spherical, the size and colour of old ping-pong balls. Usually there were three to a clutch, but some years there were as many as five and once after a particularly bad drought when the hunting had been poor, she laid only two which she abandoned after a few days. Their shells were paper-thin, and both eggs were quite hollow.

While his wife incubated the eggs, the male used to keep watch from the branches of an umvumila tree that grew a few yards back from the lip of the precipice. Very often the first sign that the owls were nesting would be the male bird suddenly swooping down on us from his tree, snapping his beak and making passes at our heads with his long, hooked claws. Julian's sausage-dog Brutus carried to his grave three, long, deep grooves down his back where the owl had raked him. Brutus was the large, coarse-haired variety of dachshund, a lion-hearted

little dog, unfailingly cheerful and dedicated to the sport of chasing lizards. I never knew him catch one, but he became remarkably clever at scaling the rocks in their pursuit, and would spend hours at the entrance to a crack, groaning with excitement and frustration, cocking his head this way and that as he heard the lizard moving about inside. The owls, however, were quite adamant that Brutus was not to set foot in the vicinity of the Little Precipice during the nesting season, and Brutus reluctantly accepted their ruling, although a number of his favourite lizard haunts were close by.

We knew of a man who lost an eye through an owl attack, and we shared Brutus's deep respect for them at this time of the year. While she was on eggs, the female would sometimes fly off if we peered down at her, but once the owlets hatched, nothing on earth would persuade her to leave the nest, and she would puff herself out, hump her back and produce an alarming fusillade of angry clicks and hisses.

So irresistibly charming were the babies that I used to wait until the mother left the nest at dusk, and then climb down on to the ledge to visit them. To begin with they were small, downy balls of white fluff, adorned with huge golden eyes, and they would sit quite docilely in my hands, wobbling their heads and drooping their absurd, little wings. Before the week was through they would have developed a full range of aggressively defensive measures, the most efficacious being a knack of tossing themselves on to their backs and presenting their talons, drawing blood in a split second from my approaching hand. Thereafter I would leave them alone, though I continued to watch their progress every day. As they grew and matured their baby fluff gradually acquired flecks and speckles until they, like their mother, merged perfectly into the lichen-covered surface of the granite ledge. One day I would find the rock-shelf bare except for a few feathers lying in the empty scrape, and that evening the whole family would be found back in the silver oaks, the young owls shorter than their parents but, in every other respect, perfect replicas.

It was some days after the owlets had left the nest that Vigi, our gardener, told me that there was 'a bird' in the long grass at

the verge of the road. He refused to come with me himself, but he
directed me to the spot from a safe distance. There lying
awkwardly on his side, and glaring up at me from the ground, I
found one of the young owls. As I approached, he clicked his
beak threateningly and floundered away, trying to hop and fly all
at once. His right wing hung loosely and it was plain that during
the night he had been hit by a vehicle. I felt sick with dismay.
Heaven knew, we had few enough cars in our road. How *could*
anyone be so careless?

I went after him and finally he fetched up in a hollow, too
tired to struggle away any further. Here he resorted to his baby
tricks, threw himself on to his back and offered me his talons.
After a few unsuccessful attempts to get past them to hold him
by his body, I decided to let him take me in his claws. Slowly I
advanced my left hand. He struck out with both feet, seizing me
at the junction of hand and wrist, and ten nails drove into my
flesh. Curiously enough, it wasn't particularly painful, and the
device worked like a charm. Evidently feeling that he had now
done everything possible in the circumstances, he meekly
allowed me to slip my other hand round him and tuck him gently
under my arm. How thin and light his body felt under the soft
cloak of feathers! I took him straight up to my room, which was
dark and cool, and patiently persuaded him to relinquish his
cramping grip on my wrist in favour of the back of an upright
chair. There he settled himself comfortably, shook out his long
loose feathers, snapped his beak and let the opaque nictitating
membrane droop tiredly over his eyes. Poor little owl, he must
have been exhausted, sprawled uncomfortably in the grass in the
full dazzle of the sun ever since dawn.

There was no visible break or dislocation of the injured
wing, so we concluded that the bones had been badly bruised
and that what he needed primarily was somewhere quiet to
convalesce. He spent the first week in my room, perched on the
back of the chair above a sheet of newspaper. Within two days
he was tame enough to step on to my wrist like a parrot, and
readily accepted pieces of raw meat, which he tossed into the air
and swallowed whole, closing his eyes with each 'mouthful'. His
grave, spectacled appearance reminded us all so forcefully of

our kindly old G.P., Dr. Burnett, that he was christened Doc by mutual consent.

Although he was feeding well I became anxious that he was not receiving the sort of diet to which his digestion was accustomed. He was still quite unable to fly, however, and we knew it would be a long time before he could rejoin his family. They continued to come hunting every night, and when they sat on my roof and called, Doc became very excited, hooting back to them and producing his strange echoing hiss. It seemed worth finding out whether his parents would feed him, if we left him out on a low branch of the fig-tree. Accordingly we set him out at dusk and watched from a distance to see what his family would do. Shortly before nightfall one of them found him, and soon the whole family were gathered in the branches of the fig above his head. After talking to him for a while, they began taking it in turns to come sweeping past him on the wing, swerving off and sailing away over the veld in a heartbreakingly eloquent entreaty for him to fly away — the one thing which Doc could *not* do. Presently the sight of his brothers and parents sailing by on soft wings was too much for him, and he valiantly launched himself off his branch, only to crash awkwardly on to his side among the rocks. It was clear that he was only going to hurt himself further. Reluctantly and with a heavy heart I took him back to my room.

The following morning I set him out on the branch once more, thinking that he might prefer to spend his days in the open, with the sounds and the sights which he knew all around him. Here, too, I encountered a problem. The small garden birds, who never mobbed the owls except in the evenings, made Doc's life a misery. It was as if they knew that he was hurt and couldn't retaliate. They tormented him without mercy, almost knocking him off his perch with the force of their attacks.

At this juncture Father stepped in and helped. He built Doc a spacious, open-air, roosting box in which he could sleep during the day. The front was partly gauzed over to discourage the small birds, and fixed in position were two robust perches made of natural twisting branches, complete with bark and lichen. Doc's claws curled round them comfortably and there was ample room for him to potter about and stretch his wings. We stood his 'bedroom' outside under the trees, and he appeared to like it in there, sitting with his face to the wall, dozing hour after hour. As the afternoon mellowed and the light became less intense, Doc turned round on his perch and began looking about, bobbling his head and shuffling his feathers. Then I would lift him out, put him on my shoulder, and the two of us would walk about in the bush until it was dark and I had to come in for dinner. I hoped in this way to keep him in touch — albeit tenuously — with his own environment.

When I went to bed, he returned with me to my rondavel, to take up his old position on the back of the chair. There he would have his dinner and sit contentedly preening his feathers with his short, black beak, or contemplatively scratching his head with one long claw. I loved to watch him yawn. His wings would droop, he would close his eyes, and his beak would open back and back until it seemed it must crack in two. Suddenly it would snap shut with a click, he would jerk upright, shake out all his feathers, sneeze, and stare about with stern defiance as if daring anyone to laugh.

To begin with, Jezebel had regarded Doc's presence in my room with a glowering mistrust. This was *her* territory and she deeply resented his intrusion. Doc, however, paid absolutely no attention to all her mutterings and face-pullings, contenting himself with cracking his beak like a whip-lash if she prowled too close. This was enough and Jezebel would stalk away, ears back, tail whisking angrily, to sit on the end of my bed and scowl, composing Oriental curses against him.

Little by little, Doc's wing improved. He was able to parachute from the chair down on to the floor without crash-landing. And then, better still, he managed to hop back up again, first on to the seat and then on to the rail. Soon he was making comparatively long flights across the room from his chair to the windowsill, and it seemed that the time had come to leave him out at night once more. As it turned out, this decision was a little premature and nearly cost Doc his life. That evening when the other owls found him, he joyfully took to the air, and I watched in delight to see him soar off over the dam wall, a dim, grey shape against the darkening bush. Next morning he was nowhere to be found, and I was distressed to observe that only two young owls were roosting with their parents in the silver oaks.

A search was mounted and Doc was finally found, cold and wet, in the long, dew-drenched, assegai grass near the well. He was completely exhausted, too tired even to grip his perch. I made a nest for him out of a hot-water bottle and a towel, and gradually he perked up and began to revive. This adventure set him back somewhat, but by the end of the week he seemed completely restored, so I put him out in the tree once more. On the following two mornings he was still there, very hungry and glad of some meat, and it looked as though he was getting the measure of his own strength. And then on the third day he was gone!

Fearing the worst, I searched the grass in the vlei and then the dam wall and the kopje, and finally in desperation I counted the owls in the silver oaks. There sat mother and father, and around them at varying distances — were *three* young! *Doc had made it*!

I was wildly excited, and tried to make certain which of the youngsters was Doc, but they all looked exactly alike, each slowly blinking its golden eyes and regarding me with grave courtesy. I hooted, I imitated the snapping of his beak, I talked to them each in turn, trying to elicit some response, some sign of recognition. I thought I could detect a slight irregularity in the way one of them held its wing, but it was difficult to be certain. At last I gave up and trailed away home, my delight that he was safe tinged with sadness. Despite the loving care I had lavished on him, it was plain that I meant less to him than his own family. It was a hard lesson, but one that was not lost on me in later years. All the human love in the world is no match for a wild creature's love for freedom.

6

Wheels

FATHER HAD THREE enduring passions in life — motor cars, cricket and wild-life photography, in ascending order of preference. As to motor cars, it was always a source of sorrow to me that I had been born in the age of the internal combustion engine, and I would have given my eye-teeth for a pony or a donkey. Father, however, who had been brought up among saddles and stables and harness, welcomed the arrival of motorised vehicles with joy, and flatly refused to have anything further to do with equitation. His father who had come to Matabeleland from Kimberley with a team of mules and a wagon heartily endorsed this view. I believe that Father's appreciation of motor cars went back to 1911 when Bulawayo held its first motorised gymkhana. Father, then aged twelve, won the Open Reversing Event in a spanking new Model T Ford.

They were robust, well-made vehicles, those early Fords and Chevs, with good, high clearance that was admirably suited to what we fondly called our 'roads'. In many instances these roads would have been more appropriately termed 'dongas' or 'excavations', or 'abandoned water-courses'. Then of course there was the dreaded dry-climate phenomenon — corrugations. These are rippled ridges of sand running across the road at right angles. Under one's bare feet they feel soft and powdery, but drive over the same corrugations in a motor vehicle, and they'll shake the fillings out of your teeth. Father, who was addicted to the use of hyperbole, used to claim that some years the corrugations were so bad that when a donkey lay down in them only its ears stuck up.

Mr. Hammond, the celebrated headmaster of Plumtree School, had a farm some miles out of the village, to which he and the family could retire for occasional week-ends. He bought Plumtree's first motor car, once again the trusty Model T. Prior to this, when the family visited the farm, they had to inspan four mules and would jolt slowly along in a sturdy, high-wheeled buggy. There was great excitement, therefore, the first time they prepared to make the journey by car. There were seven in the Hammond family — Mr. and Mrs. Hammond, four sons and a daughter, so the car was pretty well loaded down. Everything went beautifully, and they bowled along merry as a wedding-bell until they reached the drift across the Makwa River. Naturally there was no water in the river — there almost never is water in a river in that part of Matabeleland — but the banks were steep and the river bed itself was full of heavy sand. The car negotiated the downward slope without mishap, got through the sand with commendable ease, but floundered while making the ascent of the far bank. Mr. Hammond let the vehicle roll down again into the river bed, and once more charged the incline. A second time the engine stalled. After the fifth or sixth attempt, they were forced to concede that they were truly stuck. The four boys strained and pushed at it, but the bank was too steep and the car far too heavy. Despite all their efforts, there was nothing they could do to persuade the wretched, tin Judas to get them out of the river bed. At that point each and every one of them would gladly have traded in the glittering, new car for the old, mule buggy.

Finally two of the boys were dispatched on foot to the nearest farm to borrow a team of oxen. They returned later in the day with four bullocks which were roped to the car and successfully hauled them out of the river. Thereafter the kindly farmer arranged with Mr. Hammond to have the bullocks and a herd-boy on hand at the Makwa drift whenever the Hammonds wished to spend a week-end on the farm.

This arrangement had been in practice for some months when Mr. Hammond made an interesting discovery about the petrol supply of his Model T Ford. The petrol tank was situated in an elevated position high up behind the back seat. Contemplating this, Mr. Hammond had suddenly been struck by the significance of the term 'gravity feed'. So convinced was he that he had put his finger on the difficulty at the Makwa drift, that next time they were preparing to visit the farm, he omitted to put in a request for the bullocks.

He and his unsuspecting family reached the river as usual, but this time he stopped just before it, turned the car, and to their bewilderment he reversed over the bank and into the river. Then while they clutched on in startled amazement, he proceeded to roar backwards up and over the far bank, laughing and triumphant. The 'gravity feed' problem had been solved, and from that day they were able to dispense with the services of the four bullocks!

Next to motor cars, Father adored cricket, and above cricket he loved photography. He was stringently selective in his choice of subject-matter, however, and nothing was more likely to provoke his scorn and derision than what he called 'home movies'. He would spend hours, sometimes days or even weeks,

to get one photograph of a particular bird. But ask him to take a
thirty second snap of a family group and he would explode. It
maddened him to see people posing for photographs, and he was
on occasions downright rude to well-meaning friends who would
beg him to take some photographs at their daughter's wedding.
"Photograph *people*? Never!"
Such a request would leave him in a bad mood for hours, and
he'd prowl about in his workshop-cum-darkroom, muttering and
grinding his teeth and banging his huge, enamel, developing
trays.

Father's cameras were his pride and joy. They always
travelled in the best seats in the car, and they received more
careful attention than anyone in the family, apart from Mother.
For each camera, each lens, he painstakingly made a felt-lined,
fitted case which travelled packed in its own canvas bag. His
greatest enemy was dust, and so in addition to the cases of
cameras, there was a separate one which contained nothing but
an impressive array of dust-defeaters — lens caps, hoods, filters
and camel-hair brushes. His photographic stable contained a
16 mm Bell & Howell cine-camera, and three Leicas — one
loaded with colour and two with black-and-white. Then there
was a formidable battery of lenses, culminating in a huge
40 cm telephoto that looked like a bazooka. When we went on a

trip, the car became his mobile studio. Its interior bristled with an assortment of brackets and clamps so that none of the equipment could rattle loose over the rough roads. He converted the driver's door into a camera-stand so that he could 'shoot' from behind the wheel. It had a screw-in turret that would receive any one of the cameras, or the heavy hydraulic head which he used when making a long, sweeping shot of a moving animal, or a long range of mountains.

Father took a passionate delight in his equipment, but I believe that what really attracted him to big game photography was the fact that it got him into the bush. There is a magic, a poignancy, a sense of excitement about the bush that is not only gripping, it is addictive. Once bitten by the 'bush bug' a person is infected for life. Father had the disease in its severest form, and naturally passed it on to his children. Bush fever is a kind of madness that compels you to return and return — a longing which will seize you by the throat until you could gladly sell your soul for the sight of a dry thorn tree against an empty sky, a herd of wildebeest wheeling under their cloud of dust, or the deep rasping "augh!" of a lion prowling in the night. The veld has a scent all of its own too, a combination of dust and dung and sunshine, a heady fragrance that fills the lungs and intoxicates the blood like strong wine.

In spring the call of the bush exerted its most powerful magic on Father. Although we lived on the outskirts of Bulawayo and didn't come into daily contact with big game, their presence could be felt none the less, lurking like spectres just beyond our reach. Occasionally there would be a tantalising report from a neighbouring farmer who had been forced to drive a hippo out of his mealie field, or the owner of a small, domestic dam would excitedly summon the police to help him remove a crocodile. Once in a while we would hear how a lion's pugs had been found near a cattle kraal. These fragments of news always acted on Father like a goad. For a day or two he would fret and fume, torn between the anxiety of leaving his business and the tormenting desire to get away. Then one evening the cameras would appear lined up under the angle-poise lamp on his work-bench, and we'd smile at one another in perfect understanding and contentment. Another trip was in the air!

A curious feature of most of the world's great travellers and explorers is the insignificance of their ultimate goal. Stanley, for example, set out ostensibly to find the source of the Nile, but this achievement was negligible in comparison with his other discoveries. Ulysses' destination was the island of Ithaca, yet his most memorable adventures took place elsewhere. Jason, the Crusaders, Marco Polo, Thor Heyerdahl — each and every one of them is an embodiment of the worthy text: 'Enjoy the road, for all is lost to those who hurry on to journey's end.'

Father carried this philosophy as far as it would go, even a little further sometimes. It wouldn't do to set out for one of Africa's great game reserves just on the offchance of picking up a good shot or two. One had to have a specific purpose, a definite goal to add stature and direction to the enterprise. He might decide, for example, that he needed to complete his sequence of the giraffe's mating display, or he'd discover that he hadn't a single exposure of the rare red lechwe. Once, while pondering over his collection of colour transparencies, he observed that he had only half as many slides of birds as he had of animals, so we resolutely set our faces against big game, and disappeared into the trackless wilds of the Chobe swamps for an ornithological orgy.

Perhaps the best part of travel in Africa in those days was the fact that the monster called Tourism had not yet been born. Far from tourism being promoted, the opposite was the case, and vigorous attempts were made by outlying farmers and far-flung rural authorities to discourage the careless and improvident traveller from venturing too far. We would travel completely self-contained with everything from sleeping-bags to food and cooking utensils. Father had purchased the crumpled fuselage of an old Spitfire after the war, stripped out its fuel tanks and clamped them to the roof of the car, where they were used to hold auxiliary supplies of water and petrol. There was only one thing which he refused to take on a journey into the bush and that was a firearm. The guns stayed at home along with the kitchen sink.

Over the years we travelled from the Kalahari to Katanga, from the Amatongas forests of Mozambique to the Mountains of the Moon. True, I missed a great deal of school, but I gladly did without any number of hours in front of a blackboard! In all the months I *did* spend at school, I never found anything to match the sight of a herd of elephant emerging from the trees like grey ghosts, to drink at a quiet waterhole.

7

Lion Country!

Rising UP FROM the steamy coastal plains of Mozambique, Gorongoza Massif looms over a wilderness of unrivalled beauty. Probably the most scenic game reserve in all Africa, Gorongoza takes in the mountain's southern flanks, spreading eastwards towards the sea and embracing the lazy coils of the brown Urema River. It is a paradise for birds, with belts of dense palm-forest broken by wide green plains of short grass. Waterbuck, zebra and wildebeest throng the open country, while on the banks of the river, hippo stand drowsing in the sun like shiny, black boulders. The biggest croc I ever saw was on the Urema River, a huge grey-and-mustard monster who stood as high as a sports car, waddling ponderously into the water with the slow, rolling gait of some unimaginable leviathan. The original rest-camp had been abandoned after it was flooded in a year of exceptionally heavy rain. A pride of lions now used it as their headquarters, and it was quite usual to find eight or ten of them at home, lounging at their ease on the observation deck or dozing contentedly in the doorways of the chalets, paws and chins hanging over the doorsteps. The palm-forest, too, teemed with elephant, buffalo and impala — in fact the only animals which one couldn't find in Gorongoza were the true savannah species like rhino and giraffe. It was too wet for them.

The truth was that Gorongoza was too wet for people as well. The wealthy enthusiast could reach the main camp by light aircraft, but for us there was no alternative but to get there by

road over the treacherous Pungwe Flats where in the wet season the 'road' resembled something between a slime-pit and a ploughed field. The best part of arriving in Gorongoza was the prospect of a hot bath to loosen off the huge scabs of caked mud that covered our limbs after pushing the car time and again. The Pungwe River itself had to be crossed by pontoon, a rickety contraption that consisted of several forty-four-gallon drums lashed together with planks and ropes. A team of brawny men hauled it over the river by means of a steel hawser, but it was hideously unstable and if too many people stood on one side, the whole pontoon tipped up. Father once jokingly enquired of them how many vehicles had gone to the bottom of the river in that way.

"Only two," came the proud reply.

One spring we had settled in at Gorongoza for a fortnight's 'shoot' when the rains made a premature arrival. Not just rain in the general sense of the word, but a vehement, passionate outpouring from the heavens, a continuous drumming of warm water on to the land, flooding the Urema Flats and rendering every road and track completely impassable.

If we were disappointed, our loss was negligible by comparison with the plight of a vast team of cameramen and special-effects pundits who had flown out from Hollywood for filming on location. Maddeningly, the skies would lift just as the sun was setting and the light was too poor to 'shoot' the long skeins of birds that streamed upriver to their roosts. The Producer, a tall loose-limbed man with a thin, wide mouth like a lizard's and the most enormous feet, was almost out of his mind. He couldn't bear to look at them.

"I'm jest gonna close my eyes," he groaned, clapping a long hand over his face.

Father and the cameramen consoled one another round the camp fire at night, swopping yarns and inspecting one another's equipment. Under the open-sided dining-shelter the Producer and his team sprawled in their canvas chairs, morosely slapping at mosquitoes and comforting themselves with draughts of cool Portuguese beer.

"Aw, *dern* it all," the Producer burst out again, turning to Father. "It's not only filming-time we're losing. I've brought out seven crates of sound equipment to make live recordings of animal noises. The only recordings we can get here are these bleeding mosquitoes. We coulda got the whole sequence in the Everglades!" He landed himself a heavy crack on the back of his neck, bringing away a hand splashed copiously with his own blood and one squashed mosquito.

"Animal noises?" Father enquired.

"Yeah, lions roaring, wild birds screaming, elephants trumpeting — the authentic sounds of Africa."

Father looked thoughtful.

"Wait a minute," he said. "I think Rodrigues might be able to help you."

He returned presently with the Chief Warden, a brown giant of a man with a thick crop of implacable, black hair combed straight back from his forehead. I liked Rodrigues. Although his command of English was slight, he had a mobile, humorous face and a deep, contented laugh.

"So, animal noises, eh?" he enquired, his black eyes twinkling.

"Yeah." The Producer nodded heavily, and stifled a yawn. Unable to get on with his film, he was finding that time hung heavily on his hands, and the main camp at Gorongoza had little to offer in the way of night-life.

Rodrigues drew up a chair and sat down. He cleared his throat once or twice, and then without any warning he emitted a prolonged, shuddering scream. It had all the nail-tingling quality of a piece of heavy furniture being dragged across a cement floor. The members of the Hollywood team who a moment before had been lying bonelessly in their chairs, leaped convulsively to their feet. To make matters worse, a startled gecko dropped from the ceiling on to the Producer's bare arm. He let out a roar of fright, and plunged about knocking over his drink and treading on a brand-new pack of Havanas.

"Jumpin' Jehosophat!" he yelled. "What's that?"

"*Elefantes*," Rodrigues smilingly explained. "Now I make for you the hippo, yes?" He filled his lungs and began to grunt deep down in his barrel chest.

"Be-e-h, beh-beh, mm, m, m."

It was a hippo to perfection! Then before an astonished audience, Rodrigues went on to imitate all the noises of the veld which he knew so well. I wouldn't have believed that the human voice was capable of producing such a wide range of brays, grunts, squeaks, whistles and clicks. In response to an urgent signal from the Producer, the sound effects men sprang into action. Microphones and amplifiers appeared as if by magic, and Rodrigues continued his concert while the great wheels of Hollywood's tape-recorders spun silently under the stars. I sat entranced, for Rodrigues was a natural and gifted mimic whose repertoire included everything from the shrill tinkle of a tree-frog to the hoarse coughing of a lion, from the warning snort of a buffalo to the lunatic yodel of a zebra stallion challenging his rival.

After a while Rodrigues paused and mopped his sweating face. It was thirsty work. Eagerly the Hollywood team plied him with beer and exhorted him to further efforts. Red-faced and laughing, Rodrigues then launched himself into the kingdom of birdsong, reproducing with meticulous perfection the mournful mew of a kite, the grating rattle of a guinea-fowl and the haunting, liquid notes of the chorister robin. The Producer was beside himself with delight, and with just reason, for these were recordings of animal sounds which the average man would never hear.

Now, whenever I hear a sound-track that includes animal cries in the background, I am transported back to that hot, steamy night at Gorongoza when Rodrigues presented the film world with their library of 'noises off'.

Born and reared in a little town like Bulawayo, we children were very isolated from the rest of the world, very naïve and gullible. There was no television, of course, and Father disapproved of the cinema. Rare exceptions were made in favour of such epics as *War and Peace* or *The Ascent of Everest*, and very occasionally we were permitted to see a Western. The result of this was that anyone who spoke with an American accent immediately identified in my limited experience with a character from the Wild West. As far as I could judge, every U.S. citizen was a big-tough-cow-punchin'-tobacco-chewin'-gun-slingin'-hero who wore a ten-gallon hat and stood seven feet tall in his ridin' boots and spurs.

It had come as something of a shock to discover that not a single member of the Hollywood team wore spurs, let alone chaps. I clung to my convictions, however, and hastily found an excuse for them. They, after all, belonged to the artificial world of the movies, and were in no way typical of the man in the street. Thus reassured, I was able to preserve intact my image of the American Man. Regrettably for my illusions, we had no sooner left Gorongoza than we came upon another party of Americans, an encounter that left me saddened by the definite knowledge that they had feet of clay, in every sense of the word.

The rains had continued unremittingly and Rodrigues warned us that unless we moved out within the next few days, the Pungwe River would come down in flood and we would be cut off. The main road now beggared description. Its entire surface had been churned into a deep, heavy slush that dragged at the car's belly. Fresh falls of rain had added a slippery gloss to the already slimy texture of the road, and there were huge pools and troughs of brown water lying everywhere.

We lurched and skidded and slithered along, mud flying from the wheels, mud splashing up on to the bodywork and the windows, the headlights completely obliterated, our field of vision limited to the two triangular smears made by the windscreen wipers. After some miles of this, a mysterious object came into view on the road before us. Seen, as it were, through a glass darkly, it might have been anything from an elephant to a Sherman tank. Father pulled up to a cautious halt, taking advantage of a relatively firm patch in the road. The object in our path now manifested itself as a small truck with a covered back, tilted over on one side and so deeply embedded in the mud that none of its wheels were visible. It appeared to be deserted, but while we were still discussing the prospects of squeezing past it, a large piece of mud detached itself from the rear of the vehicle and started to move towards us. It appeared to be a huge, chocolate monster with two, curious white discs set into its

upper reaches.

"What is it?" I whispered, half afraid.

"It's a spider," Charles said positively. "A giant tarantula!"

"Nonsense," scoffed John. "It's a gorilla. Look at its legs."

Fascinated, we gaped through the windows in speechless wonder as the apparition drew near and finally came to rest beside the driver's door. I observed a pair of blue eyes gazing wanly out of the white discs, which I could now identify as a pair of spectacles. Could this brown and glistening object be human? To be sure, I could just make out that it had arms, legs, even hair, but the entire figure had been generously and systematically spray-painted with a ground wash of thin mud, and then embellished further with irregular clods and lumps so that the camouflage was complete. The only visible skin was that behind the spectacles. Even the clothes — what had once been a pair of longs and a singlet — were plastered to the body and indistinguishable texturally from the skin. Unless a person had been actually rolling and wallowing deliberately, it was hard to imagine how he could have got into that condition. He was obviously some kind of a comedian, and with one accord we broke into relieved shouts of laughter.

No answering smile, however, flickered under the mud-caked surface of the poor wretch's face. He simply stood there in a puddle, drooping sadly, his thin arms hanging dejectedly at his side, his skinny chest heaving with unspoken feelings. Father finally got his voice under control.

"What on earth are you doing?" he asked.

It was a moment before the person found the strength to reply. "I've been pushing our truck," he said. His voice, faint and thin with fatigue, bore the unmistakable twang of an American accent.

"What, all on your own?" Father was incredulous.

"Yes."

"How long have you been here?"

Again he took a while to gather his thoughts.

"Couple of hours," he whispered. "You're the first car that's stopped."

We could see now that he was a young man, probably not more than twenty-three or twenty-four. Clearly he was anything but robust, and it was obvious too that he was in the last stages of exhaustion. Anything less like the swashbuckling figure of the Desert Ranger was hard to conceive. I was stupefied. Father voiced all our suspicions:

"Are you part of the Hollywood team?" he enquired.

"Hollywood?" The blue eyes looked mildly outraged. "No, *sir*. I'm a missionary."

"A *missionary*? Great Scott!" Father goggled at him for a moment, and then recovering himself, he climbed out of the car, and introduced himself. We followed suit, filled with solicitous curiosity at his plight. He told us his name was Tudor and he came from Pennsylvania.

We squelched forward through the mud on foot to size up

his chances of getting out. The truck was about as badly stuck as it could be. Even the tailboard was partially submerged. Father made a quick circuit of the vehicle to assess the situation and came back looking puzzled.

"I thought you were alone," he said. "The whole cab is full of people!"

"Yeah," Tudor agreed, "but none of them are real able-bodied."

"You surely weren't trying to push, were you, with all that lot sitting inside?"

"Sure," Tudor admitted listlessly. "What else could I do?"

As for getting the truck to budge, Tudor might as well have been pushing at the Rock of Gibraltar. A new suspicion dawned on Father.

"What about your kit?" he asked. "Have you unloaded all the stuff in the back?"

Mutely Tudor shook his head, and opened the rear doors to reveal the interior crammed to the roof with crates and luggage of every description and, crowning it all, an enormous red-and-white Coca-Cola ice box.

Father's face darkened, and he went round to the driver's window once more. What he said to the inmates I don't know, but presently an apparently never-ending stream of Tudor's relations began to emerge from the truck, each one stouter and more indignant than the last. They turned out to be Tudor's parents-in-law, his wife and a cluster of small children. The father-in-law was inclined to be loud-mouthed and bossy, evidently the leader of the expedition, and it had been on his instructions that Tudor had been compelled to strain and heave in the mud, getting sprayed from head to foot by the liquid slush that flew up from the spinning rear wheels, while the rest of them sat comfortably in the cab.

Father sent them all off into the bush to collect brushwood and branches, while he and Tudor unloaded the back of the truck, and the rest of us got down on our bellies and began scooping away the mud from the wheels. It was filthy work, but not altogether disagreeable. At the end of several hours we had managed to get all four wheels on to a mat of sticks and branches and had prepared a corduroy of poles in the mud to give the truck something to bite on. It was time to see if we could get her out.

Tudor's father-in-law resumed his place behind the steering wheel. The truck's engine revved into life, and we all clustered round its bodywork like ants attacking a beetle.

"All ready?" Father called. "Let's go, gradually now, easy . . ." While we strained and slithered, the truck slowly began to move, throwing up heavy gouts of mud and chunks of wood, painfully hauling itself out of the hole like a wounded buffalo. Then, with a sudden surge of power, its feet found *terra firma*, and we all ran after it whistling and waving and shouting. There were smiles then, and laughter and handshakes all round. Even Tudor had regained a certain spring to his stride.

We travelled behind them just in case they became bogged down again, but all went well and we waved goodbye when they finally hit the main, tarred road to Beira. I had found the whole affair most interesting and educational, a widening of the horizons in the field of human endeavour. Tudor may not have enjoyed the physique or the glamour of the Lone Star Ranger, but he certainly deserved full marks for trying!

If Tudor was the quiet, modest, self-effacing American, his counterpart was the extraordinary woman we encountered on the Zambezi. Father was particularly anxious to procure some close-ups of monkeys' faces, and he was advised by the Game Warden at Victoria Falls that the very best opportunity for this existed on Kandahar Island where a troupe of vervet monkeys had become a favourite tourist attraction.

"If you can put up with the tourists," he said, "you should get some good shots."

The following day we accordingly presented ourselves at a point upriver from the Falls from where the launch set out for Kandahar Island.

At that time Victoria Falls was just beginning to boom as a tourist centre, drawing adventurous globe-trotters from all over the world, and the launch-trip up the river was a favourite attraction. The river there was very wide, running strongly between a succession of cigar-shaped islands, each wearing a longitudinal fringe of the tall ilala palms, as scrupulously erect as a line of soldiers at a military parade. Their lofty crowns of fan-shaped leaves clattered gently in the wind, like a row of giant feather-dusters sweeping the sky. In silhouette the humped outlines of the islands resembled a school of swimming dinosaurs, their spines decorated with the dorsal serrations of the palms.

All along that stretch of the river, the banks were fringed with glittering, emerald fountains of the phoenix palms that leaned languidly out over the water, trailing their fronds in the river like long, limp fingers. There was something breathtaking in all that verdure, particularly as a few steps away from the river, the bush was as dry and stony and desiccated as any other waterless tract of Matabeleland. The mighty river and its generous abundance of water was like a promise from heaven, a living token of a fuller, richer existence which was not within our experience.

The launch was relatively small with wooden-slat benches and a green, canvas awning, the engine spluttering feebly to itself as the gaily dressed knot of tourists tripped across the gang-plank and took their seats. Above the mutter of the engine, one could hear in the distance the dull roar of the Victoria Falls where it plunged over the lip, only a few hundred yards down the river. We could see not far off the great, white cloud of spray hanging in the air like smoke from a bush fire. Even here the river had an undercurrent of urgency, a sense of secret excitement, as if it knew what lay ahead.

"What if the engine fails?" someone called out. A few people laughed, but the thought must have been in all our minds. The boatman was a tall, athletic-looking fellow with red hair and freckles, and a cynical smile. He now grinned wolfishly, cast off the mooring lines and let the launch drift out sideways into the river. I felt the current pull us round, tugging eagerly at the craft as if urging us to participate in its thunderous plunge 300 feet into the gorge. The tourists fidgeted uneasily, glancing apprehensively at the boatman who continued to tinker unconcernedly with the engine. I was privately measuring up my chances of trying to swim for the bank when he appeared to find the throttle, the engine coughed importantly, the propellers bit into the water and the prow of the launch swung round slowly and began to nose up-river. In a few moments the boat-house and the jetty disappeared behind a curve of the river and we were alone on the water, the banks slipping by, thick and tangled and primeval. It was serenely beautiful and wild, the great river rippling by like blue satin, while here and there the riverine vegetation was cut by a narrow hippo path that tunnelled through the undergrowth. One had the sensation — indeed the conviction — that the river was exactly as it had been when Livingstone first approached the Falls in his dug-out canoe.

The only discordant note was struck by a harsh-voiced woman with an American accent who kept up a tiresome monologue about her experiences when navigating rivers in Malaya and Brazil. I, who had ended up sitting next to her, found myself hypnotised, stupefied by her forceful torrent of words. Her voice had the strident, penetrating quality of a buzz-saw, with a grating edge to it that almost hurt the ears. Her presence was overpowering, for she was colourfully arrayed in a red-and-black polka-dot suit with matching head-scarf, and a fascinating pair of sun-glasses with black-and-white chequered frames that were pointed at both ends like a cat's eyes. Both her arms were lavishly adorned with bracelets and bangles of wood and brass and ivory. As she accompanied her every remark with wide, sweeping gestures, she clattered and tinkled and rang like a timpanist, while I cringed back in my seat, afraid of being swept off into the river by an imperious arm. Under the blast of her voice all conversation dwindled and died and soon she had the entire launch in a mesmeric coma, addressing us all like a public meeting.

After a while I noticed that the boatman's legs were beginning to twitch irritably, and presently he cleared his throat noisily as if wanting to say something.

"The Zambezi River," he began, but his words were rapidly drowned in an avalanche of recollections about Bangkok. He drew a deep breath, raised his voice and continued ". . . is the largest river in Africa south of the equator. It was at this point that Livingstone . . ."

She gave a derisive hoot. "You call this a river? Say, where I come from we could fix a little leak like this in two minutes!"

The boatman subsided into a smouldering silence while a few of the other tourists were sufficiently roused to glare at her in an annoyed fashion. She, however, having vanquished the opposition, continued her triumphant monologue with the devastating efficiency of a jack-hammer. The boatman stared ahead resignedly, his cold, green eyes narrowed against the glitter of the water. As the launch negotiated another bend in the river, he suddenly straightened and looked alert. His hand moved quickly to cut the engines, and he took advantage of the sudden lowering of the noise level to bawl out: "If you'll look carefully in the stretch of water ahead of us, you will see a small herd of male hippo."

We all craned our necks excitedly and, sure enough, some thirty yards away, the tranquil expanse of the river was interrupted by a cluster of smooth, grey lumps like shiny boulders. We eased a

little nearer and soon made out the enchanting faces of the animals with their wide, bristly muzzles, mild protuberant eyes and neat pink ears which they flicked back and forth at our approach. Only their faces were visible, floating on the surface and watching us with gentle interest. The question that was hovering unasked on all our lips was immediately voiced by my companion.

"Say, can you tell me," she began in tones of dreadful scorn, "how you are able to tell that those are male hippos?"

The boatman turned his green eyes towards her nonchalantly. "You can tell they are male hippo," he replied with studied emphasis, "you can tell they are *male* hippo, because they all have their mouths shut."

Surprisingly enough, the unified shout of laughter that greeted this observation was enough to deflate her completely, and she lapsed into an injured silence for the remainder of the journey. The rest of us, however, were intensely thankful to the boatman for releasing us from her thrall.

8

In the Presence of the King

IT IS A SWELTERING, hot day. The horizon is dancing in a curtain of heat-haze and the veld all around us rings to the shrill cries of the cicadas. The two lions are only just visible where they are lying flat on their sides in the short, coppery grass. I can just make out the smooth outline of a shoulder and now and then the flick of a tasselled tail. They seem to have the drugged sleepiness of a pair of huge, well-fed dogs, basking in front of a hot fire. Inside the car the temperature is well over a hundred, but we sit in absolute silence, waiting, waiting,

waiting . . . Near by on the ground a yellow-billed hornbill is dissecting a pile of elephant dung, lifting out the grubs and dung-beetles with delicate precision. Father watches him for a moment, then slowly, stealthily changes the lens on his camera, and turns it on to the hornbill. Many of Father's most spectacular photographs came about in this way, accidentally almost, when reluctant to abandon the pride, yet maddened by the lions' indolence, we would be rewarded with a charming performance by one of Nature's lesser players.

Frequently at the beginning of a trip, Father used to make a firm policy statement: "This time," he'd announce, "we are *not* going to be distracted by lions, do you all understand that?" The three of us would nod obediently. No lions.

"No lions," he'd repeat in a trenchant tone. "We've wasted enough time on them already."

Yet, somehow or other, here we are again, meekly gathered at the door of the King's chamber along with the vultures and the hyenas, waiting like courtiers in slavish attention upon his Royal Presence.

Just as each person has a favourite fruit and a favourite colour, so everyone who has lived in the bush selects a wild animal which he loves above all the rest. I claim no originality of outlook, no unusual preference for the lesser-known and the neglected. It's the lion, every time. My preference, however, needs to be seen in the light of one who is prepared to worship any cat, from the scrawniest alley-cat upwards. He is at once a wanton voluptuary, abandoning himself completely to the sensual pleasure of a sun-bath, and a mighty powerhouse of phenomenal intelligence, skill and ferocity, who at the flip of a coin will be on his feet and streaking across the veld to make a kill. When we were with the lions, we were in the grip of a sensation that anything could happen at any time, and it frequently did! The difficulty and the challenge lay in having the camera ready to shoot when the action began.

One of the foremost authorities on lions was a Game Ranger called Len Vaughan, whom we first met at Kafue Game Reserve. He was a tall, stringy, twinkling-eyed man with a voice like a rasp-file and a predilection for practical jokes. For some years Len was stationed at Robins Camp at Wankie where he had ample opportunity of widening his knowledge of lions, and it was said of Len that what he didn't know about them, probably wasn't worth knowing. On one occasion Father was grumbling to Len about the fact that although he had reels of film of lions in various attitudes, nearly all of them appeared sleepy and contented.

"I need a shot with action," Father told him, "an angry lion. How would you advise me to set about it?"

"An angry lion, h'm?" Len smiled. "Tell you what, next time you find a couple of sleepy lions, let me know. I think I could help you."

Later that day we happened upon a splendid pair of lions, dozing on an anthill in attitudes of total repose. One of them slowly opened an eye to peer at us and closed it again, while the other barely twitched his ears. Father sat slumped in his seat, regarding them with disgust. "Waste of film," he growled, having taken one or two reluctant exposures. "Who wants to see a picture of a pair of lazy brutes like that? Let's go and fetch Len Vaughan, and see what he can do."

Len returned with us to the lions, riding in high, good humour on the front seat beside Father. There was about him the air of pleased anticipation of a man about to enjoy a good joke. The lions were just as we had left them, bored and soporific. Len said: "Set up your camera. Decide which lion you're interested in and get yourself focused on him."

Father set to work. He was after a good one this time. He was using his longest lens, so that the lion's head filled the frame. Every whisker looked as big as a stalk of assegai grass, and he could almost count the fleas in the lion's beard.

"You ready?" Len asked.

"Ready. What are you going to do?"

Len chuckled. "I'm going to tickle them up for you."

Len opened the door of the car and climbed out softly, while Father fixed his eye to the view-finder and poised his right index finger over the button. Slowly Len approached the front of the car, and stood there a moment, smiling into his moustache. The lions dozed on, watching him with slitted eyes. Suddenly Len stooped and picked up a stone and both lions exploded into the air, roaring! I had a vivid impression of both great beasts airborne at once, their tails straight out behind them like broomsticks, and then Len was back in the car, sitting composedly in the front seat and smiling about at us in delighted interest. "Did you get your picture?" he asked.

Father said — but perhaps on second thoughts it might be better not to repeat what he said, but he insisted on having a cigarette before attempting to drive back to camp. Len Vaughan was still chuckling about it hours afterwards.

All the same, good lion shots *were* difficult to come by. Like

most camera hunters, Father's greatest ambition was to capture on film a lion actually making its kill. It became an obsession with him, and it used to infuriate him to come across a fresh kill. Despite his frustration, he none the less took some wonderful sequences, such as the one of a lioness chasing a warthog. She was playful, rather than hungry, and the little pig simply elevated his tail like a periscope and showed her a clean pair of heels. Then there was the lioness that we discovered actually eating a live buffalo. She had merely stunned it, and commenced with her dinner, lying across its shoulders and lifting up and down as the huge animal breathed beneath her. One of Father's best comic shots was of a heavily maned lion whom we came across asleep under a clump of palms. As the camera began to whirr, he rolled over in surprise only to discover that he had the most terrible taste in his mouth. He went through a magnificent pantomime act — gagging, sticking out his tongue, gulping, licking his whiskers, and finally staggering round to the other side of the palms to flop down in the shade. Each of these were really good shots in their own way, yet Father remained dissatisfied.

However, his patience was rewarded in the end. Towards the beginning of spring, he spent a fortnight at Robins Camp,

making three or four sorties each day. On this particular morning the bush was unusually devoid of life, and we had been crawling along scanning the veld fruitlessly when Bill Miller, who was with us, tapped Father on the shoulder and pointed silently into the dense mopane forest on our left. He had seen a handsome pair of fully maned lions, lying down but not asleep. Both of them, in fact, had their heads up and appeared to be moderately alert. We watched them for a few moments, but they were a little too far off to make a really good photograph, especially as the bush was so heavy, and in any case both men had any number of shots of lions lying down. Father had started the car when one of the lions suddenly sprang up and began to investigate a hole in the ground. He crouched in front of it, inserted a long paw down the hole and scooped about inside, like a cat trying to get a cotton reel out from under a cupboard. Intrigued, we stopped to see what he was after. Presently the lion squeezed his head and shoulders into the entrance to the hole, and when he emerged again, there was blood on his muzzle.

This put a different complexion on things! However, when we attempted to get within photographic range, the second lion rose threateningly to his feet, wrinkling his lip and lashing his tail. We stopped. The lion glared at us for a moment, then as if determined to make himself quite clear, he charged. It was the first time I had been on the receiving end of a lion's charge, and I found it a fairly unnerving experience. He ended it in a great swaggering broadside, throwing up heavy scoops of sand with his enormous paws, laying back his ears and pulling faces. Every time we tried to edge nearer, he drove us back, and there was no knowing when he might decide to abandon the bluff charge in favour of the real thing.

It was a difficult position. Quite plainly the lions had trapped some creature down the hole and were going to wait there until it came out. But with one of them in such an aggressive frame of mind, it was awkward to get near enough to make photography worth while. After considerable deliberation, the men decided to go and consult Len Vaughan. For one thing, we needed his authority to take the car off the road, and for another it might help to have his advice on the lion's behaviour. Would he continue to bluff, or might he be provoked into making a real attack? We found Len in his office, snarling over a desk full of papers.

"My God, how I hate paperwork!" he roared as we entered the room. "I tell you, these monthly reports crucify me, and who reads them, anyway?"

Father wagged his head sympathetically, and then told him he had found a tricky pair of lions. Len chuckled.

"And you want me to tickle them up for you again, I suppose?" he asked, his eyes twinkling.

"Well no thanks, Len," Father replied hastily, "not this time. If anything, I'd like you to calm them down a bit."

"Some people," Len grumbled, "are terribly difficult to please. What's the problem, then?"

We told him about the lions having an animal trapped down a hole. Len raised both long arms in supplication to the heavens. "How am I expected to file a monthly report," he thundered, "with crazy photographers trying to get themselves eaten by my lions? Come on then, let's hurry," he went on, kicking over his chair and striding to the door. "I'll tell you fellows something. I've never seen a kill yet myself. This could just be IT!"

He sprang into his Land-Rover and followed us back to the lions. To our relief and excitement, both of them were still there, just as we had left them. Len put his Land-Rover in first, twisting and turning among the mopane with practised ease. The grumpy lion immediately went into his routine of crouching, snarling, lashing his tail, ending in another bluff charge. Len Vaughan laughed and took the Land-Rover round in a tight circle to come in again, closer this time. Once more the lion charged, ending his rush with an angry toss of the head and a series of deep, resentful grunts. Len drove back to us, smiling merrily.

"Safe as a house," he pronounced. "He won't touch you. Go in as close as you like."

Reassured by Len's evaluation of the position, Father edged closer, ignoring the lion's repeated attempts to drive us off. Finally he was satisfied with the range, and slowly leaned forward to switch off the ignition. (It was impossible to use a telephoto lens with the engine running, for the vibrations caused huge wobbling distortions.) Len Vaughan stayed with us for almost a quarter of an hour, but that monthly report was still awaiting completion, and with the greatest reluctance he finally decided to leave.

His vehicle was barely out of sight when both lions sprang forward and plunged their forequarters down the hole, while the cameras started to whirr. The two lions were straining at something, the mighty muscles of their haunches quivering with exertion. Presently, to the accompaniment of the most piteous screams, they dragged a struggling warthog from the hole. While one of them grimly held the warthog by the throat, the other pinned down its kicking legs and began to eat, tearing long strips of meat from the buttocks. It was a gruesome spectacle, but the lions were hungry and the worst was over quickly. Abandoning his usual caution, Father shot off a whole reel of film, and soon had to reload, crouched down on the floor of the car wrapped in a blanket and cursing under his breath. Now he switched to his most powerful lens, taking some incredible close-ups of crunching teeth, a preoccupied golden eye suddenly turning on the camera in hostile resentment, coarse white whiskers running with blood. At last Father's dream sequence had come true. The film was a winner, but poor Len Vaughan — when we returned and told him about it, his comments were unprintable!

It is one thing to view a lion with the admiring and tolerant eye of a game photographer, and another matter entirely to encounter one in the wilds when one is on foot and unprepared. I suppose that more stories have been told about lions than any other African animal, and regrettably enough nearly all of them have, to my mind, a sad ending. My sympathies are almost always with the lion, for I suspect that out of every fifty lions which have been branded 'man-eater' there will be only one which deserves the title. Every now and then it does happen that through injury or some other misfortune, a lion is driven out of the pride, and is forced to feed himself as best he can. One story, however, of an encounter between a lion and a young girl, bears repeating.

Muddy Bain was fifteen at the time, a level-headed girl, not given to hysteria or extravagant flights of fancy. Muddy's elder sister, a girl of about eighteen, had recently married and had moved to a farm near Mazoe. They had been on the farm some weeks when Muddy went to spend a few days with the newly-weds. It was wild country, and the hills and kopjes of the district abounded with leopard. The young couple had built themselves a house out of Kaytor Huts — two enormous, corrugated-iron tanks lined on the inside with mud brick and thatched above, with the space between the two tanks enclosed and roofed to make a living-room. The floor was made of big blocks of mopane wood about nine inches thick, hammered into the earth, a primitive but enduring form of parquetry. The guest cottage where Muddy slept was a pole-and-dagha hut in the garden, its fragile walls insulated on the outside by a covering of long thatch.

One night after dinner, while her brother-in-law was escorting Muddy to the door of her room, he suddenly caught her arm and said: "Don't move. There's a lion."

Ahead of them, in the dark, Muddy saw two glowing eyes. They were an eerie, silvery blue and stared fixedly at them for an instant before the creature turned its head, and vanished. It was a dark night with no moon and the feeble rays of the lantern were not sufficiently powerful to illuminate the animal's body.

"It's all right. I was mistaken," her brother-in-law said reassuringly, leading her on once more. "I thought it was a lion, but it must have been one of the dogs from the compound."

Muddy thought no more about the beast, but during the night she was disturbed by an unusual sound. She lay awake wondering what it could have been. Presently the noise was repeated, a rustle, rustle of the grass covering of the hut, followed by a scraping noise as if something were tearing and clawing at it. "It's that dog again," she thought, "sniffing about outside."

"Voetsak!" she shouted, the universal message to all stray dogs. The scratching noise stopped, and Muddy was about to drop off to sleep again when it started up once more. Irritated at the thought that this might go on all night, Muddy resolved to chase it off by giving it a good fright. She climbed softly out of bed and tiptoed across the hut to the wash-stand where a big, enamel ewer filled with water stood in a basin, ready for the morning's ablutions. The clawing at the grass continued from just outside the window, so she abruptly flung the window open and threw out the water, shrieking "Voetsak!" once more, for good measure. Then she banged the window shut and went back to bed.

The following morning, her brother-in-law left at dawn for a week's tour of the distant parts of the farm. He had been gone for

over an hour when the cook came outside with a tray of tea for
Muddy. A moment later he flew back to the house in extreme
agitation to report that Muddy had been eaten by a lion. He had
found the thatch pulled off one side of her hut, and observing a
number of huge pug marks, he had assumed the worst. Muddy
however was still peacefully asleep and was most astonished to
be woken by her sister and to find the whole household in a state
of uproar.

The two girls couldn't be sure what animal had made the
pug marks — lion or leopard, or possibly hyena — so the older
sister covered a few of them with jam tins to preserve them for
her husband to see on his return.

Later that day, two prospectors came by with their pack-
mules. It was customary to offer hospitality to anyone who
dropped in, and during the course of conversation Muddy's
sister mentioned the episode of the mysterious beast and the
footprints. The two men, having examined them, proclaimed
that they were lion and, furthermore, that it would return. They
offered to spend the night on the farm so that if it should come
back, the girls would not be alone and unprotected.

That night Muddy stayed in the main house with her sister,
while the two prospectors slept outside. At about ten o'clock the
girls were startled from their beds by the sound of a single gun
shot, and almost immediately one of the prospectors knocked
on the door and asked them to come and look. He led the girls
round to the guest hut, where a pitiful sight met their eyes. It was
a fully maned lion right enough, but very, very old and
wretchedly thin. One of his limbs had been injured and was
gangrenous. He must have been on his last legs, poor old fellow,
and would scarcely have been able to damage a frog. When they
opened his mouth, they discovered that he had only one tooth. It
was a good thing, really, that he had been put out of his misery.

A more cheerful note is struck by a story which Nick
McKisack gave me concerning a rather unusual dinner-party at
his parents' home in Zambia. At that time the McKisacks lived
in a remote area where lions were not uncommon, and the house
itself was the usual farmstead with the kitchen and wash-house

separated from the main building by a stretch of open yard. On the night in question they were entertaining to dinner a rather important guest, a lofty dignitary from Britain, and they were naturally anxious to offer him their best hospitality. When the soup arrived, Lady McKisack observed that Cook seemed more than usually *distrait.* However she put it down to the jitters that normally afflict servants when a hostess particularly wishes to put her best foot foremost. Next to arrive was the meat course. The roast bird reached the table safely, but then there was an uneasy pause. Finally Cook arrived slightly out of breath, and a trifle wild-eyed, triumphantly bearing a dish of roast potatoes. Lady McKisack caught his eye and murmured a discreet rebuke.

"Now come along, Cook, don't bring the vegetables one at a time like this," she whispered. "Bring them all together, on a tray."

"I'm sorry Nkosikaas," Cook apologised in a hoarse whisper. He glanced round apprehensively at the door. "There is lion outside. In one hand I can bring vegetables, but in other I must carry spear!"

I suppose wild bears were not an altogether imaginary peril in Shakespeare's day for him to have observed:

> In the night, supposing some fear,
> How easy is a bush suppos'd a bear.

Certainly I have many times experienced the same pheno-menon with lions, jubilantly crying out "Lion!" only to suffer the humiliation of seeing the 'lion' melt away under my very eyes, while a stump or rock or bush assumes its true identity. The converse also is true, however, and more than once I've seen a stone or a dead stump suddenly flick an ear and turn its head and lo! — a lion! I don't know why it is that there is something irresistibly funny at someone else's discomfort over some imaginary danger, but the fact remains that practical jokes comprised a very large proportion of the entertainment in the old days here. For such a solemn-looking chap, my Uncle Niels had a surprising penchant for this form of diversion.

As a youngster of nineteen in the Native Department, he was stationed at Hartley in the days when it was little more than a network of cattle-yards, a small police-station and a tiny pub. Virtually the only social life occurred on the occasion of a cattle sale, when the stockpens would be filled with lowing steers, milling nervously under a great cloud of dust. Then the small pub would come to life with the boom of men's voices, the beef buyers from Salisbury and the stockmen arguing strenuously over whether it had been a good or a poor season. It never took long for the conversation to drift away from such stern stuff to more congenial topics, and soon someone would come out with the story of a recent hunting exploit. Lions loomed very large in a stockman's life, for lions in a cattle-pen tend to run amok, slaughtering right and left, and naturally the cost of such a massacre is very considerable indeed. It was against this background that Niels used to resort to his practical jokes.

A very good facsimile of a lion's roar can be achieved by the use of a watering-can; the larger the can the deeper and more resonant the resulting roar. A little water is run into the vessel, and one then makes appropriate noises down the spout. The result is a deep, bubbling roar, rich with an eerie, echoing quality, enough to lift the hairs on the head of the most seasoned hunter.

Under cover of the dark, and once the party in the pub was well under way, Niels used to steal up to the stockpens, armed with his watering-can. A few tentative growls and grunts were enough to start the cattle bellowing, and soon the little hotel would disgorge its customers, who would pour out into the night babbling excitedly and hurrying off for their guns. Now to the east, now to the west, Niels simulated the lion, while the herd boys were set to build great fires at each corner of the kraals and all the big, white hunters would stride about excitedly brandishing weapons and issuing one another with instructions. Here was entertainment for the gods! The following morning the little village would be buzzing with the news that so-and-so had actually spotted the lion — 'a great big fella with a full mane', and another could swear there were two of them, because he'd seen a lioness fleeing past the pub at a crouching run, too quick for him to get a shot at her. Yet a third reported that he had

been up early and had found what he took to be their spoor in the sand, quite four or five of them, he judged. To add spice to the situation, these were men who *knew* a lion's roar; but then so did Niels, and it is not so much an indication of their gullibility as of the authenticity of the watering-can's sound effects!

If Rhodesian men have one flaw it is a certain lack of polish and suavity when dealing with the fair sex, a tendency to become tongue-tied and offhand. Rhodesian women who are accustomed to their menfolk's somewhat rough-and-ready ways know to look beyond the horny crust for the qualities they admire. There is no doubt, however, that many a girl encountering this peculiarity for the first time, has felt bewildered, rebuffed and even insulted by these men-of-few-words. While some women will meekly accept this casual treatment with a philosophical shrug, there are others who feel most strongly that the men ought to be brought to heel. Certainly hell hath no fury like a woman scorned, even a woman who supposes she has been scorned by default, as it were. At all events, such was the situation when Niels was called on to employ his ventriloquistic skills to defend the honour and prestige of Rhodesian manhood.

Some months after the episode of the watering-can lion, Niels had been transferred to Salisbury, and while there was a little more social life in the capital, entertainment was still of a conspicuously home-spun order. Niels had found digs in a bachelors' mess with three other young bloods, one of whom — Dick — used to spend his week-ends on his parents' farm near Norton. After one such visit home Dick returned to Salisbury in a state of gloom and dejection, and it was a while before his mess-mates could worm out of him the source of his discontent. Finally he divulged that in order to eke out the slender living on the farm, his mother used to take in paying guests — people from abroad who had a thirst for adventure and believed they would enjoy 'roughing it' in the wilds of Africa by way of a change. On this occasion Dick had arrived at the farm to find it in the possession of three young and spirited schoolmistresses. During the course of the week-end these three worldly wenches had made it abundantly clear to Dick that they were singularly unimpressed with what they had seen of Rhodesian manhood — a callow, craven lot, in their view, and Africa itself was a bitter disappointment. To think they had come all this way, expecting to find excitement and adventure, a land teeming with lions and crocodiles and peopled with brawny-limbed, hairy-chested heroes wearing bandoliers and striding about the veld in riding boots and pith helmets — and were they to be fobbed off with *this* — 'this' being Dick, whom they evidently regarded as a poor specimen. They were furthermore openly disparaging about the farm's obvious lack of lions, man-eating or otherwise.

Dick was still smarting from their jibes, dismayed at his inability to elevate himself and Rhodesian manhood in general to the heroic heights of these damsels' expectations. Something would have to be done, he said, some desperate strategy resorted to in order to adjust the imbalance of their views. After lengthy consultations they resolved upon a plan. A message couched in suitably clumsy and unpolished terms was sent to the ladies, inviting them out for a week-end's camping under the stars and conveying the hope that they might find it not quite so dull as life at the farmhouse. As the level of high adventure had, to date, fallen so far short of their expectations, the girls readily accepted the invitation.

So it came about that a few nights later the rising moon found the party encamped at the foot of a very high kopje in one of the remoter areas of Dick's farm. The cooking-fire and bed rolls were set out in a small clearing, while all around them the bush fell under the mysterious mantle of night, a rustling darkness filled with the ghostly forms of trees and rocks and the gliding shadows of things half-seen. The servants had their own fire a little distance away, and from them came an occasional snatch of song and the pleasant fragrance of skewered meat sizzling among the coals.

They commenced dinner — a rough and coarse affair to be sure — and to begin with the girls were at their wits' end to strike conversational sparks from such dullards as their slow-witted escorts. Gradually, however, in their leisurely, laconic way the men began swopping yarns.

"Did you ever hear how Toby Smeaton found a python in his pyjama-leg . . . ?"

"Yes, and remember the time when a nest of scorpions took refuge inside my sleeping-bag!"

"D'you recall how Pat Napier's horse was taken by a lion while we were at dinner, and next morning we surprised a hyena loping off with one of its hoofs in its mouth!"

From time to time one of the lads would get up to fetch a log of wood for the fire and no one particularly noticed it when Niels slipped away into the night.

As the conversation proceeded, the girls had become a little less talkative and showed an inclination to huddle closer to the fire. Dick was in the middle of a story about a lion that used to raid his father's cattle kraals when the night was sawn in half by a tremendous, grating roar from somewhere close by, a deep, full-throated sound followed by a descending series of lesser grunts.

"Wa-a-u-gh! Wah, wah, wah!"

It was sensational. The girls clutched one another, their eyes wide with fright.

"What's that?" they gasped.

"Lion, I guess." Dick picked his teeth with a straw.

"A lion? But what — but where — but what are you going to do?"

"Well, if he comes into the firelight," came the nonchalant reply, "I might take a shot at him."

"But what if —" The girls' eyes moved fearfully round the encircling shadows. Presently they jumped again as the lion's roar came for a second time, now from the opposite side of the camp. This was too much for the servants. Thoroughly alarmed, they scraped their fire together on to a piece of tin and moved their camp into the main circle. When the lion roared for the third time, now terrifyingly close, Dick stood up and deliberately loaded his rifle.

"Reckon I'd better chase him off," he declared and strode off into the darkness. Almost immediately there was a violent crashing in the bushes and a number of shots rang out in quick succession. The girls screamed and clung together. After a few minutes Dick returned smiling with bits of leaf and stick in his hair, and reported that he'd got him.

"Have to go after him at first light, though," he added, "as I fear I didn't finish him off."

"You mean — you mean there's a wounded lion out there now?" one of the girls quavered.

Dick nodded casually, glanced at his watch and said he thought they ought to try to get some sleep as they might have a disturbed night. One by one they made for their sleeping-bags, and in the general excitement none of the girls appeared to notice that Niels was once more among them, innocently pottering with his blankets.

During the small hours he was woken by the sound of something moving about stealthily, close by. For a moment the fear gripped him that what had started out as a joke might have turned into the real thing, but the shape that was moving furtively before the fire was not that of a lion. It was the most shrewishly critical of the three schoolmistresses, still fully dressed and very wide awake. The noise that had woken Niels was her feverish stoking of the fire! Shaking with silent laughter, Niels ducked his head down into the blankets once more and went back to sleep.

The following morning the girls were tousled and grumpy. They'd slept badly, they declared, and they had decided not to spend another night camping. They wanted to be taken home. Dick, whose head now poked out of his blankets, enquired if something was the matter, wasn't it exciting enough for them? They replied somewhat frostily that adventure was one thing, but that they didn't care to risk their lives by placing themselves in the hands of a bunch of incompetent clowns. Why, in any case, they demanded, hadn't Dick got up at first light to track down the lion? Dick grinned and scratched his hair. Revenge was going to be sweet!

"Aw you didn't believe that was a lion, did you?"

The girls took a lot of convincing, at first refusing to believe that the prowler in the night had been no more than a paper tiger. Finally Niels had to produce his watering-can and give an on-the-spot demonstration.

One thing can be said for schoolmistresses — when the spoken word is needed they have a ready and fluid supply on which they can draw, and they now commenced to deliver their collective opinions in shrill and forceful tones. This verbal chastisement continued unremittingly all the way back to the farmhouse, the girls at last silent and aloof and the men bloody but unbowed, continually shaken by gusts of mirth. Fifty years later Niels for one was laughing still.

9
Suicide Month

FATHER'S FIRM, J. Wightman & Son, had originally been started by Grandfather as a saddlery and leather-work business. Then, with the advent of the motor car, he had been forced to branch out into other spheres, and now the greater proportion of his trade was in the importing and distribution of fresh produce. I loved the smell of the shop, a composite odour of fruit and vegetables that changed from day to day and week to week. The bass notes were sustained by the earthy aroma of potato, onion and hessian, with seasonal overtones. In winter it was orange and naartjie and lemon, followed in early summer by the fine, clear cold-room scent of peaches and plums and grapes. These would be succeeded in turn by melons and mangoes, and in autumn the shop would be redolent with the musky fragrance of great, wicker baskets of flesh-pink litchis.

Father's shop stood on the corner of Selborne Avenue opposite the Market Square and the City Hall. Next door were the premises of Reg Hart, the auctioneer. Reg was a tall, craggy-faced man with a strong, hooked nose and a sudden way of exploding into very loud laughter. When in action on the Market Square auctioning a mountain of assorted debris, his voice would carry nearly as far as the chimes of the City Hall clock. "NOW then who's going to bid me four pound four miserable pounds for this excellent pump; it's three-and-a-half horsepower and how do I know whether it works Mr. Viljoen FIVE pounds thank you sir WHO will bid me six pounds . . ."

On days when there wasn't a sale, Reg Hart used to stand in his shirt-sleeves outside the door of his shop, wide-brimmed hat on the back of his head, his braces pulled up so tight that his waist-band was on a level with his ribs and his turn-ups brushed the tops of his socks. Hands clasped behind his back, he used to harass the passers-by with good-humoured but outrageously insulting statements about their appearance or their private lives.

Next door to Reg Hart was Pearce, the butcher, a quick-moving, spectacled, little man whose long, striped apron almost swept the floor. Whenever we entered his premises he used to put on an act of great stealth and conspiracy, surreptitiously presenting each of us with a scarlet, Vienna sausage. The last shop in the block was Bob Downing's bakery. Portly, red-faced with bright, blue eyes, Bob Downing was another of Bulawayo's impresarios whose ready wit was as famous as his confections. Every day the lovely fragrance of baking bread floated enticingly from his ovens. I used to ogle longingly at his displays of cakes — little, iced creations in delicate pink or green with fine, white piping round the edges and decorated with half a walnut or a cherry. Then there were wavy-patterned Florence cakes, their tops gleaming like polished marble; dark, moist, fruitcakes smelling sweetly of mixed spice, and thick, succulent chocolate-cakes encrusted with scrolls of chocolate flake. We seldom had cake at home except at Christmas or on someone's birthday, for cakes, like sweets, were considered an unhealthy extravagance, and Bob Downing's windows were a torment.

It was a common sight to find Father, Reg Hart, Pearce and Bob Downing each standing outside his respective door, admiring the weather and ribbing his prospective customers. After a while they would gravitate towards one another, meeting as a rule outside Reg Hart's. There they would hold spirited debates on everything under the sun from the laws of insolvency to the rinderpest, and from motor cycles to the price of flour. Such was the originality of outlook expressed on these occasions that it was always entertaining to eavesdrop, and usually their little group included a number of interested hangers-on. Reg Hart was greatly given to accosting the passers-by for their opinions, when he felt himself cornered in debate.

"Here McGregor," he'd bawl out. "You're the man we want! How much did you pay for that piece of land near Khami ten years ago?"

McGregor would cross the street to join them, fuelling the fire of the argument about property values and income tax.

One day their numbers were swelled by the addition of Andy Thompson and Doug Wells who had come to town to see Reg about some mining equipment. Andy was a huge, florid-faced man whose language was so strong and full of oaths that to me it was like listening to a foreign tongue. I used to lurk in the doorway of Father's shop drinking in his remarks with horrified relish as if he were some bloodthirsty pirate from the Spanish Main. I had to take care not to be discovered, however, or Father would banish me with a frown and a nod that meant 'be off'.

On this occasion the group of men were engaged in a heated and noisy dispute concerning the iniquities of the Press. Bulawayo boasted one solitary newspaper which represented, in the eyes of these reactionaries, the sins of the world, and there was no crime and no social malaise which could not directly or indirectly be laid at its door.

It was most unfortunate that a representative from the paper's advertising department should have selected this particular morning to come touting for business. Seeing four prospective clients in a knot, he unwisely resolved to approach them collectively, and launched himself into his set piece, pointing out all the advantages which would flow from advertising in the daily newspaper. They heard him out in ominous silence. Reg Hart was the first to explode.

"And you are *actually* suggesting that I should *pay*," he roared, "to have my good name in your abominable rag? Tell your editor," he went on wrathfully, "that I would far rather pay to ensure that it does *not*!"

"Aw come off it, Reg," Bob Downing interrupted. "Nobody goes to you anyway. We all know that advertising would be completely wasted in your case."

Reg's reply to Bob was short and insulting, rounding it off with the emphatic statement that he would rather die than see his name in the paper.

Now Andy Thompson, who had been visibly swelling with ideas, delivered a blast of such complicated and colourful invective to the Press representative that the unfortunate man wilted and tried to slink away. Bob Downing caught his sleeve. "Half a second, sonny," he smiled. "What did you say your name was? Blackwell? I'll pop in and see you this afternoon. I could use a spot of advertising."

The others poured scorn on his head, but Bob retained his cheerful composure, and the following day the Bulawayo public was treated to a half-page advertisement that read:

Come to Bob Downing's Bakery
for the best confectionery
in Matabeleland

Next door to
REG HART
in Selborne Avenue.

Bob Downing certainly was one of the Grand Masters in the art of the practical joke!

Spring came and went and still there was no rain. Exhausted by the effort of producing their profusion of flowers, the trees were reluctant to expend any more of their precious sap on foliage. A few of them allowed a meagre crop of young leaves to form a light canopy, but even these drooped and twisted in the blazing heat. The camel's-foot had a clever way of protecting itself against dehydration. In the early morning and in the evening, its butterfly-shaped leaves would be widespread to absorb its vital ration of sunlight, but during those unbearable hours from nine till four it shut each leaf together like a book, exposing its pale undersides to reflect the pitiless sun.

September drew on into October and still not a cloud flecked the heavens. Now the white and empty sky became dirtied with the smoke of grass-fires that turned the sun red and dropped curiously contorted flakes of black ash, spinning and falling like dark, silent snow. The presence of the fires hung over us, an evil spirit, and at nights we could see their glow on the horizon.

During the next weeks the temperature crawled up steadily through the nineties and over the hundred mark. Tar melted in the roads and the last dams and rivers dried up. So dry was the air that the tall jug of iced water that always stood on our lunch table carried no dew of condensation. The merest whisper of vapour would appear where a block of ice touched the glass, but it would vanish instantly when the ice bobbed away. Perspiration dried on one's skin, and continuous clouds of dust rendered everything gritty to the touch. People's hair became brittle and electric, standing out from the head like a brush. Finger-nails splintered and snapped, and one's skin burned and itched, cracking and flaking away like a reptile's. It seemed to me that people's moods were determined by the feel of their skins. Tempers were always short in October, and it was a wise precaution to try to get the important business of the day accomplished early in the morning while people were still more or less human.

In many ways I found the heat more intolerable at nights, lying wakeful and uncomfortable on my bed, all coverings kicked off, searching with my toes for a cool corner of sheet or restlessly moving my head for a fresh patch of pillow to soothe my burning cheeks. There was not a breath of wind outside, not a leaf stirred. On such a still night I could hear the tolling of the City Hall clock, its leisurely Westminster chimes reaching out over the sleeping veld in restful benediction. Nearer at hand, of course, its chimes were deafening, deep resonant clangs that set the windows of Father's shop buzzing in their wooden frames.

The wild bees, too, found October a stressful period. With the veld tinder-dry and water and nectar desperately hard to find, they became restless and irritable. On those hot, electric days it would take little more than the scent of a sweating horse or the immoderate crying of a child to start the bees off on a rampage. There came a day during an exceptionally trying

October when the City Hall clock indirectly caused more excitement and danger in Bulawayo than there had been since the Matabele disturbances.

It was a blisteringly hot Saturday morning towards the end of Suicide Month, and town was unusually thronging and active. In Father's shop, business was at fever pitch. That morning's train from the Cape had brought in the first consignment of deciduous fruit and the shop was jammed with customers who were literally buying up the trays of peaches as they were off-loaded from the mule wagons outside. Over the street in the Market Square Reg Hart's voice, hoarse with thirst, roared on as he conducted the morning's auction, the crowd of buyers and spectators moving round with him, alternately fanning themselves with their hats and jamming them on again as the sun beat down like a mallet on their bare heads. The temperature inside Father's shop was just under a hundred, while outside in the blazing sun the air fairly crackled with static electricity.

On one side of the City Hall was the Market Square, on the other was a small park, an oasis of cool green shaded by a number of stout Canary Island palms and flaunting a few bright beds of canna lilies and petunias. A very large swarm of wild bees had cleverly made their hive in the clock-tower where they were thoroughly safe from robbers, yet had ready access to the pollen and nectar of the small park. That particular day, however, the combination of the heat and the noise had brought them to the brink of frenzy. Sweating mules outside Father's shop, the auctioneer's bell, the shouting of the bidders . . . one could see the bees saying to one another, "I don't know about you, but a fraction more of this and I shall go berserk." The last straw came on the nose of twelve noon when with a tremendous grating and clanking the City Hall clock's mighty chimes began the ceremony of tolling out the hour. I suppose to the already excitable bees it seemed as if the clock would never stop. Maddened beyond endurance, they poured out of the clock-tower and attacked everything in sight.

For a moment Reg Hart gaped about in shocked disbelief as his crowd of followers who a moment before had all been listening with rapt attention began dancing about and then scattered, screaming. A second afterwards he received his personally delivered message from the bees, and moving his large form with surprising speed, he shot across the street and into his shop slamming the door behind him.

Father had just completed off-loading the last of the mule wagons and was busy signing a batch of delivery notes as the clock began to strike. The first we knew of the bees' attack was the sudden plunging of the team of mules who all began to lash and kick in their traces. The next instant they had broken into a wild gallop and the empty wagon tore off down Selborne Avenue with the frantic muleteer in hot pursuit. He didn't get far. There is nothing like a running figure to attract an angry bee and in a minute he was down, rolling and clawing as the stinging insects swarmed over his head and arms. A storekeeper dragged him indoors to safety while all down the street the shops were hastily closing their doors to keep the bees out.

From behind Father's plate-glass windows we watched the scene in the street with mingled horror and hilarity. Dogs fled yelping in every direction. A cyclist who came pedalling jauntily down the street oblivious of the impending doom, suddenly swerved violently, threw up his arms, skidded and crashed, screaming horribly. Immediately the bees were over him in a thick brown pelt. Someone rescued the cyclist, and then all eyes were drawn by the figure of a man who was plunging erratically across the Market Square. His immaculate white linen suit and elegant Panama at once proclaimed his identity, a middle-aged bachelor noted throughout the town for his bashfulness with women. He staggered across the street tearing the bees away from his face and burst into Father's shop. Before our astonished eyes he cast himself on his knees at the feet of one of the customers, a stout formidable matron, and thrust his head up her skirts. Although the woman no doubt sympathised with his plight, she was naturally outraged at his abrupt approach and, besides, the bees proved to be just as willing to sting her thighs as his face. She reacted excitably, whacking at him with her sunshade, indignantly clutching at her skirts and screaming for help. He, equally desperate, followed her about on his knees, grimly holding on to her dress and determined to keep it over his head at any cost. The two of them and their attendant swarm of bees reeled and raged about among the trays of peaches and piles of potatoes. Helpless with laughter, Father and a few other customers struggled to disengage them, and finally succeeded in restoring order.

By twelve-thirty the town was deserted. The noonday bustle and hubbub had melted as if by magic, while round the clock-tower a small, black cloud of bees still swarmed indignantly, their angry hum quite audible in the silent streets. Years later, people still spoke with bated breath of the day that the bees showed us who was boss.

In recent years the African bee has acquired a world-wide notoriety, after a South American bee-keeper, who was impressed with the African bee's hardiness, imported a swarm into Brazil. The bees proliferated and several swarms went wild, spreading up through Central America and across the Isthmus of Panama. At present they are known to have established themselves as far north as Guatemala. Their savagery and the potency of their sting finally came to the attention of the world's sensation-mongers who promptly dubbed them KILLER BEES, and many prominent news magazines carried alarming articles about farmers and livestock that had been stung to death.

In Africa where the bee's virulence is only too familiar, these horror stories were greeted with quiet amusement. Throughout the Dark Continent deaths from bee stings are a relatively common occurrence and for every man who dies as a result of wild bees, there are many more who require lengthy hospitalisation.

Not long ago there were two quite serious attacks in the Salisbury area. In one of these, fourteen people died. Angry bees descended on a chattering crowd of people who were boarding a bus. While some of the would-be travellers fled, many managed to get inside the vehicle, and the driver proceeded to take off at speed hoping to leave the swarm behind. However, quite a number of bees had entered the bus along with

the passengers, and the driver himself now came under attack. He lost control of the bus which plunged headlong over the bank of the Makabusi River. Attracted by the screams and the uproar, the remainder of the swarm followed the bus and fell on the accident victims, severely hampering the efforts of the helpers and the ambulance teams who tried to assist the injured.

It is thought that certain odours, as well as noises, excite bees and provoke them to attack. It is claimed that bees cannot abide the smell of sweat or of blood or of fear. They certainly have no respect for the Marquis of Queensberry rules, and have no compunction against going for a man when he is down. A swarm of bees had taken up temporary quarters in a thick hedge beside a school car-park where parents used to collect their children at lunch-time. When the bell rang and crowds of noisy children began running past the hedge, the bees became restless. Even then disaster might have been averted if someone had been able to quieten the children, and direct them away from that portion of the hedge. Regrettably, however, the din continued and finally one of the parents was stung in the face just as he drove in to the parking lot. He swerved involuntarily and his car collided with the bicycle-barrow of an ice-cream vendor. He, in turn, was knocked from his saddle, fell and cut his head, only to rise up bellowing wrathfully and streaming blood. As far as the bees were concerned, this was the last straw. They poured out of the hedge and set upon the luckless ice-cream man. The cut on his head was superficial, but the poor man died from bee sting toxaemia. Needless to say, many other people including a number of children were severely stung in the same episode.

There are two times of year when the bees are most likely to go on the rampage. The first is at the beginning of the hot season when the bush is dry, water and flowers are scarce and the hives are short of food. The other occurs at the end of summer when the rains leave us. Then, although the hives are full of honey, the swarms have increased in size so they feel it when the incoming food-supply suffers a sudden set-back. At both these times the swarms are under stress, and it may take no more than a slight disturbance to make them run amok.

It is strange how some people can withstand bee stings with relative impunity while others are dangerously allergic to them. It appears that allergy to bee stings is cumulative, for many people find themselves swelling more and more alarmingly each successive time they are stung.

For a man with a severe allergy, Henry Schoultz is lucky to be alive today, having had a most extraordinary experience with bees while fishing in the Zambezi valley. In the early 1960s Lake Kariba on the Zambezi offered exceptionally good sport, and it was not unusual for a small boat to bring in as many as three or four hundred bream in a day. Kariba is a bewitching place. So fierce is the heat in the valley that mirages form in the sky, shimmering stretches of silver 'water' in which the weird shapes of baobab trees float like disembodied ghosts. Sometimes the mirage in the sky links up with the real water of the lake itself, and a bewildered fisherman will sit in his boat blinking the sweat out of his eyes, wondering what has become of the shoreline. A peculiar sensation that he has gone crazy steals over him. He appears to be in the grip of a frightening hallucination, trapped in the centre of a silver bubble whose glittering, curved walls spin and revolve with the inverted images of dead trees.

Out there in the centre of the lake the heat and the glare are intense. Henry Schoultz's fishing party was in an open, fourteen-foot boat. There were six of them: three men, two women and a three-year-old child. By midday they had caught so many fish that two of the keep nets were almost full. Schoultz decided to head back to the shoreline where heavy mopane bush stood waist-deep in the water. Except for the increased danger of crocs, it was pleasant among the trees, being partly shady. The fishing, too, was excellent, as bream for some reason are particularly plentiful in that environment, especially in the vicinity of a baobab tree.

It was easy to get lost in that drowned forest, for the open lake was soon invisible as the boat twisted this way and that among the grey trunks and branches. Every few yards they tore off a piece of coloured toilet-paper and pushed it into a cleft in a tree to mark their return route. It was still and quiet and very hot.

Presently Schoultz found what he was hoping for — a baobab. This one looked particularly promising, as it had half fallen over and was reclining in the water, its stout branches offering a perfect, natural jetty on which to moor the boat. He cut the engine and they coasted up beside the huge tree. One of the men threw over a keep net which landed with a heavy splash. He quickly looped its cord round a baobab twig and made it fast. The next moment the nose of the boat struck the trunk of the tree with a soft bump and all hell broke loose.

Like many baobab trees, this one was partly hollow, and unbeknown to Schoultz and his party it was occupied by a swarm of bees. Why they were so irritable on that particular day it is hard to tell — perhaps it was a combination of the heat, the sound of the approaching boat, the splash of the keep net, the smell of sweat and the bump against their tree. At all events they poured out in their thousands, fastening on to the people in the boat and stinging wherever they could.

Schoultz says the confusion and the noise were indescribable. The women began to scream, the child was shrieking in terror, all of them stamping and slapping, the men shouting and trying to brush off the hordes of bees. One of them finally decided to risk the presence of crocodiles and plunged overboard, but the bees only settled more thickly than ever on his head and face when he came to the surface. All this while Schoultz was desperately endeavouring to restart the outboard but, as so often happens when an engine is hot, it refused to fire.

One of the women who was wearing a very wide, flared skirt now took the child and hid it between her legs, crouching over it so that her skirt made a kind of tent. In the meantime her own face, neck and shoulders were a crawling mass of bees, that even swarmed down the front of her blouse. The other woman now became totally hysterical, her shrieks only attracting still more bees so that the men finally had to dunk her in the water.

Fortunately at this point, Schoultz managed to start the engine. By now their faces and eyes were most fearfully swollen. Schoultz remembers noticing that Pieterse, one of the party and normally quite a thin man, looked like an immensely fat Chinaman. His face was puffed out to unrecognisable proportions, his eyes no more than tiny slits. The boat was inches deep in dead bees, and it was such slow work threading their way back among the trees that the rest of the swarm stayed with them in a dense, stinging cloud.

At last they reached the open lake. Schoultz pushed the throttle over to full, the engine roared and they leaped forward, gathering speed. In a few moments the swarm of bees was left behind, and Schoultz headed back for Charara fishing camp, pushing the boat as fast as he dared. *In all that time he himself had received exactly five stings.*

Why the bees left him alone is a mystery. Was it because he was so preoccupied with starting the engine that he didn't join in the dance of slapping and shouting? Was it his clothing? (He was wearing a pair of khaki shorts and a pale green, cotton shirt.) Was it because he was next to the outboard and the smell of petrol deterred the bees? Whatever the reason it was providential for everyone on board the boat that day. If he had been as severely attacked as the others, there would have been no one in a fit state to handle the boat, no one to get the engine going, and no one able to see well enough to steer through the trees. Every last one of them would have been stung to death.

As soon as they landed at Charara, Schoultz drove the rest of the party to Kariba hospital. One of the women was admitted while the others were treated and given further medication to take away with them. Ill and in considerable pain, they none the less appreciated how lucky they had been to escape with their lives. There was, however, still one fly in the ointment: in their desperate haste to get away from the bees, they had left the keep net full of bream tied to the baobab tree.

Henry Schoultz thought about it on and off during the afternoon, wondering whether he dared to go back and fetch it. Obviously neither of the other men were in a fit state to undertake this kind of rescue operation, but at the same time he was most reluctant to lose the fish and the keep net. Finally he resolved to make the attempt, and just before dusk he set out with a servant for Foster's Clearing, the area of the drowned forest.

As he approached the trees, he cut out the engine and he and his servant paddled the boat in among the mopanes as if it were a canoe, moving softly and quietly. It was most uncomfortable in there in the gathering dusk, with the knowledge that the water all around them was alive with big crocs who would be rising to the surface for the night's hunting. After what felt like an interminable time they came upon the baobab. Everything seemed quiet and peaceful just as it had the first time that they had approached the tree. The thick arms of the baobab made mute signs in silhouette against the sky as they cautiously paddled nearer. Neither of them said a word. Nearer and nearer they crept, and now Schoultz could see the twine of his keep net still fastened to one of the branches. Taking the greatest care not to allow the boat to touch the tree, he leaned over and gently untied the rope. For several tense moments he and his servant struggled to heft the weighty load over the scuppers, but at last they got it aboard and lowered it quietly into the boat. Then with the same stealthy caution, they softly paddled back through the trees and once more reached the open lake.

It was with considerable relief and satisfaction that Schoultz tied up that night at Charara. The keep net was so heavy that two men had difficulty carrying it up to the camp. In its way, it had been a good day's fishing!

There is a famous medieval painting of a castle under attack. On the battlements stands one of the defenders, poising above his head a domed beehive which he is about to hurl down among the assailants. A formidable weapon indeed, and if only he had been equipped with a hive of African bees no doubt that would have been the end of the siege. A similar story is told of an episode during the Anglo-Boer War. During the closing stages of this bitter struggle, Kitchener was ruthlessly pursuing his scorched-earth policy, razing to the earth the few, remaining Boer homesteads. A Boer woman who, without her menfolk, was endeavouring to keep the farm together somehow or other, observed the approach of Kitchener's men. She had only one weapon at her disposal — her three, treasured hives of bees, but she resolved to use them none the less. Just as the troop of horses swung into the farmyard she overturned the hives and ran for the house. The infuriated bees proved to be a stern deterrent, for they fell on both horses and men forcing their retreat, and so the farm was saved.

Wild bees have a way of choosing the most extraordinary places for their hives. Not content with hollow trees, a cleft in a rock, or a disused termitarium, they will quite cheerfully take over human habitations and expect their conquered subjects to toe the line according to the chief law of the bees, 'Tranquillity First'. Any hollow space will do — the drawer of a desk, a cupboard, the boot of a motor car, a chimney or a partly filled water-tank. In the old days of wood-and-iron buildings the bees used to favour the empty space between the corrugated-iron exterior wall and the timber boarding on the interior. During the hot weather the iron walls became too hot to touch with the hand, and the air trapped behind them was as hot as a furnace. Naturally, this made the bees particularly restless and irritable. Bob Hammond's family had a lucky escape from a swarm of wild bees which had built their hive in the hollow walls of their wash-house. As luck had it, the whole family were out for lunch, but it was a desperately hot day and something must have set the bees off during their absence. The Hammonds returned in the evening to find that the bees had run amok killing the dog, the pet monkey, a parrot, twenty hens and the horse. Their peaceful farmyard was a scene of total destruction.

Dr. John Barbour who spent many years in sisal research in East Africa had a similar swarm in the walls of his wash-house, and there was general speculation on the sisal estate as to how they were to be dealt with. In this instance, however, Nature provided her own cure, though it was somewhat drastic. During the night a column of driver-ants swarmed in through the walls of the wash-house, each ant emerging with a bee grub or a mouthful of honey, and in the morning there were only a few dead bees left on the ground outside to indicate that there had been a hive there at all.

It's one thing for a swarm of bees to occupy a building, but in 1956 bee scouts found a truly exceptional site for their hive, and such was the stir that their discovery aroused that it was reported all over the world. In April of that year Rhodesia's very first Vickers Viscount prop-jet aircraft was delivered to Central African Airways at Salisbury Airport. Within hours of its arrival bees had taken possession of the aircraft and had set up home in one of the wings. When this was reported over the BBC World Service News, advice poured in to Salisbury from all over the globe. A man in Durban suggested that the bees could be driven off by the scent of garlic. A Londoner recommended tying up a horse somewhere near by, well wrapped to protect him from stings, whilst a local housewife insisted that bruised lemon leaves were all that was necessary to discourage them. None of these measures proved effective, however, and so C.A.A. called on the advice of Mr. Jack Garratt, a Salisbury bee-keeper. He estimated that the swarm was a big one and suggested that it should be smoked or gassed out. Aircraft engineers were concerned that this might kill off large numbers of the bees while they were still inside the wing, and that these would leave a residue of acid that might damage the rubber and metal of the fuel tanks. At this point C.A.A.'s chief pilot decided that desperate measures were called for, and he attempted to frighten the bees out by taking the Viscount up to seventeen thousand feet and putting her through her paces. He executed rolls, bumps and banks, he looped the loop and flew upside-down, but all to no avail. Quite unperturbed by these manœuvres the bees contentedly continued their housekeeping. Mr. Garratt then offered a new suggestion: "Try moving the plane to a new position each day — even a few feet would be enough. Bees are easily confused and disorientated by this, and they could all be enticed into a hive baited with brood comb that was left standing in the plane's original position."

This device would in all probability have solved the problem, but the aircraft engineers were impatient to get the Viscount into operation, and so they trundled the plane into a hangar and took the wing apart. When at last they got inside, all that remained of the swarm was a tight little cluster of about

twenty bees. The others had already dispersed and moved to
new quarters.

For all her fierceness, the African honey-bee is a wonderful
little creature and it speaks volumes for the quality and
abundance of her honey that so many people persist in keeping
their own hives. My grandmother maintained a number of
swarms, each called after a Queen of England. There was the
Matilda hive and the Mary hive and the Anne hive, and so on,
but there was one which was simply called the Mad hive
because its bees used to go on the rampage a couple of times
each year. The phenomenon of a bad-tempered hive is one that
continues to puzzle bee-keepers, but there is a theory that
'ground bees' are more excitable and intractable than other wild
bees. Some authorities claim that the ground bee — that is, the
one who selects a termitarium or antbear hole in preference to a
hollow tree — is slightly smaller and darker, and produces a
superior honey to her arboreal sisters. This theory is borne out,
to some extent, by the Elcombes who had a very trying time with
a swarm of ground bees.

On their farm a few miles south of Salisbury they kept a
number of hives that stood in the garden of the homestead. One
day the Elcombe boys found that a swarm had taken over a hole
in the ground near the big forty-thousand-gallon water storage-
tank that stood at the top of a kopje. Knowing that ground bees
were reputed to have particularly desirable honey, they resolved
to lure these wild bees into a conventional hive, so they stood
some frames temptingly filled with brood comb near the bees'
hole. In a few days the ruse worked and the bees evacuated their
underground tunnel in favour of the wooden hive.

Unfortunately, however, the hive had been so placed that
after midday the sun fell full on it and each afternoon the bees
became irritable, posing a real hazard to the dairy which was
near by. Not wanting to lose their valuable dairy cows over a
swarm of bees, the Elcombes decided to bring the hive down
from the kopje to join the other five swarms in the garden of the
homestead. The boys moved it at nights, marvelling at the great
weight of honey which the ground bees had already amassed. At

last the new hive was safely installed in the shade of the garden, but now a new problem arose. Whenever the gardener started up the motor mower to cut the lawn, the new bees attacked him in a fury and he was forced to desist. With the onset of summer the grass was growing rapidly, and something had to be done if the garden was not to go to rack and ruin. They struck on the idea of stopping up the entrance to the new hive very early in the morning and letting the gardener mow the lawn in the cool of the day before the bees had a chance to get themselves worked up. Unfortunately, this did not work either because a number of bees always spent the night among the flowers and, on hearing the mower start up, they reacted like the proverbial war-horse to the trumpet and sallied forth to do battle. Once again the gardener was forced to flee in disarray. By this time the lawns were ankle high and the gardener not unreasonably refused to attempt to mow while the new hive remained in the vicinity. Someone finally hit on the scheme of kitting the gardener out in full bee-keeper's regalia, and thus attired in hood, veil, gloves, leggings and boots he was able at last to mow the lawn, attended by an angry retinue of several thousand bees who trailed up and down the garden after him.

The hazards of continuing this practice were all too obvious, and the Elcombes reluctantly concluded that the ground bees' hive would have to be moved away from the homestead. They finally found a place for it in a shady bit of woodland, well away from the dairy and from the lawn-mower, where the bees could continue their work undisturbed!

It is difficult to judge to what extent bees understand the activities of humans, but on one occasion a swarm of bees showed a keen degree of awareness and active intelligence while a hockey match was in progress. Considerable rivalry has always existed between the two Air Force stations, New Sarum and Thornhill, and the various sporting fixtures that are arranged to test their superiority in the field are keenly contested and well supported.

The 1978 hockey match was no exception. Thornhill, the hosts on this occasion, took to the field in yellow, while the visiting

New Sarum team were resplendent in royal blue. Unbeknown to the players, a swarm of bees had taken up temporary quarters in the hedge along the southern boundary of the hockey pitch. As the game gathered momentum and the pack of sweating men thundered by, panting and shouting for the twenty-seventh time, the bees resolved to put an end to these continual disturbances. Thornhill supporters agree that the bees demonstrated their loyalty to the home side by singling out the New Sarum men for their most stinging attacks. In the course of the uproar more than half the visiting team were severely affected and had to be taken to Gwelo Hospital for treatment, while only a few Thornhill men received any stings at all.

"No question of foul play," chuckled a Thornhill bee-keeper, "bees can't stand blue. And our chaps were luckily all in yellow!"

Even knowing that they are savage and unpredictable, I still love my garden bees and can think of no more restful a spectacle than a humming host of them tumbling busily among the open flowers of my climbing yellow rose. To me there is something infinitely satisfying in the sight of a furry, golden bee exploring a newly opened peach-blossom or forcing her way eagerly between the still-bunched petals of a pomegranate bud, to vanish into the dim, scarlet cave within. What a world of beauty the bees inhabit! If they grow impatient at the coarse vulgarity of the sounds and smells that attend human habitation, who can altogether blame them?

10

Wineskin Clouds

THERE IS ONLY one topic of conversation.
"When's it going to rain?"
Screwed-up eyes peer anxiously at the sky.
"Been any rain your way?"
"Not a drop."
The cattle are losing condition, fires ravage the land.
"Where are the rains, man?"
"God knows. I hear they had half an inch at Balla Balla yesterday."
"Lucky devils! It must come soon, surely."

As a child I felt none of the gnawing anxiety which plagued the adult world at this time of year. Rather, I was caught up in a sense of excited expectancy, as if I were sitting in a hushed theatre waiting for the curtain to go up. The adults knew, of course, only too well how long we might have to wait for that curtain to rise, and knew, too, the terrible cost in terms of crops and livestock and starvation if the rains did not come soon.

Every day now for a fortnight the sky had been a spacious gallery in which were displayed great, marble sculptures of cloud, titanic statuary of giant men or ships with billowing sails, massive bulls with stumpy legs and sweeping horns, or a rampant dragon whose terrible claws have raked the sky from east to west. They'd swell pompously in the midday heat, to sag and wilt as night fell, while in their shadows the veld was dying of thirst.

Around Bulawayo the horizon is ruler-straight, broken only by the abrupt, flat-topped protuberances of Mfazamiti and Thabazinduna. Flat, flat, flat — it seemed as if the very land had been ironed out by the heat of the sun, and at times my heart yearned for the cool depths of a valley, the eerie gloom of a mountain slope. None the less, in those days before the rains, the sky was filled with cloudscapes that would have put the Himalayas to shame. Why, Everest itself was a mere molehill in comparison with these soaring sierras that stretched from horizon to horizon, huge masses of cloud shouldering thirty-five thousand feet up into the heavens, their summits crisp and white like Olympian cauliflowers, their lower flanks grape-blue and shadowed with mysterious kloofs and ravines.

I used to sit on the top of Big Rock, my chin on my knees, and watch them and dream, picturing under that deep bank of cloud a real mountain-range, a magic land of rivers and great trees, unexplored and beautiful. Moreover, this celestial scenery was ever-changing and no two days were alike. One afternoon would paint the sky with a vision of the Mojave Desert — flat-topped mesas, separated by sweeping plains of cirrus. The next afternoon the heavens would be crammed with swelling thunderheads whose dramatic attitudes seemed charged with action and purpose, like an armada preparing itself for battle. The clouds added a new dimension to the world, and my imagination took wing and soared in improbable fantasies.

At nights the huge clouds used to growl and mutter with thunder, illuminating portions of the sky with nervous lightning as if a distant war was being waged with heavy artillery. Then one evening the wind would carry with it the sweet scent of wet earth, and we would all stand outside sniffing it luxuriously. "Someone's getting rain tonight," we'd agree excitedly, knowing that soon it would be our turn.

Still the heavens withhold their favour, as if brooding on man's transgressions. Then with slow and majestic deliberation the clouds gather round us, closing off the rest of the world, shutting out the sun, drawing nearer, stooping lower in sinister conspiracy with the earth. A splitting crack of thunder silences the birds. The cats lay back their ears and stalk into the house. A sudden gust of wind lifts the branches of the trees, making them dance and gesticulate in excited anticipation. And then we hear it — a distant grumble like faraway surf, a million raindrops drumming on the land. Louder it grows and nearer, and then with a swishing stinging roar it is upon us! Mother stands laughing at the back door while we shriek and caper, opening our mouths to the rain's clean sweetness, whooping up great lungfuls of that incomparably scented air. The tide of life has returned and all the veld rejoices with us.

It frequently happens that a period of drought is broken by severe hailstorms. Those towering giants of cumulo-nimbus clouds are treacherous brutes, for all their splendour and magnificence. The very hot weather appears to encourage in them the formation of fierce updraughts that carry the frozen raindrops higher and higher before allowing them to fall to earth. Frequently our hailstones are patterned with concentric rings formed by successive layers of ice as the hailstone is whirled around inside the cloud. It is customary to measure hailstones in familiar domestic terminology, as being the size of peas or of marbles, pigeon's eggs, golf balls, hen's eggs, tennis balls, grape-fruit, water-melons . . . man's exaggerations are apparently limitless. Jests aside, however, we usually have one or two hail falls a year in which the stones vary in size from peas to pigeon's eggs. The water-melon variety is extremely uncommon, although it is not unknown for several large stones to fuse together so that the final lump that plummets to earth is closer in size to a soccer ball than a tennis ball.

For the farming community, a severe hailstorm can be disastrous. I have seen whole trees stripped of every leaf in a matter of minutes, vast fields of maize flattened and beaten into the mud, beautiful gardens of flowers, vegetables or fruit smashed to pulp. The larger hailstones slaughter hundreds of head of livestock and do untold damage to vehicles and buildings. While some farmers regularly insure their summer crops against hail, for many others a bad hailstorm is nothing less than a cataclysm. Professor Geoffrey Bond told me the story of a tobacco farmer at Banket who after a prolonged drought, was desperate for rain. He had even gone to the length of purchasing a 'rain rocket', a device which is fired into a promising-looking cloud and causes it to cool rapidly and drop its load. Day after day went by, however, without a suitable cloud darkening his horizon. Then one day about a month before Christmas a fairly good cloud formation began to develop over his wilting tobacco lands. Excitedly he prepared his rain rocket for launching, and fired it into the heart of the cloud. It was a good shot and within minutes the cloud adopted a dark and threatening aspect. The farmer was rubbing his hands with quiet glee, when the cloud sailed slowly across the boundary between his fields and those of a particularly irascible neighbour where it proceeded to drop a devastating hailstorm. The neighbour's tobacco crop was totally ruined!

Aghast at what he had done, the unlucky farmer, in the weeks that followed, crept about as inconspicuously as possible, sparing no effort to avoid encountering his neighbour whose wrath was likely to be terrible indeed. Then on Christmas Eve he was astonished to receive from the neighbour a splendid case of Scotch whisky. A note appended to the gift read: "Thanks for the hail, old boy! It wasn't a good crop anyway and the Insurance Company has paid me out in full. Merry Christmas!"

Regrettably, not all hailstorms have such a fortunate outcome! One year, many people in Gwelo lost their treasured household possessions when hailstones choked the gutters, so that great sheets of water came pouring across the ceilings and down the insides of the walls, ruining pictures and carpets and other valuable goods. On another occasion Mrs. Ashley Cullinan and her family experienced a catastrophic hailstorm on their farm in the Gwelo area. In this instance it was not so much the size of the hailstones that caused the damage, as their sheer volume. After a while a great bank of ice had built up outside the back door of the house, damming up the rain-water's escape and a brown river of flood-water poured into the kitchen. The menfolk did what they could to protect their heads from the hail's onslaught while they dug and chopped a gorge through the wall of hailstones to enable the water to drain away. Even then their troubles were not at an end, for presently with a rending crash the roof gave in under the weight of hail. When at last the storm passed, Mrs. Cullinan went out to assess the damage to the rest of the farmyard. The fields and her garden had been reduced to a wasteland, and her heart ached for a poor, little bantam hen who only that day had hatched out a brood of seven tiny chicks. The ordinary farmyard hens had all been sheltered in the fowl-coop, but of the little hen who ranged free there was no sign. Mrs. Cullinan feared that she and her chicks had been swept away in the flood, but she finally found the brave, little mother crouching against the leeward side of a large tree-trunk. Branches and leaves and debris lay scattered all around, but there she was, winking her bright, black eyes, her battered and bedraggled wings still spread protectively over her little brood. All seven bantam chicks had survived!

Naturally, the rain itself is responsible for numerous disasters, and so often it is the suddenness and intensity of the tropical cloudburst that catches one by surprise. A gold assayer, Mr. M. Wolffe, told me a story about a mine where one of these fierce downpours had a strange sequel. It appeared that a small-worker had pegged some claims on a gold reef. He called his claim The Giant Mine and he worked it successfully for some considerable time. Then, as so often happens, he ran into a fault in the rock and lost the gold-bearing reef. For weeks the miner blasted this way and that, trying to locate it again, while his resources dwindled away. Charge after charge of dynamite exposed nothing but barren formation, and there was no sign of the longed-for quartz vein. Almost at the end of his money, the miner was underground one day with a team of drillers preparing blasting holes for yet another charge of dynamite, when a tremendous rainstorm broke overhead. The storm-water drains on the surface were unable to cope with the volume of rain, and the mine workings began to flood. With great difficulty the miner and his men struggled out into the open air, grateful to be alive, as the mine filled with water behind them. Sadly he realised that he no longer had sufficient funds to pump the water out of the mine, nor to continue to search for the lost reef. He regretfully decided to abandon the claims.

For some years The Giant Mine was forgotten, and then one day another small-worker investigated the shaft and found that the underground workings had all dried out. He even came across the last batch of holes which the former owner had drilled just prior to the storm. This new miner pegged the abandoned claims, charged the old drills with dynamite and blasted the rock face. When all the rubble was cleared away he found that he had broken through into the lost reef! What's more, the rediscovered vein proved to be even richer than before. It seems very hard on the former owner that a mere rainstorm should cheat him of success when he almost had it within his grasp, but there it is! — what are we but pipes for Fortune's finger?

Speaking from a purely selfish point of view, there is nothing I enjoy so much as a good thunderstorm, especially at night. There is something exhilarating in all that release of energy and violent sound, the sudden flash of lightning that illuminates in an instant the garden bending and straining under the wind, the abrupt plunge back to darkness, together with the tearing crack and boom of thunder that sets the windows buzzing in their frames and reduces poor, old Josephine, the Labrador, to a cringing bundle of misery. Dear old Jo is no gun-dog. The mere sight of a toy balloon is enough to make her wretched. At the first growl of thunder she comes slinking into the house, guilty and abject, seeking the security of human companionship. Perhaps to her it sounds like some huge and menacing species of dog whose growl fills the sky. If she only knew it, the lightning is the real killer! All children in this country are drilled in the hazards of lightning — "Don't stand under tall trees during a storm. Don't shelter near a wire fence. Don't swim or take a bath if there is lightning about." For all this, lightning regularly takes its toll of two to three hundred lives each year.

As a child in Bulawayo I saw five men killed by lightning during a cricket match. The bolt actually struck and split a jacaranda tree at the edge of the cricket field on the far side of the pavilion. Two of the outfielders performed a frightful kind of *danse macabre,* leaping convulsively and tearing searingly hot coins from their pockets and flinging them away before dropping to earth.

Only last year a cattle rancher near Nyamandhlovu lost thirty head of cattle in a single lightning strike. The herd had taken cover under the spreading branches of a wild fig, and that was the end of them!

In a country that experiences drought for seven months of the year the rain is always welcome, even with its attendant drawbacks, and I can never suppress a feeling of pleasure and excitement at the commencement of a deluge. This attitude is, I know, incomprehensible to someone who has been brought up to regard the rain as a nuisance, and even my husband, who comes from Natal, finds this preoccupation with the rains a little bewildering. Only last week we had sweltered through an oppressively hot day with thunder growling round the sky all afternoon. Just at sunset a few large drops began to fall, so as usual I hurried outside to see what size of storm we could expect. A shaft of sunlight had pierced the cloud bank on the western horizon, illuminating with brilliant, yellow light the underside of the giraffe-thorn outside the back door. The huge umbrella of the tree looked weird, lit from below like that, with the sky dark behind it. It reminded me of an extravagant stage-setting for *Under the Sycamore Tree,* with the footlights casting the branches into dramatic relief. As I tilted back my head to see the sky, I observed that the last rays of the sun were also flashing off the falling raindrops. They came spinning out of a high, gauzy cloud like a sparkling cascade of crystal beads, each drop twinkling against the stormy sky. Then as the light deepened from gold to orange, and finally a fiery red, so the raindrops turned from diamonds to a swarm of golden bees, and at last to thousands of ruby sparks showering down from some great blast-furnace in the sky. The children came out to admire it too, and Tom said he felt as if he were standing underneath a volcano. As if this were not enough, Tracey turned and saw that the entire eastern horizon was spanned by a vast, double rainbow. While the sky outside the rainbow was a glowering charcoal grey, that within the huge semicircle was a rich rose-pink that gradually deepened to lilac, lavender and heliotrope before fading into night. I felt giddy with all that splendour, humbled by a knowledge of the inadequacy of all our puny strivings towards perfection. At this point Doug's head and shoulders appeared framed in the lighted window of the sitting-room. He was holding a glass of whisky and soda in his left hand.

"Why on earth are you three standing out there in the rain?" he demanded.

"Oh, did you see the colour of the raindrops? And look at that rainbow!" we chorused.

Doug peered at the dark sky where the last, faint ghost of the rainbow was still just visible.

"Yes," he said, "very nice. Now come inside for heaven's sake, before you're all soaked to the skin!"

Just after the Second World War, Rhodesia received a flood of new immigrants to whom the summer storms were a frightening experience. It was at about that time, too, that Bulawayo began to expand its telephone service, reaching out the hand of civilisation to the outlying areas. The advent of the telephone heralded an altogether new era for us. All at once we found ourselves the object of harassment from a host of total strangers who, it seemed, were living in terror of their lives on account of our small dam. Heaven knows it was a modest enough little pond, with no pretensions to holding water throughout the dry season. The wall was simply constructed of earth, but fully twenty feet wide at the base and strongly bonded together with kikuyu grass. When full it was perhaps seventy-five yards long by fifty wide, just enough for a flock of ducks and one small canoe. The little tributary of the Matsheumhlope which supplied it, only ran after a storm or during prolonged periods of rain, and it usually took at least two good downpours to fill the dam. From about the middle of December it was usual for the dam to overflow gently from one or both spillways, and the water would continue its course down the little stream bed and into the Matsheumhlope. Our phone was no sooner installed shortly before Christmas when we received the first of what were to be innumerable, hysterical telephone calls. Our phone stood on a little shelf in the dining-room, which was fortunate because, for some reason, nearly all these calls came through in the evening while we were having dinner, and so the entire family was able to enjoy them to the full. As the phone began to ring, interrupting the steady drumming of the rain, Father would push back his chair, plod over to the phone and lift the receiver.

"Hello," says Father.

"Is that Mr. Wightman?"

"Yes."

"Is that the Mr. Wightman with a dam?"

"Yes."

"I'm phoning to tell you that your dam has burst, Mr. Wightman," the voice goes on rising to a gabble. "There's a sheet of water pouring across my garden, it's reached the level of the front door and in another minute it will be into my house! I am holding you directly responsible for this. My house and family are in the greatest danger!" The man's voice cracks with excitement and emotion.

"Where do you live?" Father enquires tolerantly.

"Kildare Road."

"Oh yes," Father says, "Kildare Road. I thought so. Tell me, why did you build your house there? You're right in the bed of the valley, aren't you?"

This line of argument maddens the caller even further, and his voice begins to tremble with rage.

"Yes, I know we're in a valley, but . . ."

"And water tends to flow down a valley, doesn't it?" Father goes on remorselessly.

"Yes, but . . ."

"So either you should sell your house, or you must dig a channel for your storm-water," Father concludes.

"But I tell you your dam has burst!" the man protests, his voice rising to a scream.

"No," Father corrects him patiently, "my dam has not burst. And it's a good thing for you that I *have* a dam. Otherwise you probably wouldn't have a house."

"Now listen to me," the infuriated caller continues, trying to get his quivering voice under control, "I intend to take this up with the police!"

"By all means," Father agrees equably, "but might I suggest that before you do so, you put on a raincoat and come up and see the dam for yourself. Good-night." Father replaces the receiver, and returns to his dinner breathing heavily and darting angry looks at the telephone. Two minutes later the phone rings again, this time from someone half a mile further down the valley, and the whole rigmarole has to be gone through once more.

Our dam never broke. It never suffered so much as a wash-away, but this did not deter the people downriver from assuming the worst each time it rained. We children naturally loved these phone calls, and used to sit around the dining-room table stifling our snorts of laughter as they came through, one after another. Intermingled with frantic calls about the dam bursting were others which we received for the local police station. By a quirk of fate it so happened that their number and ours had the same figures, although the last two digits were transposed. It was a never-ending source of interest to discover the trivial nature of the complaints which the police were expected to handle. Not once, fortunately perhaps, were we involved in anything in the way of an emergency, although the callers were almost invariably in a state of excitement over their grievance, whatever it was. Father always tried to indicate early on in the conversation that he was not the Member in Charge, but frequently he would get no further than 'hello' before a torrent of impassioned words would issue from the other end of the line.

"Madam, I think you . . ." Father begins.

"Let me speak, please." It is one of the imperious breed. She continues her tirade.

"Yes, but you ought to understand . . ." Father tries again.

"I *haven't* finished!" she snaps. Evidently she is a woman accustomed to say unto men 'Come' and they come, and 'Go' and they go, and Father subsides into silence while she resumes her flood of recriminations. When at last all the wind is out of the bag, Father who has listened to the whole story with patient and attentive interest, is at last able to get a word in: "Is that all?" he enquires cautiously.

"How do you mean, is that all?" she squawks indignantly. "I would have thought that was enough!"

"Yes, yes, quite enough," Father agrees hastily. "It's just that I wanted to be sure you understood me when I said that this is not the Hillside police station."

There is a stunned silence.

"Not the police station? Don't be absurd! Of course you're the police. I *rang* the police!"

Patiently Father explains the similarities in our phone numbers. An angry outburst follows: "Why on earth didn't you say so before? Here I have been wasting valuable time telling you all this and meanwhile . . ." For several more minutes Father stands solemnly holding the receiver to his ear while the woman vents her spleen. There is a final squawk and click, and Father returns to the table to champ savagely at the cold remains of his dinner.

From our point of view, the most entertaining call came from a woman who phoned one evening to inform us that our dam had burst, and receiving no satisfaction from Father she then commenced to phone the police, as she thought, to complain about him. Father's rage was awful. Having held himself in check for the duration of both calls, he finally banged down the receiver and exploded: "Blasted telephone! I'd like to pluck the instrument out by the roots and drown it in the dam!"

The irony of it all was that we could always tell, even in the dark, when the dam was full and had begun to spill. The frogs told us. To the hundreds of toads and frogs and platannas which inhabited the dam wall, the filling of the dam was THE event of the year and they always signalled their delight in a deafening chorus of croaks, grunts, squeaks, pops and trills. It was like the continuous clangour of a busy iron-foundry and it continued all that night and through the following day. Thereafter the frog fights would begin. These were a form of semi-organised aquatic contest in which the opponents struggled for the coveted position of Chief Frog in our small pond.

Curiously enough, it was the female frogs who took to the ring. Although they must have lived in the vicinity of the dam all the year round, we only ever saw the bull frogs during the first few days after the dam filled, when they would congregate in the shallows to do battle. They were formidable Amazons, those bull frog ladies, with their bottle-green backs, daffodil-yellow bellies and egg-yolk orange throats. Their eyes were particularly striking, being vertically striped in black and white like a piece of zebra skin, and their wide mouths were amply supplied with fierce, triangular teeth. Their husbands, by contrast, were small and retiring, preferring to hide away in the more secluded reaches of the dam where they could avoid the noise and hubbub of war. Once the fights got under way no holds were barred. They would hop and leap at one another's throats, jaws gaping savagely, grunting and belching and snapping, and it was amazing to observe the skilful manner in which they delivered their upper-cuts, karate-chops and leg-throws. Between rounds they would sit facing one another in the water, gulping angrily. On one occasion I seized a lull in the fighting to rescue a frog who seemed to be getting rather the worst of it. Her lower lip was torn and she was bleeding from a long gash on her hind leg. However, she reacted angrily to my advances, drawing blood on my hand and all the while gurgling savagely and inflating herself until she was the size of a large pumpkin. With her squat body and downturned mouth she reminded me of a stout duchess who had just been insulted by a footman and was still too angry to speak. On several occasions we had as many as six or seven of these huge frogs assaulting one another simultaneously, fairly churning the shallows into a froth in their zeal.

How they arrived at a final decision as to who was the Victrix Ludorum I never discovered, but after two or three days they would quietly disappear and peace would reign once more. Soon the beds of flooded grass and the bank along the dam wall would be festooned with long skeins of shiny, black frogs' eggs, and not long afterwards the shallows would come alive with shoals of darting tadpoles.

These, of course, in turn attracted a wide variety of predators, and during the rainy season there was never a day without new visitors at the dam — a pair of Goliath herons, perhaps, standing motionless among the weeds, a flock of snow-white egrets scattered along the dam wall like pieces of windblown paper, or a solitary hamerkop, busily stirring up the mud with his feet. We had our resident pair of dabchicks, too, shiny little rust-and-brown bundles of fluff like miniature geese, each adult bird no bigger than a tea-cup. To me, their rippling whinnying cry in the early mornings was the very embodiment of summer.

In Matabeleland it is not so much the spring that brings the dry earth to life as those first summer rains. The land is transformed overnight. Newly washed, the veld sparkles in the sun. The air smells fresh and sweet while every tree and plant looks greener, released from its net of dust and spiders' webs. Dead grass and leaves are swept away, herded together into moraines by the imperious storm-waters. They pattern the veld like twisting, brown snakes or eskers in a glaciated landscape. Grass shoots appear as if by magic, a soft, green mist covers the parched vleis and an urgent sense of purpose is in the air. The rains have come, and every living thing has to get on to the bandwagon and make the most of it for the few brief months that they are with us.

First to jump on board are the white ants. It never ceases to fascinate me how they know in advance that it is going to rain. How do they know to prepare their wings and to be waiting in readiness at the entrance to their tunnels? The moment the first drops start to fall, the flying ants emerge, their four satiny wings folded neatly against their bodies. The lip of each termite hole is a bustle of activity.

Leading the procession come the soldier-ants, shiny and

red with huge nippers and hard, round heads the size of a pea.
They fan out over the ground to keep away the dangerous
enemies like toads and chameleons. Now a dry rustling is heard
deep within the earth as thousands of winged ants, each in her
bridal robe, come jostling and pushing up the twisting tunnels to
launch themselves on their maiden flight. They take to the air in
clouds, streaming away in erratic, precarious flight, their wings
so fragile that a single cannon-ball raindrop will send them
plummeting to earth. Many white ants never reach the upper air
for they fall victim to the more formidable predators like ratels
and antbears who take up their stations at the entrances to the
termitaria and lick up each tasty morsel as it comes to the
surface. Those in the air, too, are swooped on by the birds,
everything from an owl to a sparrow seizing the opportunity to
enjoy a rich, protein-packed dinner. Even so, countless
thousands escape, and in the mornings after the flight of the
white ants, the house is strewn with shed wings that lie in silky
drifts in the bath and along the skirting-boards, while mating
couples of termites trundle to and fro across the floor like
articulated trucks and trailers.

The rains bring with them a new wave of insects which are
predominantly nocturnal, and for a few weeks it is futile to
attempt to read at night under a standard lamp. A million flying
creatures zoom round the globe, clattering ominously inside the
lampshade, dive-bombing the written page and plopping preci-
pitately down one's neck. Even the most exciting thriller fails to
grip under these circumstances, particularly when the insect
horde contains iron-clad giants like the longhorn beetles. These
huge brutes come whirring in from the night to scuttle round the
room with frightening speed, clashing their serrated nippers and
rattling their wing-cases like hideous creations from a science-
fiction fantasy.

Even so, the longhorns are not the largest of the insect
invader force, this position being held by the stick insect, the
Goliath of the mantid clan. Twelve to fifteen inches long, he
resembles in repose a shrivelled twig with his legs and arms
folded neatly along his body. When alarmed, however, he opens

out his bodywork to reveal a pair of spectacular wine-red wings, rustling and rattling them threateningly before taking to clumsy flight.

I am fond of the mantids as a whole, for they have such intriguing ways of camouflaging themselves. There is the soft, grey, flat arboreal species whose furry body looks exactly like a piece of lichen-covered bark. Another resembles a ghostly figure from a fancy-dress ball, wearing a turbaned head-dress, grotesque shoulder-pads, a weirdly twisted tail-coat and scalloped leggings. His extraordinary outfit comes in shades of jungle green, burnt sienna and chocolate, rendering him completely invisible when stalking about on tiptoe among a bed of dry leaves. Yet another member of the family wears an extraordinary, harlequin costume of candy pink and apple green, with chequered wing-cases and peppermint-stick striped leggings.

While the mantids are useful creatures to have about on account of their hunting skills, there is not much to be said in favour of the rose-beetles. After the first rains, the leaves of my vines and runner-beans are reduced to lacework, and the roses are chewed right down to the stalk. It's a common sight in November to see torchlights bobbing about among the rose-beds all over town, each agonised gardener doing the rounds of his rose-bushes armed with a torch and a tin of paraffin. The beetles themselves are hard and shiny like varnished coffee-beans, and in the torchlight their eyes reflect a ruby glow. Even so, they are difficult to catch being so quick and cunning. They drop guiltily off the flower the instant the light is flashed on to them, and hastily burrow into the earth.

Among the more engaging diurnal creatures are the chongololos, or giant millipedes. All through the winter they lie curled under the earth like weird tertiary fossils. Then as the topsoil softens under the rain, they uncurl and struggle up to the sunlight. Their gleaming, black bodies glide swiftly over the ground, the fringe of legs rippling in successive bunches like wheat bowing before the wind. Young chongololos tend to startle easily when touched, casting themselves on their backs and wriggling about in a frenzied manner, in an evident attempt to emulate a snake. Older and more portly ones prefer to curl up into a neat coil or spiral, and wait in passive resignation until the danger is past.

Universal favourites are the toktokkie beetles. Their bodies are roughly the size of a cherry, hard and black, with neatly jointed white legs and small heads. They employ an enchanting form of bush telegraph to communicate with their mates. Reversing on to a dry leaf, the toktokkie will hammer on it with his posterior, bobbing up and down rapidly like a Morse transmitter. The dry, tapping noise carries for a surprising distance, and presently he is rewarded by an answering message from a long way off. The two toktokkies hurry towards one another, bustling among the leaves and tapping out messages as they go, until they finally meet face to face with a shy and joyful touching of antennae.

The boys at Plumtree School used to collect toktokkie beetles for their toktokkie farms. Fierce rivalry existed between the various 'estates', which were fully equipped with stalls and pens, kraals for the 'cattle', even dip-tanks. The most intelligent toktokkies were harnessed up in spans of sixteen to participate in wagon races. The wagons themselves were made of matchboxes, the skeis from matchsticks and the riems of cotton-thread. Whenever a toktokkie race was in progress, huge crowds of boys used to congregate around them, cheering on the winning team.

Christmas beetles, too, were highly esteemed as pets at Plumtree. They have earned the title of Christmas beetle because, like so many other insects, their presence is associated with the heavy rains that arrive in December. They are known to the rest of the world as cicadas, being famous for their ability to produce the most penetrating noise in relation to their size of any living thing. The Christmas beetle is a handsome creature very like a large, glass moth. He will sit invisible on the bark of a tree, trembling at the force of his own music, while the air all around splinters under the bombardment of his steel needles of sound. At close quarters the zing of a Christmas beetle is positively painful, so naturally the boys at Plumtree found it wonderful sport to take these creatures into the class-rooms, concealed inside their pockets. The cicada's voice is not only deafening, it possesses as well a mysterious ventriloquistic effect that makes it extremely difficult to trace the source of the sound. Experienced masters knew only too well the humiliating consequences of attempting to locate the culprit. Hammond, the headmaster was far too wise to fall into the trap of asking, "Who is the boy with a Christmas beetle?" He was, none the less, fond of relating the story of how even he was unwary enough to be goaded into committing an indiscretion through the presence of a Christmas beetle. It happened on a Sunday when the whole school was in Chapel. The service had no sooner commenced than a Christmas beetle began to make its presence felt, and the acoustics of the Plumtree Chapel being particularly good, the Christmas beetle put its best foot forward and filled the vaulted nave with its shrill, pulsating cry. For a while Hammond soldiered on, hoping that the first hymn would deter the insect, but the cicada joined in joyfully with the singing and its voice continued its triumphant solo long after the last chords of the organ had died away. Presently, after a particularly trying prayer, Hammond took off his glasses, laid them down and addressed the school quietly: "Will the boy," he said, "with the Christmas beetle, kindly leave the Chapel."

One after another the boys got to their feet and made for the door. The service was concluded with only half the school present!

Least attractive of the wet-weather insects are the maggot flies. Fat, brown and sluggish, it is their hideous practice to lay their eggs on the laundry as it hangs moist and warm on the line. Unless the eggs are killed by a hot iron, they will embed themselves in a person's skin when the newly washed garment is put on. The egg burrows down, developing into an itching, suppurating sore in the flesh, and a bad infestation of maggots can cause severe blood-poisoning. Doug Wells told me the story of an Irishman who was employed as a blaster during the construction of the Otto Beit Bridge over the Zambezi River at Chirundu. The Irishman had found the conditions of service at Chirundu extremely trying. For one thing the heat had been far worse than he had been led to believe, for another the workmen under him couldn't make head or tail of his Irish brogue, and to cap it all, he had been forced to spend two weeks in hospital receiving treatment for a severe maggot infestation that had erupted all over his arms and torso.

"Sure 'tis a terrible bloody country, this," he confided to Doug, "where the maggots are into a man even before he's dead!"

11

Bush Babies

ON THE LEVEL land below Grandmother's kopje and near the circular stone enclosure of her cattle kraal there stood a curious rock. It was about as high as a man and was shaped like a loaf of bread propped up on end, giving it the almost solemn aspect of a ceremonial monolith. We called it The Rubbing Rock, for one side of it was quite smooth and shiny where wild animals had rubbed themselves against it. I wonder why certain stones or rocks win such favour as scratching posts — their height, perhaps, or the texture of their surface? Whatever the reason, The Rubbing Rock was a tangible reminder that the land we occupied had once been populated by great herds of game. Indeed, the bushman paintings in the rock shelters told the same tale. We still had duiker and leguaans, hedgehogs and mongooses, snakes and squirrels, but the larger mammals had all moved away. Even so, a small but persistent trickle of young wild animals was continually brought into town to be reared as pets. Appealing as they are as babies, the sad fact is that wild animals very seldom make satisfactory household pets, and there is something depressingly dismal about a monkey or a stembok caged up in a run in someone's backyard.

Now and then one would come across a fellow with a lion or a cheetah cub sitting beside him on the seat of his car. The little creature is lovable and soft, with round furry ears and a baby-face. I always used to stop and stare, and finally say enviously: "He's so sweet! I wish I had him. Where did you get him?"

"Nice little chap, isn't he?" the man replies breezily. "Takes a lot of feeding, mind you. Where'd I get him? Oh, I found him in the bush. He'd been abandoned by his mother."

As a child I mercifully accepted this explanation, ignorant both of the power of the maternal instinct and of the excesses of man's greed. It came as a sickening shock in later years to learn that for almost every baby animal I had seen cuddled in someone's arms, there was a mother in the bush who had been shot and robbed of her young.

The worst of it is that in nine cases out of ten the people who initiate these kidnappings lose interest after the animal begins to grow up. Even where a young animal finds itself in the hands of the most kind-hearted, well-meaning and compassionate foster-parents, its life frequently ends in tragedy. At best the creature is simply an unbearable nuisance, at worst it becomes a hazard to the neighbourhood. The young baboon, for example, that was sweet and appealing at three weeks old, at a year is a fearsome tyrant, with teeth that would put those of a Dobermann to shame.

It is one thing to remove an animal from its natural environment and to teach it to be dependent on and trustful of man. It is another matter altogether to train that animal in the reverse process, so that it will be received once more by its own kind, and be able to fend for itself satisfactorily. As an illustration of this, I should relate the story of my Grandpa's baboon.

During the early years of this century, it was Grandpa Greenfield's practice to attend the weekly auctions on the Market Square. These Saturday morning auctions were perhaps the principal social event of Bulawayo's week. Everyone who could, used to attend, both for the entertainment and in order to meet up with friends from the outlying farms. The unfortunate thing was that Grandpa was generally unable to resist buying up at least one small bargain in the course of the sale. He repeatedly incurred Grandma's displeasure over this, when he'd bring home some frightful white elephant — an odd fruit plate, a set of bagpipes, or a faded reproduction of *The Last Supper*, somewhat eaten by white ants. On this occasion her wrath and indignation reached new levels, for Grandpa's trophy proved to be a very old and very wretched baboon.

This poor animal had been put up for auction, and naturally nobody wanted her. In those days there was no S.P.C.A. to care for neglected and unwanted animals. She was ugly and in frightful condition, chained up dejectedly and abandoned by her former owner. Grandpa bought her for five shillings as he couldn't bear to see her plight.

He called her Jenny and she became completely devoted to him. She had one failing, however. Having been cheated of her natural existence, Jenny had never been able to have babies of her own, and consequently her maternal instincts were still unsatisfied. She obviously yearned for a little baboon that she might cradle in her arms, for she used to seize upon any small child and carry it off to croon over it in the branches of a tree or on the roof-top. This naturally was a terrifying experience for the child and would send its mother into paroxysms of alarm. The problem was partially solved when Grandma made Jenny a rag doll. Jenny loved her doll and carried it about with her everywhere, sleeping with it at nights cuddled up to her hairy bosom. On rare occasions, however, she would still pounce on and carry off human babies, and after one of these events Grandpa finally realised that he would have to get rid of her.

Sorrowfully Grandpa drove Jenny out into the kopje country near Khami, some distance out of town. The rocks there were full of baboons and Grandpa confidently expected that Jenny would be overjoyed to see them. Such was not the case, unfortunately. The old baboon was terrified by the others of her tribe, showed no interest whatsoever in regaining her freedom, and only clung the more firmly on to Grandpa, refusing to be left behind. After a number of unsuccessful attempts to rehabilitate her, Grandpa was reluctantly compelled to shoot her — an event which upset him very considerably.

In its way, this melancholy tale is typical of the fate of all too many wild pets. Occasionally, however, these orphans from the bush do manage to achieve a reasonable life in spite of captivity, and I am reminded in particular of a young baboon which was presented to Reay Smithers when Reay was Director of the National Museum in Bulawayo. Naturally enough, Reay didn't want the baboon either, but like Grandpa he took pity on it. It so happened that shortly afterwards he received a request from San Diego Zoo to try to supply them with a male baboon, and it occurred to him that this young fellow might usefully fill the post. San Diego Zoo enjoys the reputation of being the best in the world — the best from the animals' point of view. No effort is spared to simulate a creature's natural environment, even to the extent of growing the kinds of trees and plants which would normally surround it in its wild state. Reay notified them that he had their baboon, and he proceeded to make the necessary arrangements for its emigration. These formalities took quite a while to accomplish. A great variety of innoculations were required, and naturally it had to be established that each of these had been effective. And then there was the question of the baboon's diet. Reay wished to satisfy himself that the baboon had adjusted to the kind of diet which he might expect it to receive in California. All this took several months, by the end of which Reay had become very fond of the baboon.

At last the day of departure dawned. As usual there were a number of unexpected last-minute matters to attend to, which delayed them, and it was accordingly in something of a hurry that he set off with the baboon for the airport. Reluctant to chain him up for their last ride together, Reay gave him the free run of the interior of the Land-Rover. Almost at once the baboon spied the licence disc stuck on to the inside of the windscreen and before Reay could stop him, he had peeled it off and popped it into his mouth. It would have involved a further delay and an upsetting tussle to get it away from him, so Reay decided to let him have it. Fate was against him, however, for at the very next traffic lights he was stopped by a sharp-eyed policeman who strode over and tapped the windscreen. "'ere," he said briskly, "where's your licence, then?"

"Look, I'm terribly sorry, Officer," Reay stammered. "I *had* my licence only this morning, but I'm afraid it — it's been eaten by a baboon."

The policeman's face flushed angrily.

"Are you tryin' to make a monkey out o' me?" he demanded belligerently.

"Not at all, Officer," Reay hastily assured him, "only I'm running late and I've got to get him to the airport and look — see for yourself, there he is in the back now!"

Reay jerked his thumb over his shoulder. The policeman thrust his head inside the Land-Rover, and there squatting on a box in the back was the baboon. His jaws were munching up and down rapidly, and protruding from his mouth was a half-moon shaped piece of paper — all that remained of the licence disc. A slow smile spread over the policeman's face.

"Go on!" he said incredulously. "I thought you were pulling my leg!" He turned back to Reay. "You'll get yourself fixed up with a duplicate licence tomorrow, won't you?"

Reay assured him he would, and resumed his dash to the airport. He was confident about one thing, anyway — the baboon was not going to present the San Diego Zoo with a feeding problem!

My sister-in-law Peggy used to have a pet vervet monkey, a

dainty little beast with a velvety, black face, soft grey fur and a
wasp-waist that would have been the envy of any sixteenth-
century belle. In those days Peggy and Lloyd, her husband,
lived in Natal on a large plot of land, half of which was covered
with a tangle of tall old mango and banana trees. The other half
was occupied by the house and garden, and the premises of the
family business — a small factory where Lloyd manufactured
refrigeration equipment. When Jacky the monkey was a baby she
used to accompany Peggy and Lloyd to work, but as she grew up
she became more independent and preferred to remain at the
house, pottering about among the mango trees. One feature of
the factory routines had impressed itself on her memory,
however, and each morning and afternoon when the hooter
sounded for the tea-break, Jacky would go flying down to the
factory for her mug of milky tea. During the rest of the day
her time was her own, and this enabled her to indulge in her

hobby of spying on people. She took a keen interest in all visitors, scrutinising their cars and handbags in the minutest detail, following with observant eyes everyone who set foot on the premises, from the postman to the vicar.

During this period Doug had to make a hurried visit to Natal. He knew nothing of Peggy's monkey, but arrived late at night, utterly exhausted having driven non-stop the twelve hundred miles from Salisbury. He had collapsed gratefully into bed in the spare room, secure in the knowledge that he would be able to sleep late the following morning.

Jacky the monkey discovered him shortly after dawn. Now, whether she was prompted by a purely clinical interest in Doug's apparently lifeless condition, or whether she simply wished to ascertain the colour of his eyes, we shall never know. At all events her curiosity got the better of her, and Doug was dragged up from the depths of sleep by the feel of sticky little monkey-fingers delicately lifting his eyelids by their lashes. Still three-quarters asleep, he found himself confronted by the black and puckered face of a vervet monkey, not two inches away from his own. Her little amber eyes were peering intently into his with a look of gentle concern. Of all the rude awakenings which he has experienced from time to time, Doug claims that the least congenial was to have his eyelids hauled open by a monkey.

Shortly after this episode, Jacky began to extend the field of her endeavours. Curiosity is generally considered to be the particular preserve of the cat family, but Jacky exceeded the most inquisitive cat in the pursuit of her researches into the private lives of Peggy's neighbours. She was particularly assiduous over the activities of a pair of middle-aged spinsters who lived next door. No aspect of their daily routine was too dull to escape Jacky's quick-eyed scrutiny. I recall that at the age of four or thereabouts I was fascinated by the question of what people's pyjamas were like. If ever we had guests to stay, and we frequently did, there was only one thing about them that interested me and that was what they wore when they went to bed. I would spare no efforts to catch a glimpse of these mysterious garments, lurking in the dark, outside their rondavel in the hope of discovering whether it was striped flannel, blue

canvas or white crêpe de Chine. Once this point had been
cleared up, my curiosity about their wardrobe was satisfied, and
as far as I was concerned our guests could have appeared for
breakfast wearing a grass skirt and a swallow-tail coat without
exciting the slightest interest. Perhaps Jacky was spurred on by
some such motive — who knows what strange thoughts go on
inside a monkey's head? At all events she spent hours at the
spinsters' house, peering in through the windows and pulling
faces at them whenever they appeared. It began to prey on their
nerves, this face at the window. Soon they were dropping things
in the kitchen or scalding themselves with their tea as they sat on
the sofa. They became as jumpy as victims of the Gestapo,
knowing that their every move was being observed. Finally, one
of them made a formal complaint to Lloyd, protesting that the
monkey's activities were an invasion of their privacy.

Fortunately they were spared the necessity of chaining her
up because at this point Peggy's dachshund, Mitzi, produced a
litter of puppies. Prior to this, Jacky and the little dog had been
the best of friends and used to play boisterous games together,
taking it in turn to chase one another pell-mell through the house
each evening. With the arrival of the puppies all this changed.
Absorbed in her babies, Mitzi lost interest in games with the
monkey, and no doubt Jacky felt lonely and rejected. Added to
this, something about the puppies must have triggered off the
monkey's own maternal urge which had been dormant all this
while, for she ceased spying on the neighbours and persistently
attempted to fondle the pups. Mitzi used to drive her away with a
volley of angry barks, and if the monkey so much as approached
the puppy box, she would get up and stand over them growling
savagely and wrinkling her lip. Time and again Jacky was put to
flight and had to content herself with watching them longingly
from the safety of the pelmet or the top of the kitchen dresser.

Then one day, while Mitzi was out of the room, the
monkey seized her opportunity. When a few moments later
Mitzi returned, she saw Jacky in the nursery box with one of the
puppies in her arms. Mitzi froze in the doorway and every hair
on her back bristled up on end. Stiff-legged and menacingly she
approached her litter, never taking her eyes off the monkey. For

a while Jacky held her ground, cradling the puppy and stroking it with her quick, rubbery little hands. Then under Mitzi's baleful glare, she guiltily and reluctantly laid the puppy back among the others and hopped out of the box. Mitzi's hackles subsided at once and from that moment the tide turned in favour of the monkey. It marked the beginning of a new relationship between the dog and the monkey. From then on Mitzi allowed Jacky to take charge of the puppies. She cleaned them and flea'd them, comforted them and cuddled them like an attentive nursemaid. As if relieved of the burden of these duties, Mitzi contented herself with feeding her puppies and left all the other chores to Jacky.

When at last it was time for the puppies to leave home, Peggy observed that Jacky was even more disturbed by their loss than Mitzi. So much did she appear to pine that Peggy resolved to do something about getting Jacky a mate. When at length she succeeded in obtaining a young, male vervet monkey, it was a case of love at first sight! The pair adored one another, but from that day there began a noticeable deterioration in

Jacky's relationships with her humans, and even with Mitzi. It was not that she grew savage; she merely became aloof and cool. Quite plainly it had been monkey society which she had craved all along, and the others had been no more than second-rate substitutes. The pair of monkeys became progressively more wild, spending their days in the trees in the garden, eating their fill of Peggy's bananas and mangoes and only coming into the house if lured in with something specially tempting, like a mug of milk. Even the factory tea-hooter had ceased to exert its former attraction.

To complicate matters, the spinster ladies now renewed their complaints, protesting shrilly that since there were now *two* monkeys at large, the position was twice as bad. They remarked furthermore that as one of them was a male, this made their espionage all the more outrageous. In point of fact, Jacky and Jacko were not in the slightest interested in the neighbours now, being completely absorbed with one another. Peggy decided, however, that the time was ripe to return them to the wild. One hot day towards the end of January she and Lloyd took the monkey couple up the coast to a wild stretch of forest adjoining the sea. Peggy felt racked with guilt, like the father of Hansel and Gretel, but the only alternative was to cage them up and that seemed so much worse. She knew besides that the kloofs all along there were full of wild bananas, and the low scrub next to the beach was a continuous hedge of amatungulu, the wild jasmine which at that time of year was laden with its pointed plum-like fruits. Her hunch was justified, because the monkeys made no attempt to return to their adoptive parents, but accepted their new environment at once and soon disappeared into the forest.

'Pregnant woman in rabies scare', the headline announced excitedly. I leaned over Doug's shoulder to read the short article. It was a typical five-minute sensation story calculated to round the eyes and purse up the lips of the casual reader. A young, pregnant woman had been disturbed by the furious barking of her two Alsatian dogs. On going outside to investigate she had found them harassing what appeared to be a tiny

Alsatian puppy. She called them off, and picked up the pup which immediately bit her in the hand. It was then that she realised with a shock of horror that the little animal was not an ordinary puppy, but a young jackal. She dropped it, screamed and ran into the house to telephone her husband and her doctor. It would have been normal medical practice for the woman to receive a course of rabies serum injections. However the fact that she was pregnant complicated the picture somewhat, for the injections might cause a miscarriage. The Government Veterinary Department, which was asked to comment on the situation, recommended that every effort be made to locate the jackal so that it could be established without doubt whether or not it was infested with rabies. If it were rabid then the woman would have to receive the injections, regardless of her condition, but if not, then neither she nor her unborn child were endangered. The article was accompanied by a photograph of the young woman looking suitably thoughtful and depressed.

Jackals are notorious rabies carriers, and the mere presence of a jackal in an urban area was highly suggestive of an outbreak of the disease. By the following day a major rabies alert was under way, and the story now merited a two-column spread. The police had been dragged into the affair too, and had put out an urgent appeal for anyone seeing the jackal to report its presence immediately. It had now been established where the jackal came from. It appeared that some people had brought a young jackal back with them from a cattle ranch in the Nuanetsi district. Interviewed by the Press as to how he had come to have a young jackal, its owner had replied: "Well it was just a youngster, you see. It had been abandoned by its mother and the wife and I took pity on it. We thought we'd keep it as a pet, like, but now it's run away, and there's all this trouble about rabies . . . "

As I read this I felt the first stirrings of indignation and distress. While I sympathised with the woman who had been bitten, I was upset by the thoughtlessness of the people who had shot the mother jackal and exposed the pup to this sort of situation. My misery was increased when the next morning's front page carried a large close-up of the baby jackal itself. He had been found and captured and, when the photograph was taken, he was imprisoned in a tiny budgie-cage pending delivery to the Veterinary Department for clinical observation. The sight of that poor little scrap of fur crushed up in a cage and terrified out of its wits was more than I could stand. I telephoned the Government Veterinary Department and asked them what they proposed to do with the baby jackal, once all the excitement had blown over. An extremely harassed vet explained that as far as he was concerned the less he had to do with the jackal the better it suited him.

"But if he turns out to have rabies, of course," he went on, "he'll have to be destroyed."

"How long will it take you to find out?" I asked.

"A couple of days," he said. "Within a week, at any rate, we should have established whether or not he has the disease in its active form. But then you must remember that rabies is a very difficult disease to diagnose when it's not active. An animal, or a human for that matter, can be infected and actually be incubating the disease for anything from six months to a year without showing any symptoms. You also have to take into account the fact that even rabies in its most infective period — the fulminating period as we call it — can take two forms. Either it can make an animal crazy, you know the well-publicised condition where the creature runs about yapping and biting and foaming at the mouth — or it can assume the paralytic form, as it's called, where the animal is very quiet and apparently docile. In cattle, for example, they may do no more than go off their food, become listless and die. It is definitely too early yet to determine whether this little chap is dangerous or not, but we've taken samples of blood and saliva, and as I say, we'll know the results in a few days."

"If the blood tests show that he's clear," I said cautiously, "what will you do with him then?"

"Theoretically we're obliged to give him back to his original owners," the vet said, "that is, the people who brought him back from Nuanetsi. I understand, however, that they don't want him any more. They would prefer us to put him down."

"If that's really the case," I said, wading out deep into trouble, "may I take him?"

I had not yet asked Doug what he would think of a jackal in the house, and I had an awful suspicion that he would be far from pleased. The vet laughed.

"You don't want to keep a jackal," he said. "They're not good pets, you know. And remember, even if his tests say he is clear, he still could be incubating rabies. It would not show up in his blood or saliva at this stage."

"Even so," I replied doggedly, "if no one else wants him, I'll take him."

"Why, what will you do with him?" he asked.

"I don't know," I replied truthfully, "but I'll think of something. I can't bear to think of him being put down when none of this is his fault."

The vet laughed again, took my telephone number and promised to let me know what transpired.

I put down the telephone with the sinking feeling that I had done something silly. Here I was with two young children of five and two, and for all anyone knew I might be exposing them or myself to the very real risk of contracting rabies. In an attempt to reassure myself, I went to the study and drew out Volume 18 of the encyclopedia. "Rabies or hydrophobia," it began cheerfully, "is an acute, ordinarily fatal, infectious disease of the central nervous system and is, as a rule, propagated in domestic dogs and wild carnivorous animals such as the wolf, jackal, coyote, fox, mongoose and skunk." It went on to detail the symptoms and the course of the disease, a gruesome page-and-a-half dripping with such ghoulish phrases as 'nerve tissue', 'fresh wounds', 'convulsive seizure', 'maniacal behaviour' and finally 'paralysis and death'. I put the book away, feeling sick at what I had done.

I clutched at the hope that Doug would forbid me to get the jackal, but when I told him about it in the evening, he simply raised his eyes to heaven and offered the opinion that I was out of my mind. For a week I heard no more and gradually assumed that the little creature had been found to be rabid and had accordingly been destroyed. Then shortly after lunch one day, the phone rang. It was the Veterinary Department.

"Is that Mrs. Dibb? Ah yes, I'm phoning to let you know that the tests we did on that little jackal are all negative. He's clear. You can have him."

Instead of feeling pleased and excited, my heart sank into my boots.

"Thank you for letting me know," I said miserably. "Where shall I collect him?"

"We've returned him to his owners, but they're most anxious to be rid of him. I'd go right away, if I were you. We've told the people about you, and they are expecting you."

I thanked the man and hung up thoughtfully.

"We're going to get a jackal," I told the children, "a baby jackal."

They hopped up and down excitedly, bursting with questions.

"But there's just one thing," I went on seriously. "He's wild and he bites, so until he becomes tame I don't want either of you to handle him or touch him at all."

They were disappointed, but even so their eagerness and enthusiasm had rekindled my hopes. Together we cleared out the big, wicker clothes-basket, lined it with an old towel and set off.

The jackal's owners lived in a ramshackle, red-brick house that stood in a waste of neglected garden. When I knocked on the back door, a woman opened it fractionally and eyed me unsmilingly through a narrow crack.

"Good afternoon," I said, "I've come about the little jackal."

The woman continued to regard me unwinkingly. Then she turned her head and addressed an invisible person inside the house.

"She's 'ere," she said. The door opened a little wider, and now the woman was joined by a bedraggled-looking elderly man. They stood shoulder to shoulder staring at me as if I'd escaped from a lunatic asylum. Neither of them said a word.

"Er, where do you keep him?" I asked, to break the spell.

"Keep 'im?" the man snorted. "We keep 'im locked up, that's where we keep 'im!"

He led the way through a dark passage to a dim and dusty spare room, explaining: "I'm taking no chances this time, I can tell you. I've put 'im in a trap for me carrier pigeon, and that's where 'e can stay." He indicated a small, wire pigeon-cage on the floor. "There 'e is. 'e's all yours."

In the darkness of the house I could just make out a tangled ball of fur, a pointed nose and a pair of frightened eyes. The jackal was so tightly jammed into the pigeon-cage that there was no room for him to turn around. He was covered with his own dung and dirt, his thick, furry coat so matted and filthy that he smelled like a badly kept zoo. I bit back the angry words that rose to my lips, and opened the lid of my clothes-basket.

"'ow yer goin' ter get 'im out?" the man asked in sepulchral tones. "Yer can't 'andle 'im. 'e bites."

"Yes," I said, "I expect he does."

As I lifted the trap-door of the pigeon-cage, the man and his wife shrank back to the doorway. There was so little room inside the cage that I literally had to force my hands past the jackal to get them round his body. As soon as I had hold of him and began to draw him out, he whipped his little head round and sank his teeth into the index finger of my left hand.

"Oooo, look out!" the woman cried. "'e's biting you!"

"Yes," I agreed, "he is."

The jackal made no attempt to struggle or change its grip on my finger. He simply clung on with his little puppy teeth and I felt it was preferable to let him do so, than to attempt to tear my hand away.

"Look at that!" the woman hissed in a horrified whisper. "She doesn't *mind* if 'e bites 'er!"

The instant I lowered the jackal into the dim interior of the basket, he let go and cowered away from me. I tied the lid on quickly and carried him out to the car. My finger was bleeding from half a dozen punctures. The man followed us out.

"Wot about rabies then?" he asked with the grisly relish of an onlooker at the scene of an accident. "You'll get rabies from that there bite, won't yer?"

"I hope not," I replied grimly. "I'll let you know if I do."

Unfortunately he took this to mean that I would hold him responsible, for he began to shout: "It's not my fault if you get bitten!" he cried heatedly. "If I'd 'ad my way, I'd 'ave 'ad 'im put down, I would. He's a nasty, dangerous, little . . ."

Hastily I started the car and drove away before I said something rash.

On the way home the children found a name for the little jackal. They called him Henry.
"Why Henry?" I enquired, smiling at them in the rear-view mirror, where they sat solemnly on the back seat with the washing-basket between them.
"He looks like Henry," came the cryptic reply, and so Henry he remained.

Henry was without exception the most miserable, frightened, pitiful, little animal I have ever seen. When we took him into my bedroom and let him out of the washing-basket, he bolted under the bed and from there into the cupboard where he hid, shivering with fright. There was almost nothing of him. He was no larger than a four-month-old kitten, his huge, pointed ears unnaturally large on such a tiny body. I was most anxious to clean his fur, but he was so terrified by my every movement that I was at my wits' end to know how to help him without frightening him to death. In a way, the worst of it was his utter silence — he had not uttered a single sound, not a growl, not a grunt, not a whimper. After all he had been through at the hands of humans, his cowering terror was not so very surprising. The first thing he was going to have to learn was that I would not hurt him. While the children went outside to play, I sat with Henry, talking to him softly and letting him get used to my voice. After a bit I leaned forward and touched him, stroking his matted fur. He shrank away from me, screwing himself up into his corner. He didn't attempt to bite, or to make any hostile gesture, but watched me fearfully out of his smoky-blue puppy's eyes, and trembled in every limb. It was too awful.

I withdrew my hand and moved back, sighing inwardly and wondering how to proceed with him. Presently I became aware of a snuffling at the crack of the bedroom door. It was Josephine, the golden Labrador. Overcome with curiosity, she had ventured into the house. Now Josephine is an 'outside' dog and this was a grave breach of discipline. All the same, I resolved to overlook her misdemeanour, and let her into the room to see what she and Henry thought of one another. I felt certain that Henry would be safe with her, for Josephine is the most gentle and motherly creature who has never so much as growled at, let alone bitten, anything in her life. She came bustling into the bedroom like a fussy, old housekeeper, sniffing here, there and everywhere, and in a few seconds she had found Henry cowering in the cupboard. Josephine lifted her head in surprise, cocked her ears, glanced up at me and gently wagged her tail as if to acknowledge a fairly good joke. And then Henry did an astonishing thing. Ignoring me, he scrambled to his feet, trotted swiftly out of the cupboard and ran under Josephine's belly, pressing himself against her hind leg! There, lifting his sweet little pointed face, he spoke to her. It was such a high, thin, fine needle of sound that it was almost inaudible, a tiny whine of welcome. Old Jo looked down at him benignly, wagging her tail, and Henry raised himself up on his hind legs and tried to suckle from her. I found my eyes filling with tears. I had not stopped to consider how, through all his terrifying adventures, the little jackal was still missing his mother.

Although Jo had borne a litter of pups within the past year, her dugs were dry and naturally she wouldn't let him suckle, nosing him off gently but firmly and wagging her tail in an apologetic fashion. I tiptoed off to fetch a saucer of warm milk.

As I put it down on the floor, Henry lifted his head and narrowed his eyes, sniffing the air, but he clearly didn't know what to do with the milk. I managed to persuade Jo to lie down, placed the saucer close up to her belly, and that did the trick! Then of course I had to fetch another saucer of milk for Josephine, who by this time was beginning to feel a little bit 'put upon'.

So far so good! Next, I fetched Henry some raw meat. He devoured two or three pieces of it very hungrily indeed, snatching the meat from my fingers and swallowing it at a gulp. And then he did another strange thing — while he continued to take the meat from my hand, he didn't swallow it, but hoarded it up until his mouth was quite full. He then trotted back into the cupboard and pushed all his meat deep into the toe of one of Doug's best black shoes! When at last he had satisfied himself that his hoard was safely buried, he came out once more and began to explore the room.

His movements were as silent as a cat's — very rapid, very soft. He moved everywhere at a quick, noiseless tripple and could change direction without a second's pause. He trotted restlessly round the room, skirting along the walls and disappearing under the furniture, bolting across the open spaces and lingering wherever there was cover. This cautious exploration went on for some time and presently Jo became bored and indicated that she wanted to go outside. The instant she disappeared, Henry shot back into his cupboard and curled up tightly once more in his corner.

I could see that if I were going to be able to handle him at all, it would have to be with Josephine's assistance and under the comforting influence of her presence. Now Henry's eyes were beginning to droop tiredly, so I crept out of the room, closed the door and left him to have a good sleep.

All afternoon I puzzled over how I was to clean his fur. His coat was so matted and caked with filth that I knew he would never be able to make any impression on it himself. Towards five o'clock when the sun streamed into the bedroom, I summoned Josephine and marshalled together the items necessary for Henry's ablutions — a small bucket of warm water, a flannel, a cake of soap, a pair of nail scissors and a comb.

Once again Henry ran to Josephine, greeting her with his tiny whine of pleasure and pressing himself against her leg. He was noticeably less timid than he had been only hours before, allowing me to touch him and stroke him without cringing. All the same, it was difficult to know where to begin the herculean task of cleaning him up. Finally I decided to start on his hindquarters as they were the worst, so I dipped the flannel into the warm water, wrung it out and mopped softly at his fur with what I hoped might simulate his mother's licking actions. Henry turned his head and watched my hand in surprise, but he stood quite still and submitted to my ministrations with docility. After a bit he became skittish, poking the flannel with his nose and pretending to nip my hand. And then as if in an ecstasy of pleasure he rolled on to his back and presented his tummy to be cleaned, dabbling at the air with his little, pointed paws and clicking his jaws open and shut with obvious delight. I couldn't help laughing at him. Some parts of his fur were so heavily encrusted that I had to snip them away with the scissors, but even this he endured with the greatest good humour, positively turning himself this way and that so as to enable me to get at the awkward places.

I consider that an animal's willingness to clean itself is a barometer of its spiritual and physical well-being. A sick or an injured animal that yet has the will to wash itself, is hopeful of its own recovery. I was therefore enormously cheered when Henry began taking a hand with the task of tidying himself up. Perhaps the 'licking' movements of the flannel had triggered off some neglected instinct in himself, or perhaps he felt less daunted by the magnitude of the job, now that he was getting some help with it. At all events, he set to work with a will, nuzzling at his fur and clicking his teeth together in the most practical way.

After thirty minutes of our concerted efforts, Henry was a different creature. His coat that had at best been a dingy brown, now shone in rich tones of apricot and gold, while the thick silky 'saddle' on his back emerged as a gleaming charcoal-grey, flecked with silver. Groomed and combed, his beautiful brush of a tail puffed out behind him like blue smoke, and altogether with his slim, black forelegs, large pricked ears and fox-like face, Henry was exquisitely lovely.

That evening I proudly presented Henry for inspection, when Doug returned from work. Doug was relatively non-committal. He conceded that Henry had a sweet face and a beautiful coat, but he was frankly displeased with the story of the meat in his shoe, and I could see that he was worried about the bites on my finger. Henry was very good during the night. He didn't whimper or scratch or make a disturbance, but shared Jo's blanket with her in the spare room. By the following morning it was quite plain that Henry was a member of the family.

Next day I made the discovery that Henry was very badly infested with worms. I bought him some cat-sized worm pills, and after the eradication of these parasites, a further improvement was noticeable in his appearance and demeanour. His little belly which had been hard and round, grew soft, smooth and supple and his whole aspect became more jaunty and confident. His aplomb was very easily shattered, however, and if Henry had a failing it was his extreme timidity. Any sudden noise, or the unexpected appearance of a human being was enough to send him flying for cover. His favourite place of refuge remained the bedroom cupboard, and I always tried to ensure that it was left open for him.

Henry came with us each evening, when we took Josephine for her walk, but whereas she was allowed to trot at heel, I kept Henry on a lead. The first time he accompanied us, I almost lost him when he took fright and bolted away from the deep growl of a lorry. With Josephine's help I found him again, hiding quivering in a hedge, but I couldn't bear to think what would happen to him if he were to become a fugitive once more, so from then onwards he stayed on a lead. For the rest of the day, Henry clung closely to Josephine, following her wherever she went, lying down where she did, drinking when she drank and cleaning himself when she did her *toilette*. The only matter over which he demonstrated his individuality was on the question of food.

Whereas any normal puppy will gorge itself to bursting

point, Henry was extremely fastidious, eating only a little of his dinner and reserving the rest for later. I wondered if this tendency had developed as a result of the jackal being a natural scavenger. I had always imagined that a scavenger was only a scavenger because it possessed neither the skill nor the temperament to hunt for itself. This would appear to be only part of the picture. I suspect now that jackals scavenge simply because they do not enjoy large quantities of food. Henry's appetite was literally satisfied with the tiniest scrap of meat or bone, and he emphatically preferred to eat little-and-often rather than all at one fell swoop.

Not that he was wasteful. Any surplus dinner he would collect neatly into his mouth and hide, usually in a shoe, with the result that we never knew what we might find in our footwear. Many times someone dressing in a hurry would suddenly let out a roar or a shriek on pushing their toe into a mess of meat, and we were forced to devise a strategy to protect our shoes from this abuse. Eventually I hit on the idea of leaving one of my old shoes in the bedroom cupboard, and this became Henry's favourite burial-ground for his excess food.

Henry's beauty and confidence grew day by day. He even became playful, executing airy leaps and twists and somersaults round my bedroom in the evenings, or dropping his head down between his forepaws and looking up at me with a roguish expression. He knew his name and responded to being stroked by drooping his ears and wagging his tail. All appeared to be going well when an unexpected situation developed — Josephine came into season. I had been so taken up with Henry that I had completely forgotten that this event was looming on the horizon, and the first we knew of it was the arrival of the neighbourhood swains. Naturally each of these young bloods was eager to show off in front of his lady-love, and what better way than by chasing off an impudent young jackal. Henry was much alarmed by these visitors, and as our plot was not fenced or gated we finally decided that the best thing would be to put Jo into kennels for the duration of her season.

Josephine's disappearance had a profoundly demoralising

effect on Henry. I had thought that after all these weeks he would have gained sufficient confidence in himself to take it in his stride, but such was not the case. He became pitifully timid once more, hiding away in his cupboard at the slightest noise, or if in the garden, bolting headlong for the nearest cover. I became most alarmed that he might take fright over something when I was not right there to call him back. By now he would come to me when I called, but shyly, hesitatingly, starting and cowering at every little sound.

During the previous few weeks it had become increasingly apparent that Henry was a predominantly nocturnal animal. He would spend most of the day-time sleeping in the cupboard, only waking up towards late afternoon. Then for the rest of the night he would trot restlessly through the house, from one end to the other, hunting for spiders and moths. Due to my renewed anxiety that he might take fright and run off, and my concern that he was bored by being cooped up in the house at nights, I decided to build him a large run where he could stay until Jo returned.

We constructed a spacious, hexagonal enclosure, that took in a good-sized granite outcrop and was shaded by a number of dense, indigenous bushes. Knowing how much his bolt-hole meant to him, I dug Henry a burrow, lining it at the end with an oil-drum into which I placed an old sheepskin rug. Henry loved his burrow and used to spend nearly all day inside it, fast asleep, only emerging in the evenings to hunt about among his rocks for beetles. In many ways this run improved Henry's lot because there was far more for him to do at nights. He obviously enjoyed scrabbling in the earth after grubs and insects, and he made little tunnels and hidey-holes for himself in the thick, tussocky grass between the boulders.

All this while Doug had continued to regard Henry with something of a jaundiced eye. He despised his timidity which, he claimed, was nothing more nor less than jackal cowardice, and he was still genuinely concerned about the rabies aspect. Then one day something occurred which presented Henry in an altogether different light. It had been one of those trying days for both of us and we were tired and grumpy with one another. Doug had had problems at the office, the children had been unusually fractious and, to crown it all, the dinner which I had so painstakingly prepared was a disaster. I don't quite know what went wrong with it, for it was nothing more complicated than an oxtail stew, but after a few mouthfuls Doug pushed his plate away and refused to touch it.

"It's frightful," he said. "Quite uneatable. You might as well give it to the dog."

"My dog isn't here," I retorted, almost on the brink of tears. Good old Jo. She'd have eaten it without a word of protest, relishing every drop.

"Well in that case I suggest you give it to that blasted jackal of yours. One thing's certain. It's unfit for human consumption."

"Very well then, I *will* give it to my jackal," I snapped. Thoroughly hurt and annoyed, I scraped off all the oxtail into a big enamel dish and took it outside to Henry. A full moon had just risen, bathing the garden in a wash of silver. Henry was standing on the top of one of his boulders, nose lifted to the sky, sniffing the air. I called him gently and he came to his gate to greet me. I slid through the door and joined him in the run, fondling his ears and talking to him.

"Look at this, Henry. See what I've brought you. Lovely, lovely oxtail stew."

Henry sniffed it cautiously, then ran around behind me and came to sniff the meat from the other side. For a long while he hung his chin over the dish in a contemplative fashion, and at last he made up his mind. Neatly and deliberately he picked up each knuckle of oxtail until his mouth and gorge were quite full. Then, holding his head high, he trotted off on silent feet to the end of the run furthest from his burrow, and began to dig. Still holding the meat in his mouth, he set to work scraping away at the soil with his claws until he had excavated a deep, narrow tomb. Finally satisfied that it was big enough, he ceremoniously deposited all the oxtail into this burial chamber and nosed over the loose soil, patting it down firmly with the end of his snout. Then, with the pleased air of one who has solved a particularly trying problem, he sneezed, wiped his face with his paws and resumed his vigil on the top of his rock.

I had of course realised myself that the stew was somewhat sub-standard, but I had certainly not expected Henry to give it the thumbs down in such emphatic terms. Thoroughly crushed, I slunk back to the house like a whipped puppy. Doug heard me opening the kitchen door.

"Well?" he shouted cheerfully from his armchair in the sitting-room. "Did he eat it?"

"No," I replied shortly. "He didn't."

"What's that you say?" Doug's voice sounded incredulous. I heard him get up and come through the house. A moment later he appeared in the kitchen, where I was washing out the enamel dish.

"So even your *jackal* wouldn't eat it, eh?" Doug exulted. "Why, what did he do with it?"

A giggle escaped me. I suppressed it sternly.

"He buried it," I said, trying to look offended.

"He buried it?" Doug shouted delightedly. "My word, he's got more courage than I thought! Sensible animal! So he buried it, did he?" Doug laughed boisterously, and now a new gust of giggles tore through my assumed air of grief.

"Yes," I shrieked, now laughing openly, "he dug a great pit and put it all at the bottom and covered it over!"

"Ingenious little fellow!" Doug exclaimed, wiping his eyes. "What taste! What discernment! You might think," he went on more soberly, "that a jackal being a scavenger would eat just anything. But no! Even a jackal will draw the line somewhere!"

From that day Doug was Henry's sworn ally, championing his cause and that of all jackals.

"Let me tell you something," he'd say reprovingly to anyone who disparaged the jackal family, "they're very fine animals, very fine indeed," and he'd go on to relate the ignominious fate of the villainous oxtail stew.

Henry was about six months old, very handsome and almost as large as a spaniel when he began to exhibit symptoms of wanderlust. I had for some time been expecting this, for it was natural that as Henry matured he would yearn once more for the society of his own kind, and for the freedom of the wide open spaces. Fond as he was of Josephine, he obviously knew in his heart that he needed something else. He became more adventurous during the days, venturing out on to the road, and at night when we shut him in his run, he used to pace restlessly up and down his fence. I knew now that the time had come to contact Robin Hughes.

Robin and I had known each other as children in Bulawayo, and I remembered him as a shy little boy with sparkling green eyes and shiny black hair. What had made him memorable and set him apart from everyone else was his conspicuous compassion for all wild things. Where every other little boy yearned to own a pellet gun and would spend each week-end bird's-nesting, Robin used to keep an animal hospital in which his patients were anything from a toktokkie beetle to a tortoise. After growing up he had for some years been with the

Department of National Parks where he earned the reputation of being one of the finest Game Rangers whom the country has ever seen. More recently he had set up his own private game reserve on a farm near Ruwa on the outskirts of Salisbury. When I told Robin about Henry, he was very eager to have him, for he wished to breed jackals as a link in the natural chain of predator and prey. He envisaged that Henry would continue to be fed and sheltered for as long as he required it, but that he would, at the same time, have the opportunity of rehabilitating himself in the bush.

We were all sad to say goodbye to Henry. Robin and his wife Gretl came to collect him one week-end, and our little jackal went off curled up comfortably inside the old oil-drum with its sheepskin lining. We heard from Robin that within a

very short time Henry had established himself successfully in a large, three-acre pen, and was ready to be given the run of the entire farm. After such an unpropitious beginning, Henry was after all destined to lead a normal life.

And the rabies? Long after Henry had gone, I used to look at the little scars on my finger where he had bitten me the day we first got him, and I used to wonder if I was incubating the disease myself. Six months to a year, the vet had told me . . . It is now nine years since Henry left us, and though on occasions the family complain that I am rabid when I snarl and snap, we all agree that it can't be Henry's fault. Doug, in particular, won't hear a word against him. A few weeks after Henry left us I noticed a tempting advertisement in the Kennel and Pets column of the newspaper.

"Good home wanted for young white-backed vulture," the ad said. I showed it to Doug.

"Certainly not!" he exploded. "How can you think of having a repulsive creature like a *vulture* as a pet! Imagine what the neighbours will say when they see a dirty big vulture roosting on the roof of the house! People will think I'm running an undertaker's shop, and next thing I'll have the Municipal health authorities breathing down my neck. Now listen here," Doug went on firmly. "Jackals, yes," he said, "but vultures, no!"

12

Makulu & Company

BEHIND OUR HOUSE IN Bulawayo we had a large fowl-run shaded by a group of wild mimosa trees. Mother disliked the hens. While she readily admitted that there was something restful and contented in the gentle symphony of clucks and cackles that emanated from them, she felt an antipathy towards their collective personalities.

"The trouble with hens," she used to say, "is that they have no sense of humour."

Indeed, poultry in general, and hens in particular, do seem to take themselves rather seriously, and perhaps this is why I always find them so entertaining.

At one time we had a splendid white leghorn cockerel called Makulu — 'The Great One'. It was an appropriate name for he possessed not only the stature but also the presence of a chieftain. Makulu practised the art of crowing as assiduously as Caruso, and like the golden-voiced tenor, he too began his musical studies at an early age. As a gawky-legged, scrawny-necked adolescent he learned to hop up on to the roof of the hen-house where he would beat his wings and cry: "Cock-aw, cock-aw, cock-aw!" with fierce concentration. These earliest attempts at crowing resembled the convulsive, gurking squawk of an old-fashioned Klaxon horn, but after each utterance Makulu would blink his eyes and tilt his head to one side as if giving careful consideration to the quality of his recitative.

As he matured, his comb grew larger and more luxuriant

and a rusty gold mantle began to spread down from his neck to his shoulders. Now his song had sprouted another syllable and he was able to produce a very creditable 'Cock-a-do'. Even this did not satisfy him, however, and after further weeks of practice he had augmented his repertoire to include first a 'doodle', and then an extra 'doo' on the end.

By the end of his first year Makulu had grown a magnificent train of arching tail-feathers in glowing shades of copper and bronze, and was a force to be reckoned with. He pranced about the hen-run flexing his muscles and puffing out his neck, his scarlet comb now so large that it curled over on itself and dangled before one eye. Most impressive of all, his song had now expanded to a bell-like six-syllabled aria: "Cock-a-doodle-doo, aah!"

The final 'aah' was actually a desperate gargling intake of breath that activated his larynx and produced a long trailing tail-note, a minor cadenza as it were, tacked on to the main theme. Makulu certainly was cock-of-the-walk in every sense of the word, having used his clarion call to cow into submission every rival in the neighbourhood.

In those days Father used to do a lot of trading in live poultry as well as in eggs and fresh produce. He kept a large fowl-run near his shop in town, where he would accommodate new intakes of poultry as they were delivered. There was only one problem about this arrangement, and that was the regrettable way in which the roosters used to fight one another. The other birds had no peace on account of the repeated skirmishes that went on between the newcomers and the cocks which had been in the run for several days. Not uncommonly, these fights resulted in one or both birds having to be disposed of, in order to restore the peace. Noticing the tranquillity that prevailed under Makulu's rule of iron, Father decided to take our cockerel to the fowl-run in town in the hope that he might impose some form of law and order among the discordant elements there.

It was a tough assignment for any rooster, but Makulu was not one to be daunted by a change of scene. He strutted into the arena like a prize-fighter, bristling with aggressive self-confidence. Within a few days Makulu had taken charge of the

situation and established himself as the undisputed King.
Thereafter he followed a systematic procedure whenever a new
cock was admitted to the company. If the newcomer submitted
to him at once, so much the better, and he would escape with no
more than a cursory scragging. If, on the other hand, he showed
an inclination to put up a fight, then Makulu would puff out his
chest, roll up his sleeves and thrash him. It was an admirable
arrangement, because once one cock had established his
authority, all bickering ceased between the others and the whole
community was able to go about its business in peace and
harmony. Father's fowl-run became familiarly known in the
town as Makulu & Company.

The inevitable day came, however, when Makulu met his

match. In a consignment of assorted birds that came up from Bechuanaland, there was a single Muscovy drake. He was a powerfully built old fellow, with the lumpy and scarlet complexion of a heavy drinker, a fierce blue eye and a formidable beak that had a grip like a wolf-trap. If Makulu had left the drake severely alone, I suspect that all would have been well. The Muscovy after all had no desire to dominate the fowl-run or build an empire of chickens, but neither was he prepared to kotow to some cocky young rooster. The fight when it came was very short and very brutal, and the gallant Makulu was killed.

We all mourned his passing, Father more so than the rest of us, because now of course all the old trouble started up once more and there were cockfights going on all day. Finally, in desperation, Father got rid of the whole lot of them, all but the Muscovy drake. As a tribute to his independence of spirit, Father brought him home and released him on to our dam. After a while we acquired a wife for him, and the two of them led a quiet life, eating frogs and snails and keeping very much to themselves. As a small child, I was a little afraid of the Muscovy duck. Year after year she made her nest in the thick grass at one end of the dam wall. During these periods she used to become

ill-tempered and pugnacious, and if I approached she would suddenly burst from her nest weaving her head to and fro just above the ground, like a snake, and uttering a witch-like hissing and mewing. I was distinctly intimidated by these displays, and took pains to keep out of her way.

Muscovies certainly have forceful personalities, a fact that was brought home to me some twenty years later when I grew to know a pair of them extremely well. Doug and I came to have the ducks through a curious chain of circumstances. At that time I kept a small flock of hens who ranged freely round the garden. At the head of the pecking order was a splendid, matronly, old black Australorp called Angelina. She was dignified, lady-like and good-natured — within the limits of her position — and, furthermore, she was as beautiful as she was gracious. Her heavy black plumage had a metallic sheen, so that in the sun each feather glistened with green and purple highlights. With her sweeping black skirts and proud carriage, she had the portly elegance of a middle-aged flamenco dancer. I was very fond of the old hen, and often referred to her affectionately as Angelina Galina, a name that suited her well.

It came as a thunderbolt from the blue when one summer shortly before Christmas, Angelina went broody. Prior to this she had regularly laid a lovely, brown egg for three hundred and sixty days out of the three hundred and sixty-five. I couldn't understand it, and could only conclude that something had snapped inside what she called her brain, and she had said to herself: "I refuse to lay another egg or to move off this nest until I hatch out some chickens." The fact that she *had* no eggs appeared to make no difference. She refused all food and water, ignoring a bowl of grain put down in front of her as if it didn't exist. Day after day she remained hunched up in her bed of straw, becoming noticeably thinner, her eyes lack-lustre, her feathers dull and dishevelled. I grew so anxious at the way she was losing condition that I telephoned a leading poultryman to get his advice.

"Not much you can do with a broody hen," he said dispassionately. "Best thing is to knock 'er off. A broody hen's no use at all in this age of incubators and batteries."

"Well, but isn't there *some* way I can get her off the brood?"
I quavered.

"Aw, I dunno," he replied morosely. "Some folks say you
should throw water over her. I've known it work. Course, the
sure-fire way to cure her condition is to give her a clutch of fertile
eggs. But then, maybe, you're not wanting more chickens."

"No, I'm not," I agreed. "Six hens is about enough for us."

"What about a couple of duck eggs, then?" the poultry-man
suggested patiently. "If you have young children, they always
enjoy a few ducks messing about the place, and they're useful
too — eat up the snails and slugs in your garden. I can let you
have a couple of fertile duck eggs at any time."

I knew the children would adore a pair of ducks. After a
moment's thought I thanked the man and accepted his offer.
That night, after it was dark, I crept into the fowl-run and knelt
down in front of Angelina's nesting-box. One by one I gently
slipped four, large, pointed duck eggs beneath her feathers.
She gave a shrill crooning noise as each egg went in, but made no
attempt to peck either me or them. In the morning I went out to
see how she was. It could have been my imagination, but I
fancied that she was holding her head a little higher, and there
was a decidedly defiant gleam in her black eyes. As I knelt down
in front of her, she puffed herself out importantly and uttered the
same high trill of indignation.

"You funny old hen," I laughed at her. "You're thrilled to bits,
aren't you?"

Within a few days she was eagerly taking food, pecking the
grain from my outstretched hand, and when I placed a bowl of
water near her, she would scoop up a beakful and let the cool
fluid trickle down her throat, her eyes closed ecstatically. Once
or twice she floundered off her nest to totter out into the
sunshine. There she would stand swaying unsteadily on her feet
for a moment, before deliberately loosening all her feathers and
shaking them out like a bundle of ragged dusters. Then, croaking
anxiously, she would stagger back into the nesting-box and
arrange herself over her eggs with the fussy and delicate
precision of an old lady setting out her best china tea-cups.

One afternoon, four weeks later, Angelina came stalking deliberately out of her nesting-box, lifting each foot carefully and proudly, and clucking continuous encouragement to two, little balls of yellow down that obediently followed behind her. The other hens gathered outside the wire of the fowl-run and ogled at the babies enviously. Angelina was as pleased as Punch. Presently she squatted down, spread out her wings and tucked a duckling under each one. The babies peeped out through her feathers with their bright, little, black eyes and cheeped excitedly at the world around them. Presently one of them spied a fly on the edge of the water-dish. He dashed out of his ambush among Angelina's feathers, snapped up the fly, tripped over his flabby, webbed feet and fell headlong into the water-dish. Angelina rose majestically and came forward, clucking a stern rebuke. The duckling however was in no hurry to get out of the water, and in a moment the other one had joined him. The other hens exchanged significant glances, as if to say: "Poor old girl. She's produced a couple of half-wits." Angelina was a trifle flustered, but she obviously wasn't going to exhibit symptoms of panic in front of all the other hens. She attempted to look nonchalant, while keeping her eye firmly on her two delinquent offspring, and when they had finished their swim she very pointedly took her little family back into the nesting-box and put them to bed.

A fierce rivalry existed between Josephine and the hens as to who was entitled to the scraps that were flung out of the kitchen door. As the two ducklings grew, it became apparent that they led the field at this game. As they grew bolder and more independent they used to take up their station on the back doorstep where they would be sure to be first in line for any hand-outs. Josephine took this as a personal slight. The back doorstep was traditionally her particular place, and she was quite emphatic that no duck was going to usurp it. She used to dislodge them by putting on a vigorous display of good humour, cavorting and curvetting, snorting and prancing around them until the ducks lost their nerve and sidled off with outstretched necks and rolling eyes. Josephine would then lie down on the step and go to sleep.

This worked well enough while the ducklings were quite small and easily frightened, but they grew rapidly and began to develop the red faces and fierce blue eyes of the adult Muscovy. The larger of the pair had a thick cap of black feathers which he would elevate into a crest when excited or annoyed, and after some weeks it became apparent that Angelina's ducklings were a pigeon pair. We called them Samson and Delilah.

The power struggle between Josephine and the Muscovies reached new heights the following summer when Delilah selected Josephine's kennel as her nesting-box. Now Jo didn't really like her kennel, and only went into it when in disgrace, which was very seldom indeed. None the less, she knew it was her property and she resented the arrogant way in which Delilah had appropriated it. The two of them used to glower at one another, Delilah inside the kennel and Jo just outside it, while Delilah uttered the shrill, whining witch's mew that I remembered so well.

Hearing his bride's cries of distress, Samson would come steaming into action, hissing and puffing and sizzling threateningly. With his crest fully extended and his face reddening angrily he looked like an apoplectic Regimental Sergeant-Major who has just discovered a slovenly recruit on parade. With complete disregard for his own safety, Samson would seize the dog by the ear or by the scruff of her neck and attempt to murder her on the spot.

I was continually compelled to drop whatever I was doing in order to separate the combatants. The two of them would flap and flounder about the backyard, Josephine trying to shake the drake off, and Samson beating his wings and hissing through clenched beak, determined to hang on to the bitter end. I could usually dislodge Samson by clapping my hands together smartly and telling him to shoo, but sometimes he would get himself so worked up and inflamed with anger that I was compelled to lay hold of him and force his beak open with my fingers.

After a bit Josephine gave up haunting around the kennel, but by now Samson had developed a taste for dog-baiting, and was continually on the war-path. While searching for a new *casus belli* he renewed his claim to the back doorstep, and numerous pitched battles took place outside the kitchen. The instant Samson caught sight of Josephine, the blood-lust would darken his eyes and he would come strutting up, hissing like a steam-engine and lunging out for Jo's ears. She would crouch down to face him, lying on her elbows with her hindquarters in the air, having learned by experience that the most successful ploy was to seize his head in her mouth and hold it until help arrived. We marvelled at her self-control, for she could have killed him with one crunch.

"Samson, old chap," Doug used to say to him, "you don't know how lucky you are. If Jo were any other kind of dog, you'd have been a gonner months ago."

There was only one thing which Samson really feared, and that was the kitchen broom. For some reason he held its greeny-yellow bristles in abhorrence and the mere sight of them emerging from the back door would send him scurrying off ignominiously. Even with the aid of the kitchen broom, however, the simple act of giving Jo her dinner developed into a complicated military manœuvre. When her meal was ready I would go to the back door and whistle for her. Immediately Samson would shoot up his crest and draw in a long, awful gasp of horror, like a severe Presbyterian elder who has caught one of his flock playing cards on the sabbath. Then as Jo cantered into sight, I would seize up her dinner in one hand, the broom in the other, and the chase was on! The great thing was to get a headstart on him, so we would hurtle round the corner of the house with Samson after us in hot pursuit, his great flat feet slap-slapping on the ground. Where the two wings of the house met, there was a sheltered corner with defences on two sides, and here I would hastily fling down Jo's dinner and then stand on guard with the kitchen broom to parry off the drake as he bore down upon us.

Jo has always been a very methodical eater. First she lifts out her bone and lays it carefully beside the dish. Next she wolfs down the pieces of meat and licks up the mash. Finally she takes the bone in her mouth and trots off to gnaw it at leisure and in private. With Samson continually trying to dodge past the broom to get at her, this whole process was accelerated like a

Charlie Chaplin movie, particularly the 'getaway' with the bone, when she would snatch it up, plunge past Samson and tear off out of sight as if fifty devils were after her. Samson habitually took this as a sign of his complete victory. He would flick his head scornfully, stand up on tiptoe to beat his wings, and then march solemnly back to the kennel with the swaggering air of a conquering hero.

During all these alarums and excursions Delilah, in the meantime, had been diligently laying an egg a day, and had now accumulated no fewer than sixteen in her nest in the kennel. Each day when she hurried off for a quick snack and a drink, I used to check on the eggs, and was amazed to discover how interesting an egg can be! I was thunderstruck to learn that an egg can communicate! A good, fertile egg has quite a number of little ways in which it can declare its vitality — for a start, it has a warmth of its own, literally an inner glow, so that a good-sized clutch of large eggs like a duck's will keep one another warm while the mother is off the nest. The single, addled egg in the nest cooled off at once, as soon as Delilah left the eggs exposed. From the third week, the fertile eggs developed a firm, strong heartbeat that was perfectly audible when the egg was placed against one's ear, sounding like the workings of a tiny waterpump — squish, squish, squish. As the days went by this throbbing pulse was reinforced by numerous, little clickings and scrapings as the embryo moved about inside. I had never before paused to consider that a sitting bird would be able to feel and hear life within her clutch, much as if she were sitting on a collection of ticking bombs! On the twenty-seventh day there were determined, tapping noises from several of the eggs, and one of them actually produced a muffled 'peep-peep'. I found it all tremendously exciting!

Delilah had by now become so accustomed to my handling her eggs that when on the twenty-eighth day they began to hatch, the children and I were able to witness the whole fascinating process.

It is a well-known fact that a new-born human baby is anything but glamorous — at the moment of birth it is blotched and bruised and bloodstained, wet and wizened and wrinkly. Even knowing this, one still somehow imagines that a newly hatched chick or duckling steps from the pieces of its shell in a state of immaculate cleanliness, soft and downy and golden. It was a staggering revelation to discover that the terrible struggles of a baby duck's birth are, if anything, more arduous and fraught with danger than those of a mammal. It was an eye-opener to find that a newly hatched duckling is wet and gruesome and hideous.

Each little creature literally had to fight to free itself from its egg-shell prison. So prolonged were some of their struggles, that the moisture of their bodies dried before they had freed themselves, and they stuck fast on to the insides of their broken shells. It is hard to imagine anything in a less advantageous position than a chick inside its egg. Each duckling was in a different attitude, but all were hampered by want of air and by the constricting tissues of wet membrane that clung about them like strings of gluey latex. Far from being yellow and fluffy, the ducklings were slimy and transparent so that we could actually see the coils of their internal organs through the skin of their abdomens, and the quills of their wings looked like soft pencil-leads. Through the cracks in the eggshell we could see that each duckling was smeared and streaked with blood and mucus, and after each wild spasm of struggling it would collapse with exhaustion, barely breathing, its throbbing pulse the only visible sign of life.

I removed one of the hatching eggs from the nest in order to study the method that a duckling employs in cracking its shell. The egg in my hands was almost intact, with just one small hole at the wide end. Through this hole I could glimpse a tiny pink beak with a little spike on the end of it, like a blunt rose-thorn. From time to time the duckling would chip away at the hole with his spike in order to increase his air supply, but the major work of cracking the shell was being accomplished by huge convulsions of his whole body. Splits began to radiate outward from the hole, gradually extending the entire length of the egg.

After a while the beak was joined at the aperture by a long, hooked claw. Peering in, I could just make out that the duckling

had somehow managed to get one of his little webbed feet up to
the hole, and now with the next convulsion his foot tore out a
section of shell about an inch square. This improved his lot
enormously and from then on things began to move more
quickly. Using his claws he was able to rip away jagged bits of
shell one at a time, while each violent struggle extended the
cracks and splits. Finally, when he had levered off more than a
third of his casing, he managed to twist himself round and lift out
a wobbly head. Bit by bit he hauled himself into a sitting position
with his legs gathered under him, but this effort so taxed his
strength that he collapsed once more, wet and limp and
bedraggled. At this point I gently replaced him beneath Delilah's
warm feathers so that the spiky, yellow quills that dotted his
body could begin to dry out. When I peeped at him again in half
an hour, he had freed himself entirely from the shell and had
been transformed into the classic baby duckling, a glorious
cloud of golden fluff with two, bright, black eyes above a pertly
smiling beak.

Later that day Delilah took her brood for their first swim in
the duck-pond. Samson was immensely proud of his fifteen
offspring, and strutted along in the rear of the procession with a
lordly air, muttering and hissing under his breath as if enumerating
the things he would do to Josephine if she dared to put in an
appearance. For her part, Josephine was only too glad that
Samson had something else to think about besides persecuting
her, and enjoyed a few days of comparative peace.

A crisis arose later in the week when Delilah invited her
ducklings to disport themselves in the swimming-pool. The gate
had inadvertently been left open, and she had been quick to seize
the opportunity of exercising her family on this larger stretch of
water. I had to admit that Delilah looked rather lovely sailing
over the mediterranean blue of the pool with her fifteen golden
babies strung out behind her, but they ran into grave difficulties
when it was time to leave the water. Delilah herself was able to
hop out with comparative ease, but the coping stones of the pool
formed an overhanging lip which was too much for the
ducklings. Their little peeping cries of distress were altogether

piteous, but their mother could do nothing to help them. The children mounted a rescue operation, and I then firmly shut the gate of the pool area to keep Delilah out.

Half an hour later I was transfixed to see Samson and Delilah right out in the centre of the street with all their babies trailing behind them. Some of the ducklings were completely exhausted, tripping and falling at every step. Delilah in the lead was setting a cracking pace, having plainly resolved to find a way into the pool area through the hedge. One of the children ran for the kitchen broom, and we shooed them all home once more.

Delilah proved to be a most inconsiderate mother, unlike old Angelina. She walked her babies too far and too fast without giving them sufficient opportunities for rest, and she became obsessed with the desire to get all her ducklings into the swimming-pool. By exerting continuous vigilance I was able to keep them out, but once the young birds had grown their wing feathers there was no stopping them. The entire flock of seventeen ducks would take to the air, skim over the pool fence, and alight on the water with a joyous chorus of hissing and quacking, each bird celebrating its arrival by depositing a huge squirt of liquid manure into the pool. I could see trouble looming up, for while the filtration plant could comfortably keep pace with specks of dust and grass, it did not have the capacity to handle industrial quantities of sewage. As I had anticipated, when Doug came home and found the flock of Muscovies cavorting in the pool, he registered a firm protest.

"I thought this was a swimming-pool, not a duck-pond," he objected. "If this continues we shall all go down with typhoid and cholera." He turned to me. "You'll have to think of some way of controlling them, I'm afraid, or the ducks will have to *go!*"

At this point, as if matters were not sufficiently complicated, Delilah began to incubate a second clutch of sixteen eggs. These too all hatched out in what seemed an impossibly short space of time, and there we were with over thirty ducks. They ate me out of house and home, they trampled the flowers with their great flat feet, they persistently flew over the fence and swam in the pool, Samson still fought continuously with Josephine and,

worst of all, the whole crowd of them used to congregate outside
the back door so that the entire area had to be hosed down
several times a day.

"They're disgusting brutes," Doug protested. "Every time I
want to step outside I have to draw on a pair of waders in order to
negotiate the pools of guano. Something's going to have to be
done. Two ducks were fine, but thirty ducks — sheer lunacy!"

The obvious solution, of course, was to eat them, but they
had such sweet, smiling faces and were so trusting that it was
quite out of the question. I presented the whole flock of
Muscovies to a bird sanctuary where they settled in without any
difficulty, revelling in the wide reaches of water and the
abundance of snails and tadpoles. Josephine watched them go
with undisguised delight, and even today the word 'Samson' is
enough to make her lift her head and glance about uneasily. I
loved my Muscovies, but I wouldn't be tempted to keep them
again!

Among the lesser hens in Angelina's flock was a white
leghorn called Pollen. It was she who distinguished herself by
swallowing a whole snake. Pollen was an excellent layer, but
she was a troublesome hen in a way, because she had a
particular hatred for strange children. Tracey and Tom, of
course, knew how to handle her, but she was the instigator of
many an awkward fracas when friends with children dropped in
for tea. Pollen had a mean, cunning streak in her. She would lurk
close to where the children were playing, innocently pecking at
the lawn or scratching at the edge of a flower-bed, until she had
aroused her quarry's interest. This was the moment to chase her
off, but sometimes my attention would be diverted and Pollen
would succeed in luring her prey away to a secluded part of the
garden. There she would suddenly turn on the unsuspecting
child, advancing sideways and uttering a hideous droning in her
throat. The instant the child took fright and fled, Pollen would
fly at its legs, pecking and raking at them with her claws.

It was a beastly habit, and I was not altogether sorry when
one night Pollen was caught by a neighbour's collie dog. She set
up a tremendous squawking and flapping and although we

succeeded in driving the dog off, Pollen had been badly bitten and appeared to have collapsed. I felt certain that she wouldn't last till morning, but when dawn broke she was still more or less alive. She now lay hunched on the ground in a clump of long grass, with her head sunk between her shoulders and her eyes half closed. Two weeks later she was still in exactly the same place. She hadn't moved. I had picked her up and examined her, but there was nothing visibly wrong. The dog bites had healed, her limbs were uninjured, but she had simply gone into a state of deep shock and nothing we could say or do would snap her out of it. I had heard of people inducing hypnotic trances in poultry, mesmerising them with straight lines and circles, but I had never heard how they reversed the process. It was altogether most puzzling, and I was strongly inclined to make an end of her when a farmer friend presented me with a small clutch of guinea-fowl eggs. They were as round as golf balls with very hard, pitted shells, like small fossilised oranges. It seemed unlikely that the eggs would hatch, but there was nothing to lose by the experiment so one night I slipped all five eggs under Pollen to see what would happen.

I feared that in the event of any of the eggs hatching, Pollen would either kill them or ignore them completely. Then one afternoon Pollen rose to her feet like a phoenix from its ashes, stepped out of her grass slowly and unsteadily and clucked encouragingly at two tiny, almost circular pompons of silver-grey fluff that stood uncertainly in her nest. The other hens who had ignored Pollen completely all the time that she had been sitting, now gathered round and gaped incredulously at the fruits of Pollen's immaculate conception. Pollen fussed round her babies with the smug satisfaction of a mother whose offspring has just won the Beautiful Baby Competition. Pollen herself underwent a complete psychological transformation. Her shrewish disposition mellowed overnight. She became good-natured, friendly, almost jovial at times, and fell into the habit of bestowing patronising looks on her less fortunate sisters. From the day the guinea-fowls hatched out, Pollen never chased another child.

It was immediately apparent that the little chicks were

guinea-fowl through and through. A grown guinea-fowl has a
strongly characteristic gait, a jaunty, bouncing way of trotting
over the ground. These two tiny balls of grey silk bobbed along
behind Pollen, perfect miniature replicas of their real parents.
They were the tamest and most fearless chicks I have ever
reared. When Pollen came to the back door for her handful of
grain, the little guinea-fowl used to fly up on to me, perching on
my arms or shoulders or, if I sat down on the doorstep, they
would roost on my knee. This habit of sitting on my lap persisted
even when they were fully grown, when they would perch one on
each knee and preen contentedly for as long as I was prepared to
sit still. We called them Shilling and Pound, and so friendly did
they become that they used to follow me into the house,
slithering about on the polished floors and uttering tiny, tinkling
noises of encouragement to one another.

Perhaps one of the most rewarding things about getting to
know wild creatures on familiar terms is that one discovers the
more intimate ways in which they communicate with one
another. Everyone in Africa knows well enough the guinea-
fowl's usual cry, a harsh rattling churr, or the monotonous 'tik-
cloop, tik-cloop', which a large flock will chant when keeping in
touch in long grass. I learned that in addition to these, they
employ a very wide range of lesser calls — a clear, metallic 'tink'
that is a warning note, a very soft high trill that indicates
excitement and pleasure, and when feeding contentedly or
taking a sand-bath they speak to one another continuously in
little, whispered clicks and whistles and tinkles that are quite
inaudible a few feet away.

The chicks developed plumage on their wings at a very
early age and lost their silky, grey down. When about four
inches high they were strangely nondescript-looking birds of a
drab ash-brown, their polka-dots not yet visible, but ghostly
suggestions of them speckled their feathers here and there with
flecks of white. At six months old their wings were crisp and
neat, the browns had melted and given way to an austere gun-
metal grey, and they began to develop the lovely cobalt blue on
the soft skin of their cheeks and throats. The white specks on
their feathers grew into bold circular dots and their plumage was

so beautiful that they looked as though they had had their ensemble specially designed by a Paris *couturière*. The feathers lay crisp and smooth over the wings and the back, dissolving into soft silky billows on their chests and bellies. The scales of their legs were a gleaming pearl grey while the hooked scimitars of their claws shone as if they had been varnished.

They were very affectionate birds, both with one another and with us. If I were delayed indoors for any length of time, Shilling and Pound used to come into the house to look for me. From my bedroom I would hear their claws scratching and clicking across the parquet floor and there would be a series of clinks and trills from the dining-room. For a while they would wait for me patiently, each perched on the back of a dining-room chair, but if I didn't put in an appearance within a reasonable time, their polite tinkles gradually rose in volume to the full-blooded cry that will carry from hilltop to hilltop.

One of the disadvantages of our house is that the dining-room, sitting-room, hall and playroom are on an open plan, interleading with one another through an intricate series of steps and stairs. It makes the house interesting architecturally, but it gave rise to a most embarrassing situation the day I had a rather important guest to tea. I had been to great lengths to tidy the house and drill the children. I had set out the best china in the sitting-room and had baked my most successful cake. Everything was shipshape, except that I had forgotten to close the stable door from the dining-room into the garden.

Mrs. Anolick arrived. I escorted her upstairs to the sitting-room, the children said a polite good afternoon and vanished, and I had just poured the tea when I heard the familiar click of claws and an enquiring series of trills and tinkles from the dining-room. Shilling and Pound had come to look for me. Inwardly cursing my negligence, I excused myself from Mrs. Anolick and hurried to intercept them, knowing that they would soon weary of waiting for me and begin to make a hideous din. I tried to shoo them outside quickly and quietly, but they decided I was having a game with them. They leaped into the air with whistles of excitement, to alight and go skimming about under the table and chairs, while I hissed at them and made sweeping

actions with my hands.

The game seemed to go on for ever. They simply *wouldn't* go outside. I could hear Mrs. Anolick clear her throat and begin to stir her tea. This was ridiculous. I couldn't abandon my guest to have a game of tag round the dining-room with a pair of naughty guinea-fowl. The children had followed their instructions to the letter and had disappeared completely. I decided the best thing to do was to leave the guinea-fowl alone and pray that they might go outside by themselves. Accordingly I turned my back on them and resolutely marched out of the dining-room. Shilling and Pound were determined not to be ignored. The two of them took to the air and flew up the stairs, arriving with me in the sitting-room amid a flurry of beating wings and shrill clinks of delight.

At this point I gave up all pretences of trying to conduct a

dignified tea-party, and confessed to Mrs. Anolick that I would
have to allow them to perch on my knee so that I could capture
them. Crimson-faced with embarrassment, I resumed my seat
while my delinquent guinea-fowl hopped contentedly on to my
lap and began to preen. As soon as they had settled down, I
tucked one under each arm and carried them out into the garden,
taking care to close all the outside doors on my return!

Fortunately, Pollen never joined them on these sorties into
the house. Even before they were fully grown, the guinea-fowl
had exhibited a callous independence of spirit towards their
foster-mother, preferring human society to that of the other
poultry. I think one of the reasons for this was nothing more
complicated than cupboard love. The poultry pundits had
assured me that guinea-fowl were almost exclusively insecti-
vorous. This was far from the truth, for they proved to have the
most exotic taste in food, relishing anything that was highly
flavoured or scented. They adored sweet-pea flowers, and used
to jump at the rose bushes to snatch off the petals. Each morning
when I made my rounds of the rose beds to snip off the faded
heads, Shilling and Pound used to follow close at heel to pounce
on the petals as they fell.

Although they continued to roost with the hens at night,
during the day they kept to themselves, and discovered a
number of favourite vantage-points from where they used to
survey the whole garden. Shilling used these as his 'calling
points', opening his beak and throat as wide as he could, and
aiming his head at the very zenith of the heavens. In particular,
he favoured the top of a large, solitary, granite boulder that
commands a long view down the drive to the gate.

Shilling spent a lot of time on top of the boulder and was
very useful as a sentry, for the instant anyone set foot inside the
gate he would challenge them with his loudest churring cry. This
aggressive tendency developed into a fierce dislike for motor
cars. The moment guests turned into the drive, Shilling would
fly down from his rock and chase the wheels of the car, skimming
along beside them and striking at the hub-caps with his spurs. To
make his attacks all the more sensational, he perfected a
spectacular repertoire of warlike postures and attitudes, hump-

ing up his back, fanning out his wings and performing a skilful sideways pirouette and flourish.

This was all very well when he was showing off to a motor car, but decidedly alarming when he took to pursuing people. For some reason, he singled out the milkman as his particular enemy, and as the milkman ran down the drive, Shilling would pursue his retreating figure on swift, silent feet, springing high into the air just behind him and raking the poor fellow's back with his spurs. The speed and silence of these attacks were uncanny and unnerving.

Having rid myself of the necessity to protect Josephine from Samson, I now had to be on the *qui vive* to defend the milkman from Shilling, and it was no easy task. He became frighteningly adroit at dodging my efforts to intercept him, skimming around behind me in a wide, swift circle or leaping ten feet into the air just as I was about to lay hands on him. To make matters worse, the more he was persecuted, the fiercer Shilling became, and he extended his attacks to include the butcher, the postman and the vegetable-monger. He appeared to regard the arrival of each one as a test of his strength and skill.

All this sabre-rattling was, of course, no more than a sign that spring was in the air. For most of the year the wild guinea-fowl in the veld are peaceloving birds with no loftier ambitions than to make their nests and rear their young. Come spring, however, and they undergo a sinister character-change. During August and September they begin to congregate in huge flocks, where skirmishes between the cock birds go on all day long. In any group of guinea-fowl at this time of the year, there will be four or five fights in progress at once, with pairs of combatants puffing up their backs at one another, posing and pirouetting, standing on tiptoe to scrape arrogantly at the ground, and the entire flock grating the air to shreds with their raucous, rattling din. This was the stage Shilling was at now. Pound was completely devoted to him, and he to her, but none the less he felt the compelling desire to swagger and strut in front of the other lads. On moonlit nights Shilling used to communicate with a flock of guinea-fowl that belonged to Bob MacIntyre, a distant neighbour of ours, and after a while the temptation to visit this larger flock overcame him and he flew off to flex his muscles before an admiring audience of guinea-hens. Next day we fetched him back again, but a week later the same thing happened once more. Pound was disconsolate in Shilling's absence, and I worried that someone might take him for a wild bird and shoot him for the pot while he was making his way from my garden to that of Mr. Mac. He and I discussed the best way of handling this situation, and it transpired that he was hoping to breed guinea-fowl commercially, but had so far been unsuccessful in obtaining any fertile eggs from his hens. Shilling, who was as aggressively masculine as a matador, had impressed Bob MacIntyre as a promising stud, and he offered to buy him from me. I could no more have sold Shilling than I could have sold one of my children, so finally I gave him both Shilling and Pound. We can still hear him on moonlit nights, pouring out a defiant and boastful declaration of his own magnificence. I miss my guinea-fowl very much, but it is plain that if I were to attempt to keep these birds again, it would be necessary to have considerably more than two. Quite obviously, their gregarious instincts are too powerful to be offset by any artificial ties of man's making.

It must have been something to do with spring in the air, for we had no sooner lost Shilling and Pound when Angelina became broody for a second time. I felt like the sorcerer's apprentice, who had tampered with his master's magic and now didn't know how to persuade the enchantment to stop! I was on the brink of despair when Ruth Wells telephoned me.

"You don't have a broody hen, by any chance, do you?" she asked.

"As a matter of fact, I do," I laughed. "Why do you need one?" Ruth and her husband had recently started up a cattle ranch near Ruwa, and she was now looking into the possibility of trying turkeys as a sideline.

"The problem with turkeys," she explained, "is that the chicks are delicate and difficult to rear by hand. Supposing I were to get the day-old chicks, would you let Angelina bring them up for me?"

It seemed like the answer to a prayer and I readily agreed, little knowing what was in store.

The turkey project got off to a flying start. Angelina accepted the nine chicks without any hesitation, fussing over them as attentively as the principal of an old-fashioned school over her children. They were a soft, fawn colour, larger and a great deal more active than ordinary day-old chicks. It was a lovely sight to see Angelina settle down with her brood in a damp scoop of earth, all of them fluttering their wings together to get the cool black soil under their feathers. I decided that they were a great improvement on the ducks, being just as decorative and considerably less troublesome. That was just before the episode of the flamboyant trees.

Salisbury's streets are famous for their avenues of flamboyants — gracious old trees whose umbrellas of crimson flowers and feathery leaves form complete archways over the racing traffic. After flowering, the flamboyants produce great numbers of seed-pods that hang downwards like green leather sword-scabbards. After some months they ripen to a dark mahogany-brown, and the speckled seeds inside are each about an inch long and as hard as iron. I yearned to have flamboyant trees of my own, and had repeatedly tried to grow them from seed, but without success. I had almost given up when I heard that the secret is to BOIL the seeds for a few minutes in order to promote their germination. This sounded like a proper old wives' tale, for I understood that boiling a thing was a proven way of destroying life, not encouraging it. None the less, I was sufficiently intrigued by the idea to give it a try. Next time we went to town, the children and I sought out the most beautifully coloured flamboyants and collected a handful of seeds from under each. Some I boiled for ten minutes, others for only one or two, and a few I dropped into the water as it came off the boil and left to soak for a few hours. By the following morning all the seeds had swollen to twice their former size. Gleefully I planted them out in rows in three seed-boxes, and waited eagerly to see what would happen.

Within two weeks the boxes were a forest of young flamboyants, and I used to daydream about how they were going to look when they were fully grown. My hopes raced ahead several years, and in my mind's eye I could visualise an avenue of stately flamboyants up the drive, and others out in the street. I planned to pot them out for friends and generally spread my good fortune far and wide. These pleasant dreams were shattered one afternoon when, as I was working in the kitchen, a small movement outside caught my eye, and I burst from the back door flourishing a tea-towel, but I was too late ... The nine turkey chicks had found the flamboyant seedlings and were contentedly perched among them, devouring the young leaves and pulling them up by the roots in their greedy relish. I drove them off in a fury and surveyed the wreckage. Out of some fifty young trees there were about a dozen left. Sorrowfully I pricked them out and replanted them in a new box which, for safety's sake, I placed on the flat tin roof of the garage.

As they grew, the turkey chicks became progressively more unmanageable, and Angelina went frantic trying to get them to behave. Although by now they were larger than her, still all nine of them used to try to shelter beneath her wings. Poor Angelina would be jostled this way and that while her unmannerly brood pecked and squabbled and fought among themselves like spoiled children. This bickering seemed to go on all day to the accompaniment of the most piercing chorus of protest. Naturally, not all of them could fit under Angelina at once, and those out in the cold used to complain bitterly and stridently, uttering a loud plaintive 'Choop, chrroop, cheeep, choop', a refrain which always rose to a crescendo at night when they retired to roost. One quiet Sunday afternoon their cries rose to such clamorous intensity that I abandoned the idea of a siesta and went outside to investigate. There I found Angelina bustling about distractedly in front of the garage, while her evil chicks stood in a disconsolate row on the edge of the roof, peering down at her and cheeping piteously. Nearby were the remains of my last box of flamboyant seedlings. It had been stripped bare. I have never entertained particularly tender feelings for turkeys since then, and it was with a feeling of intense joy that I saw all nine of them taken off to the farm the following week.

I dare say it is very wrong of me to harbour bitter and

vengeful thoughts against turkeys in general, for there may be well-behaved and conscientious turkeys who are a credit to their race. All the same, I derived a certain fierce satisfaction from a story which Bob Hammond told me. Apparently the Hammonds used to keep an exceptionally bad-tempered old turkey tom whose practice it was to lie in wait for people as they went to the wash-house. As was usual in those days, the wash-house stood a little way behind the main bungalow, separated from it by the backyard and vegetable garden. This bird used to patrol up and down outside the kitchen door, and the minute anyone emerged he would gobble out a challenge, and advance on them threateningly with dragging wings and inflated chest. He looked very formidable puffed out like that, with his red face and long dangling nose and gleaming bronze feathers. He stood as high as a man's waist and used to enhance his imposing presence by rattling his quills and emitting a deep drumming noise in his chest. The Hammonds knew that he was all sound and fury, but nevertheless they kept a stout stick in the kitchen with which to fend the turkey off when they went to the wash-house. It so happened that on one occasion when they had a guest to stay, the stick could not be found. Being of a somewhat bashful disposition and not wishing to draw attention to his errand, the guest unobtrusively helped himself to a golf-club from the hall cupboard. Thus armed he attempted to make a dash across the backyard. The turkey tom was waiting for him, however, and such was the speed of the creature's attack that the poor man found himself engaged in a prolonged and spirited duel in self-defence. Step by step he fought his way backwards through the vegetable beds until finally nearing his destination he took one last swing at the turkey. Unfortunately this time the club caught the bird on the side of the head, and now the guest's cup of embarrassment was full to the brim. He was forced to confess to his hostess that while attempting to get to the wash-house, he had killed her turkey with a golf-club that he had filched from the hall cupboard.

Mrs. Hammond rose to the occasion like a perfect hostess, made light of the affair and pointed out that he had saved her the trouble of wondering what to serve for dinner that night!

13
Pigs in Paradise

ACCORDING TO Mohammedan legend, there are ten individual animals which have been admitted to Paradise. The largest of these privileged beasts is Jonah's whale, followed by Mohammed's racing-camel Al Adha, which is reputed to have made the journey from Jerusalem to Jedda in four bounds. Then there is Mohammed's white mare Al Borak, and Balaam's ass. Also included among the chosen few is the ox of Moses — the one he sacrificed at the foot of Mount Sinai, blood of which he sprinkled on the altar and over the children of Israel as a sign of their covenant with God. The ram which Abraham sacrificed instead of Isaac is likewise received into Paradise, as is Tobit's dog. The birds are represented by the dove which brought the olive-leaf to Noah, and Queen Balkis's lapwing that found the water. Last of all is Solomon's ant 'which having no guide, overseer or ruler, provideth her meat in the summer and gathereth her food in the harvest'.

Strangely enough, heraldic beasts like lions and eagles are not represented, a preference being shown for creatures of humbler origins. Without in any way disparaging the choice made by the authorities who drew up the list of finalists, I still yearn for the inclusion of some of the neglected species. What, for example, of the cat? Or the owl? Or the pig? On second thoughts, perhaps not the pig — and yet, in his way, the pig is a singularly engaging and humorous animal despite all the unfavourable propaganda that has been put out against him. But a pig in Paradise? Well, maybe not — and as for the cat and the owl, they were catered for respectively by the Egyptians and the Greeks.

I'm glad, at any rate, that the ox receives honourable recognition. He, after all, has been associated with man's endeavours for as long as records exist, and it seems somehow churlish and ungrateful that in return we always think of the ox as being a kind of dullard, an oafish clumping brute endowed with little intelligence or personality.
"You great ox," we say to someone who has made a stupid blunder.

Although neither exalted nor gifted with Divine inspiration, and hitherto quite unsung in the annals of history, there were two oxen at Umbogintwini in Natal which, I feel, deserve to be remembered.

As a young mathematics graduate, Doug's first employment was in the work-study department of the huge African Explosives complex at Umbogintwini on the Natal south coast. Like most first jobs, it seemed to involve a lot that was dull, laborious and humdrum, and after the freedom and gaiety of student life, Doug found the strictures of big company routine very confining. In this connection he identified his spiritual lot with that of the pair of bullocks who were employed by African Explosives to shunt their goodswagons. It was a formidable task, for the factories and their feeder railway systems spread over some two hundred acres. The two oxen were highly efficient. They were considerably quieter and infinitely quicker than a small locomotive, since they could be unhitched from one goodswagon and led across the rails to another, without the necessity of shunting right back up the line to the nearest spur junction.

In order to reach Umbogintwini in time for work, Doug had to start out from home shortly after 4 a.m. when it was still dark, arriving at the factory just as the bullocks were knocking on for the morning shift. With lowered heads they plodded dejectedly into the shunting-yards, the very picture of despondent resignation. In much the same frame of mind, Doug dragged himself up to his office and commenced the day's work.

All morning the pair of bullocks could be seen towing the

goodswagons up and down the line, but when the hooter blew for lunch at one o'clock, no power on earth would get them to move another inch until they had been unyoked! They had studied their Union Rules and they weren't going to work one second of their lunch-break! No matter if their truck came to rest in the middle of a level-crossing, they wouldn't budge, not for all the threats and imprecations in the world. Come two o'clock, however, and they would grudgingly consent to be yoked up once more, and would continue their tasks with their usual show of bored resignation.

At the close of the day, as Doug made his way back to the station, he would pass the two oxen returning along the dirt road to their pasture. Like a pair of schoolboys on a half-holiday, they would gambol and caper and frisk their tails, chasing one another at a playful canter, kicking up their heels and tossing their heads in a very excess of well-being and good humour.

Doug felt a profound kinship with the two creatures, a spiritual sympathy which he could not somehow extend to the busy black steam-engine that succeeded the oxen the following year. In the post-war boom the bullocks were abandoned and forgotten, to fall behind in the wake of the greedy god Progress.

I observe that the goat is excluded from Paradise, a sensible precaution for one shudders to imagine the fearful depredations which a goat, even a sacred goat, might inflict on the heavenly lawns and gardens. One recalls that various regiments have adopted the goat as their particular emblem, but I question the wisdom of this, for the goat has a mischievous temperament and refuses to show a proper sense of reverence for anything, man or god.

My father-in-law used to keep a large brown billy-goat called Hamish. This was many years ago when he used to live in Port Shepstone, Natal, and conducted a trading concern, buying sheep from the farmers in the Transkei and selling them up the coast. The most difficult part of the business was transferring the sheep from one truck to another. They were nervous and suspicious of the loading ramps, and they *would* balk and bunch and back off. This is where Hamish came in. Once the flock of sheep had mustered ready to load, the goat would step forward and confidently lead them up the ramp and into the truck. When he reached the back of the wagon, he would turn in a neat circle and jump out, just as the last sheep climbed aboard. The whole operation was accomplished without any fuss or stress for the sheep.

One day the goat developed a sore on his leg. It was probably caused by a tick, but like most Natal sores it swelled and became infected, making the whole leg very painful. Hamish was such a favourite that my mother-in-law made much of him, dressing his wound and bringing him into the house at nights until he recovered. In the course of this pampering the goat discovered the larder, and in particular he noted the location of the sack of hominy chop — a kind of stamped corn which was thrown out each day for the chickens.

One afternoon, while my mother-in-law was entertaining

friends to tea in the living-room, she heard a mysterious sound from the kitchen and the passage — a slithering and a snorting and a subdued scuffling of many feet. She went through to investigate, and found that the goat in his generosity had led the whole flock of sheep through the house to share with him the joys of the hominy chop!

Less amiable than Hamish was the billy-goat that belonged to Muddy Bain's father. Probably part of the trouble was that as leader of his own flock of nanny-goats, he felt that he had a 'Position To Keep Up'. He evidently suspected that it reinforced his authority to demonstrate his dominion over the smallest of the Bain children. Muddy was terrified of him. He had sharp horns, a long beard, and evil yellow eyes with weird, oblong pupils like a pair of domino bricks. The goat seized every opportunity of terrorising Muddy and her little friend Freda, belching and snorting and chasing them from one place of refuge to another.

On one occasion, after a particularly narrow scrape with the goat, the little girl entreated her father to get rid of him.

However, the goat was a great favourite of Mr. Bain, and besides, he needed him in order to propagate the herd. He told Muddy reassuringly that the goat would leave her alone once she grew a bit bigger. This was no doubt true enough, but it offered small comfort to a little scrap of four or five.

In those early days there were no toy-shops in Salisbury, and the Bain children had to make all their own playthings from the materials available round the house and garden. Muddy's brothers used to dig a hole and fill it with water. Then they would all stamp about inside it to make a smooth, pliable clay. Little wonder that Muddy's name stuck, for she loved these revels, and used to join in as enthusiastically as any of the boys. Afterwards the children would mould the clay into elephants, giraffes, lions or cattle, baking the little earthen creatures in an oven hollowed out of an antheap. Finally, they would collect gum from the wild mimosas and use it to stick on tufts of chicken feathers as manes for their lions and tails for their horses.

Muddy and Freda used to manufacture their own dolls, too, using a mealie cob as the body, a mango pip for the head and sticks for the arms and legs. The two little girls would spend hours making their dolls' clothes, using the left-over snippets and scraps from Mrs. Bain's sewing-basket.

One day Muddy and Freda were sitting outside under the scented shade of the frangipani tree, stitching clothes on to their mealie-cob dolls, when round the corner of the shed came the billy-goat! Spying the two little girls, he gave an angry snort and pawed the ground, tossing his beard in a gesture of defiance. Next moment he put down his horns and charged straight at them! The children fled, leaving behind in their haste their precious dolls, still uncompleted. Having driven the girls as far as the verandah, the goat emphasised his signal victory by eating the mealie-cob dolls together with all the treasured little scraps of coloured material. Muddy's heart burned with hatred and disappointment, but there was nothing she could do to save her doll from its terrible fate.

That afternoon, however, a most curious event took place. The billy-goat suddenly leaped into the air, turned a complete somersault and fell down dead! Mr. Bain was thunderstruck;

indeed nobody could imagine what had caused the animal's abrupt demise. The snakebite and button-spider theories were rejected for want of the necessary evidence, and finally Mr. Bain instructed his sons to conduct an autopsy. To everyone's amazement, the cause of death was ascertained to be a long sewing-needle in the goat's heart! Muddy never breathed a word about her doll, but she secretly rejoiced that its awful fate had been so justly avenged!

I console myself over the pig's exclusion from Paradise, because it seems to me that pigs on the whole have an exceptional talent for making the most of their lot on earth. I can think of no living creature with such a zest for living as the warthog, with such an ebullient sense of humour, such a cheerfully philosophical approach to the world at large. He is the veld's most lovable clown, not only in his behaviour but also in his very appearance. The adult warthog is bewhiskered like an ex-Indian Army colonel, tusked like a walrus, and the whole effect is rendered ludicrous by a collection of hideous wart-like protuberances under his eyes. These grotesque facial features are combined with a squat, grey, dumpy body, a sparse mane, absurdly short legs and a stringlike tail with a tassel at the end, which when carried vertically in the air conveys much the same rude message as two fingers.

The warthogs' natural genius for humour reaches new heights and attains a wider scope when they are introduced to the human way of life. Vincent Fick, a farmer at Beatrice, was given a baby warthog by a friend who had been involved in road construction-work in the Zambezi valley. They called her Suzie and brought her up in the homestead, little knowing what was in store for them!

Suzie was very quick to adapt to the Ficks' household routine, and before long she demonstrated her willingness to take a hand in running the establishment. At first she made the shoes her primary concern. She couldn't bear shoe-laces, and made it her responsibility to creep up on Mr. Fick's boots at night as they sat on the boot-rack. Surreptitiously, she would draw out the laces and then dash off with a bunch of them in her mouth, to hide them about the house or in the garden. She was quite prepared to perform this simple service for guests, too, dashing at their feet and rooting out their shoe-laces before they realised what was happening.

Suzie found that the beds required her constant attention. She felt very strongly that the proper place to sleep was on the ground, not elevated at some inconvenient and unsafe height. She became expert at 'making' the beds, hauling the pillows and bedclothes on to the floor and then sleeping on them, as if to demonstrate how much more comfortable they were that way. One day she found the bed-linen billowing on the line, an altogether ridiculous place for it to be, according to her. It was plain that absolutely no one could have achieved any degree of comfort on a clothes-line, and so in order to teach the sheets and pillowcases a stern lesson, she tore them all off the line and ripped them to ribbons.

She grew very friendly with the dogs, and would spend long hours dozing with them in the sun. When the Ficks went duck-shooting at the week-ends, Suzie would accompany them, plunging off with the pack of hounds to help retrieve the game. If, in the heat of the chase, she became separated from the others, she would squeal frantically until she found them again. She was most gregarious and adored company. When guests arrived she used to hurl herself at them with a show of exuberance and enthusiasm that was positively overwhelming. She would execute a special welcoming dance in their honour, jumping round the guests in a circle, with all her four feet leaving the ground at once.

Her greatest interest in life, however, proved to be mechanical engineering. She was fascinated by motor cars, especially their undersides. After greeting a guest and ripping out his shoe-laces, she would turn her attention to his car or truck to see if there were any improvements and modifications which she could make to it. After scraping about underneath the vehicle for a while, she would discover the glaring defect of open wiring. This, at any rate, was easy to remedy. Twisting her tusks round the wires to the rear lights, or ignition, she would reverse slowly out from under the car, trailing a tangle of cables after her. To

Suzie's way of thinking, petrol caps were another eyesore, not quite so easy to get rid of, but given enough time she was usually able to lever them off and render them unfit for further service. All these 'repairs' were carried out in a spirit of such cheerful philanthropy that it was impossible to remain angry with her for long.

She loved to 'help' Mr. Fick on the occasions when he was required to attend to his tractor or car, grunting interestedly round the open tool-box and eyeing the radiator with undisguised suspicion. With both hands inside the cylinder-head, Mr. Fick would call out to his assistant to pass him a spanner.

"William, please give me number thirteen spanner, there."

William would rummage through the tool-box.

"It's not here, Boss. Shall I look for Suzie?"

"Oh hell, yes! Quickly, before she eats it!"

Sure enough, Suzie would be found lying in the long grass at the edge of the garden, contentedly chewing up the number thirteen spanner! Having Suzie about the place was like enduring the attentions of a resident poltergeist, and the Ficks never knew what she would be up to next.

Considering the amount of mischief of which *one* warthog is capable, one shudders to think what two of them could accomplish. Mike and Christine Johnson did in fact rear a pair of these endearing little pigs, though some of their porcine exploits were not only bizarre and imaginative, but downright dangerous.

At that time the Johnsons owned the Lodge at Mlibizi, a very wild and out-of-the-way place at the western edge of Lake Kariba. The Zambezi valley is a strange place. One man will love it, while another finds it intolerable. The heat, the mirages, the lonely cries of the fish-eagles affect different people in different ways. Some who have been to Mlibizi are overpowered by its intense solitude and grow uneasy, sensing the underlying fragility of what we call civilisation. Others fall completely under its spell, and won't hear of going anywhere else. To the Johnsons themselves it is the only place in the world, and they brush aside the boastful claims made by those who favour the domesticated beauty of the Costa Brava, Acapulco or Cape St.

Francis. Indeed the grandeur and wild enchantment of Mlibizi set it in a class all by itself.

One day, when Mike Johnson made a visit to a neighbouring tribal area to purchase meat, a man offered to sell him a pair of baby warthogs, explaining that he had intended to fatten them up and eat them himself.

"They were *so* tiny," Christine recalls, "the size of rats, and we couldn't bear the thought of them being eaten. We finally swopped them for a pair of sheep, and took them home with us."

That night the fun started. "They almost killed each other to get to the bottle," Christine relates, "and so we had to use two bottles in order to feed them both at the same time. They slept in a whisky box on Mike's side of the bed, and when they woke during the night, he would feed them." (The Johnsons had a standing arrangement, that if their children required attention during the night, Christine would see to them, while Mike would attend to the nocturnal needs of their animals!) "When Mike put the little pigs back in their box after their first feed of the night, they objected to being left alone, and so he had to lie in bed with his arm over the side and his hand in the box to keep them happy. They'd screech and squeal if he took his hand out, and he could only remove it *slowly* after they had fallen asleep. This same procedure had to be followed after each of the three-hourly night feeds!"

The little warthogs were brother and sister. The Johnsons called them Mark and Clare. Soon they were too large for the whisky box, but by this time they no longer required to be fed during the night, and had found a lovely warm place to sleep, pressed right up against the side of the wood stove in the kitchen. The Johnsons tried to interest the pigs in a burrow which they dug for them in the garden, but Mark and Clare knew when they were on to a good thing and stuck to the wood stove. Naturally, a pair of growing warthogs in the kitchen didn't make it any too easy for the cook, particularly when the hotel was full, and the cook wasn't all that nimble on his pins, having one wooden leg. To make matters worse, the pigs now discovered an even better place, right *inside* the huge warming-cupboard next to the wood stove! Many times the unsuspecting cook would open the warming-oven and bend forward with his arms loaded with forty or fifty plates, only to be bowled over by the pigs. They would shoot out of the oven and make him overbalance. Once they knocked him clean off his feet, sending the pile of plates crashing to the floor.

"We had enormous crockery accounts," Christine remembers ruefully, "constantly having to replace things which the pigs had broken."

Despite their naughtiness, the warthogs were very friendly and affectionate and loved to be scratched on their backs with a rough stick. They enjoyed playing with Mike in the shallows at the edge of the lake. He would throw bunches of Kariba weed at them and they'd run away and shake it off, only to come back for more, flicking their heads up and down and squealing with excitement. They wouldn't go in deeper than about a foot, and were suspicious of the lake if Mike wasn't with them. However they found their own water-supply beneath a leaking tap on the lawn, and this became their favourite wallowing-hole. They made a pretty mess of the lawn in that place, digging up the grass roots and rolling ecstatically in the mud.

"When we took the dogs for a walk," Christine went on, "more often than not the pigs would follow us, making short detours to

forage for roots and grass, and then catching up with us again. On one of these sorties they came upon a culvert under the road. This was a tremendous discovery, and the culvert became one of their favourite play-places, where they could practise reversing in and out."

They also favoured the ladies' toilet at the Lodge. Clare, in particular, used to reverse into it and go to sleep there. Many a guest received the fright of her life when on entering the P.K. she found herself confronted by an enormous grey pig. On one memorable occasion a guest was occupying the P.K. when Clare arrived for a snooze. Annoyed that her private hidey-hole had been taken over, she lay down and pressed herself against the door so that it wouldn't open. When the poor woman tried to get out again, the door wouldn't budge, and every time she pushed against it she was greeted with an angry grunt from Clare. Much alarmed, but too embarrassed to call for help, the unfortunate guest stayed there for nearly an hour. Finally, in desperation, she scrambled on to the cistern and had managed to get one leg through the tiny window at the back, when a friend came to look for her and found Clare holding the fort. The warthog was lured away with a dish of delicacies, and the prisoner released at last!

They once got into somebody's caravan and could hardly believe their luck. They made short work of the eatable supplies, and then proceeded to open and unpack almost every drawer and cupboard. At last, exhausted by all this exertion, they climbed on to the bed and fell asleep. Shortly afterwards Mike walked past, and seeing the open door of the caravan, he thought he'd close it in case the pigs got in. His eye was caught by the mess of clothing and so forth that was strewn about on the floor, so he poked his head inside. There were Mark and Clare fast asleep, heads touching affectionately as they rested on the pillow. At Mike's "Hey!" the delinquent pair leaped off the bed and shot past him like lightning, screeching and squealing with guilt.

On another occasion, Mark somehow got into the chalet of John Pearson, the parachutist ace. John had done a spectacular jump that day and was in the bar celebrating when Mark commenced his inspection of John's kit. First of all he unpacked the 'chute and then, sniffing about further, he came upon a pair of John's shorts on the floor. To the pig's delight there was a cache of peppermints in the pocket, but try as he might he couldn't get them out. At last he got down on his knees, the way warthogs do when feeding, and sucked and sucked at the pocket until eventually the peppermints disintegrated and dissolved inside his mouth. At this point John Pearson returned to his chalet and discovered Mark at work. He shooed him out and began to tidy up his room, first repacking his 'chute and then turning his attention to his clothing. When he picked up the pair of shorts he found the pocket hanging down like an elongated teat, about four inches below the hem of the trouser-leg!

By the time they were eighteen months old, each pig weighed nearly two hundred pounds. Now their tusks began to grow, and romps with them became progressively more hazardous. The warthogs still adored human company, however, and had also developed a fondness for the malty flavour of beer. If the pub was busy, they'd come right in to join the fun, kneeling down and squealing for beer. Their needs would be explained to the fascinated crowd of tourists, and beer would be bought for them, served up in a huge ashtray. They'd merrily slurp up every drop, nosing the ashtray along the floor in case any of the precious fluid had been spilt. If they didn't get what they considered a reasonable helping, they would take the law into their own hands as it were, and flip over one of the small tables in the bar. They would then kneel down and enjoy the mixture of whatever that round of drinks had been — perhaps a few gins, a beer or two and a Scotch. On several occasions this had disastrous consequences because the mixture went to their heads, and the whole pub rocked with laughter to see them trying to find their way outside once more, an erratic process involving one hesitant step forward and two tottering steps sideways. Eventually reaching the verandah, they flopped off on to the lawn and keeled over to sleep, either back to back, or with feet or snouts touching. It was one of their most endearing habits that they always slept close together, touching one another.

When the trick of flipping over a table became a habit, they were banished to the fenced garden round the Johnsons' own cottage. Life was not so much fun for them there, but the Johnsons were concerned that one day they might cause a disagreeable accident, as the pigs were now almost mature and were beginning to exhibit the aggressive behaviour patterns of adult animals. Very sadly, Mike and Christine decided that it would be best to take the pigs to live on a nearby island in the lake. The island was well treed, and already supported a considerable game population. They took them over by boat, dug them a burrow and did all they could to help them settle in happily.

To begin with, they used to take food over to them every day. Clare developed a runny eye, and this, too, necessitated a daily visit in order to treat her with ophthalmic ointment. "When we arrived on the island, we'd whistle for them," Christine recalls, "and they'd come running out of the bush and almost bowl us over with delight. Often we'd take a pack-lunch or sundowners to the island, and sit with them for hours, talking to them and scratching their backs. They cried and squealed every time we left, and this was so heart-rending that gradually we spaced our visits out at wider intervals. It was plain that they had settled in very well, and were finding their own food. Weeks and months went by, and then one day when we went to call on them, they did not come to meet us as usual. Puzzled, we searched the length of the island trying to catch a glimpse of them. At one place we came across their spoor, and among those of Clare and Mark there were the prints of several tiny little pigs! It was wonderful to know that now they had their very own family, but we also had to accept that in the future they might be hostile towards us. Since then we've kept away," Christine concludes wistfully, "but we often think about them, our two hooligan children, Mark and Clare."

14

Pythons and Peacocks

THROUGHOUT AFRICA the python is surrounded by a penumbra of weird superstitions, a dark and uneasy mist of extravagant fantasies in which sorcery and witchcraft flicker like bolts of lightning. A number of tribes believe that the python is the reincarnation of some great ancestral spirit, and treat the snake with profound respect, even taking it votive offerings of such delicacies as a small pig or a rock-rabbit. In this country pythons are royal game and may not be killed except where life or livestock is actively endangered. I know of many farmers who positively encourage pythons on their premises, for they are of great use in ridding the tobacco barns and grain sheds of rodents. The only python that I have ever seen in the wilds was sleeping under water in a small stream. He looked like a twisted branch, lying submerged in the shallow water, his beautifully marked skin offset by the yellow sand of the stream-bed.

Though not as large as the Malayan python, nor as spectacularly coloured as the green arboreal python of New Guinea, none the less the African rock-python is a whopper, a modest-sized specimen measuring a good eighteen feet and attaining the thickness of a man's thigh. Hideous tales are told of how a python will kill a man, first stunning his prey with a hammer-blow from his blunt snout, and then commencing to salivate all over his unconscious victim before swallowing him whole. While pythons do, in fact, use the power of their strike to immobilise their larger prey momentarily, they actually effect their final destruction by crushing them to death. This process breaks down the skeletal structure until the whole body acquires the consistency of a soft sausage which can easily be swallowed.

On account of their fondness for rats, pythons are quite frequently caught in farm buildings, and make not unattractive pets. Some years ago one of the boys at Plumtree School had a tame python which he kept in a piano case. There came the day, however, when the python managed to get out and naturally its owner raised the alarm. Mr. Hammond instructed the whole school to search the grounds in order to find it again.

Not many years before, the Anglo-Boer War had come to an end and a number of prefabricated wood-and-iron buildings which the British Army had used in Mafeking were dismantled and trucked up to Rhodesia by rail. Two of these buildings were presented to Plumtree School, their peculiarity being that they were raised up on piles, about a foot above the ground, leaving an open space beneath, through which the air could circulate. The python was finally discovered under the floor of one of these 'Mafeking Houses', and it appeared that she had taken up permanent residence there, for she refused to be dislodged.

While she was perfectly visible, and thoroughly audible, hissing vigorously at the rows of boys who crouched down to peer at her, no one could be found who was prepared to creep in under the Mafeking House and actually get her. Although they are not venomous, pythons are equipped with powerful jaws and savage teeth, so that a python bite is every bit as serious as that of say, a bull-terrier or a mastiff.

Mr. Hammond, the headmaster, finally hit on the idea of sending to Bulawayo for an acquaintance of his, the Indian gully-gully man. After a few days the Indian arrived with all his paraphernalia of baskets and pipes and flutes, sat himself down cross-legged outside the Mafeking House and began to charm the snake out. It took some hours for this magic to work, but in the end he charmed her into one of his largest baskets which he presented triumphantly to the Head. What it is to know the right people!

Just to illustrate that there is more to some of the African myths than one might suppose, I should relate an experience which my aunt, Jane Greenfield had while rock-climbing in the Matopos. She and a party of other youngsters had been picnicking near Mchabesi Falls on the edge of the Matopo Hills, and an old, old man had pointed out a particular kopje to them, saying that this was where Mzilikazi the great Matabele Chief lay buried. They expressed a desire to see the place, but the old fellow was horrified, and explained to them that the spirit of the dead king still guarded the grave, and that they would be running the gravest possible risk in going there.

Not to be put off by such tales of ju-jus and guardian spirits, three of the girls set off to explore the forbidden kopje. The place definitely had an eerie atmosphere, with its numerous narrow caves and deep fissures between the lichen-splashed granite boulders. At last they came upon a place where the crack between two massive rocks had been walled up with stonework and daubs of dagha. Jane, who was the tallest, stood on tiptoe and peered over into the gloom of the cleft inside. Her eye was caught by a gleam of silver, and reaching in as far as she could she managed to grasp what was the hilt of a long, shining sword.

She was on the point of drawing it out to show to her companions, when one of the girls gave a piercing scream. Not ten feet away on a sunny shelf of rock lay coiled an enormous python! His head was raised, his tongue was flicking in and out and he was watching them intently with glittering eyes.

Hastily and with a beating heart, Jane replaced the sword, and the three girls scrambled down the kopje as fast as their trembling limbs would take them. And so after all, Mzilikazi's guardian spirit *was* there, just as the old man had said!

Although many of Mother's cousins and aunts and uncles still lived in Scotland, several of the more enterprising ones used to come out to Bulawayo to visit us from time to time. We always enjoyed having them to stay, especially as most of them were at pains to impress on us that these journeys were undertaken in a spirit of intrepid determination and high adventure. As John and Charles were for the greater part of the year away at boarding-school, it was usual for these guests to be accommodated in the boys' rondavel. One year we had a prolonged visit from a charming middle-aged couple called Billy and Mary. Billy, in particular, won our affection by professing a keen interest in wild life. All the same, it was probably a mistake on Father's part to have kept them up late on their first night with us, showing them his best films of lions and crocodiles and elephants.

When at last they got to bed, Mary was inclined to be nervous. Billy assumed an air of cheery confidence and did all he could to persuade her that the rondavel was absolutely safe and she had nothing to fear from snakes, leopards, spiders or any other horror of the night. At last he succeeded in getting her to go to sleep, and was on the point of dropping off himself when he was suddenly transfixed, feeling a heavy weight descending stealthily on to the foot of his bed. He lay there in the dark, absolutely rigid, mentally going through the list of predators which he knew inhabited our region. Surely it couldn't be a lion. No, altogether too silent, too slow in making its pounce. For the same reason he dismissed the leopard and the hyena. Now the creature, whatever it was, commenced a creeping advance up

the bed towards him, and all at once Billy realised what it was —
a python!

He longed to leap from his bed, to cry for help, but
somehow he managed to keep a grip on himself, remembering all
the reassuring things he'd been saying to his wife only a short
while previously. Scarcely daring to breath, Billy sl-o-w-ly drew
his left hand out from the bedclothes and groped about beside
him in the dark, trying to find the switch of the table-lamp. By
now the creature had crept right up the bed and had settled on his
chest, poised — as he imagined — to strike. At last his trembling
fingers found the switch and with a convulsive jerk he turned the
light on!

Billy found himself staring right into the round, golden eyes
of Little Ike, our enormous black cat, who was on the point of
settling down for the night. The following morning both Billy
and Mary looked decidedly drawn and haggard. I was detailed
to be sure to capture all the cats before dark and to keep them
with me, to prevent a recurrence of this regrettable incident!

Dogs are an integral part of farm life in Zimbabwe, even
where there are no sheep or other livestock to watch over. On
their farm near Sinoia the Robbs always kept a pack of assorted
hounds to guard the homestead and help to keep baboons out of
the maize lands. Their farm, Robbo, was the very last in the line
of agricultural development — beyond lay the Zambezi
escarpment, and virgin bush as far as the eye could see.
Naturally under these circumstances their fields of lush, green

maize were a temptation to the many wild animals that inhabited the adjoining bush.

At the beginning of the season when the maize seed began to germinate, the guinea-fowl would fly in at dawn to scratch up the sprouting grain. Later when the young plants were soft and tender, the locusts would arrive. Ame Robb recalls one Christmas Day when one of their labourers ran to the house to tell her father that locusts were in the lands. Every hand was needed. The whole family put down their knives and forks and abandoned their Christmas dinner to which they had looked forward for so long. Armed with tins and sticks and primitive rattles, they spent the whole day driving the clouds of locusts from one field to another in a desperate bid to save their maize crop from destruction.

If the young plants survived the ravages of the insect world, and providing there was enough rain, the maize reached the stage where it would tassel and cob. Then, when the sweet white milk began to swell the grain, the wild pigs would arrive. The bush-pig is different from the warthog, being a heavier animal more like the European boar, and endowed with a long bristly mane. While the warthog prefers to rootle for its food and will indeed do great damage to crops like sweet potatoes, the bush-pig has learned to trample down the maize plants in order to get at the juicy young cobs.

During this period the Robbs used to send out a trusty old man called M'dara to keep watch over the maize lands at night. He was armed with a shot-gun and a 'simbi' — a metal clanger which he used to strike at each corner of the field to drive out the pigs. One of the dogs always accompanied M'dara on these patrols, and the two of them made a very fine team. The dog was a red Irish terrier called Stinking George. (He earned his name on account of his dislike for water. Try as they might, no one was ever able to catch Stinking George when a bath was in the offing!)

On this particular morning Stinking George and M'dara were making their last round of the maize lands before sun-up. Stinking George had trotted ahead and was quartering about in the bush at the edge of the cultivated land, when all at once he began barking in a frenzied manner. M'dara broke into a run, sensing that Stinking George was in some kind of trouble. After the first volley of barks, the dog had fallen silent. M'dara searched here and there in the thick bush, and finally under a big msasa tree he discovered Stinking George tightly wrapped in the coils of an enormous python. Already the dog was practically done for. The python's head was resting between the dog's ears, and M'dara pranced about the two of them, trying to find a way of shooting the python in the head without injuring Stinking George. At last he forced the barrel of the gun under the reptile's jaw and pulled the trigger.

The first rays of the sun found the pair of them approaching the farmstead, Stinking George trotting ahead, his tail waving gaily, and behind him M'dara striding along with a jaunty air, and dragging the python which was fastened to a twisted thong of wet bark. The python measured twenty feet in length, and his track in the sand was over a foot wide.

The drama of the situation was not lost on old M'dara who entertained the entire Robb family and all the farm hands to an account of what had happened, now simulating the python and twisting himself in coils about the dog, now returning to his human shape and capering about with his shot-gun to illustrate the difficulty of finding the right position from which to fire, and finally falling down on the ground, unfolding his limbs and thrashing about in a spirited pantomime to imitate the python's death throes. M'dara was well rewarded for his bravery, while Stinking George went on to fight another day.

That day came sooner than anyone imagined. Later in the season when the mealie cobs turned dry and hard, the bush-pigs lost interest in them. The robbers-in-chief at this stage were the baboons. A troop of forty or fifty of them could do untold damage, not only plundering the maize but also stealing water. The river was some distance off, and the only water at the farmhouse came from the well, which was a mile away. The water was painstakingly brought to the surface by windlass, bucket by bucket, and tipped into a huge drum that stood in the back of a scotch cart. The cart was then driven up to the house, and used to stand outside the kitchen door. At nights, and sometimes even during the day if no one was about, the baboons would steal down from the high granite kopje behind the house, and drink the water from the barrel. More often than not a fight would break out and they would succeed in tipping over the whole drum, and all the water would be lost.

Ame Robb's elder brother John used to take Stinking George with him whenever he needed to chase off the baboons. The dog was completely fearless and would dash in among them, barking and snapping and chasing them until the whole troop were put to flight. While John was there to back him up with his rifle, Stinking George was reasonably safe, but a baboon is a terrible enemy to a dog if it catches him. Several of them will hold the dog fast in their powerful hands, and rip him open with their dreadful fangs.

One evening Stinking George did not come in for his dinner. John immediately became concerned, for Stinking George was his favourite. The lad stayed out whistling and calling long after dark, but Stinking George did not return. Next morning as there was still no sign of him, John gave the instruction that every man was to down tools in order to join in the search for the missing dog.

Stinking George was found at last among the rocks at the back of the kopje behind the house. He must have undertaken a baboon hunt on his own, but this time they got him. He was on his side, his belly ripped open from the ribs to the groin so that his entrails had spilled out and were lying in the sand beside him. He was still alive when John knelt down at his side.

Ame heard her brother shouting before he reached the house. He was calling for his mother to find a long needle and some thread. Soon afterwards John arrived, carrying Stinking George's limp body in his arms. Gently John laid his dog on the kitchen table and washed the grains of sand off the soft bag of the peritoneum. Next he moistened a piece of cotton wool and squeezed a few drops of water through the dog's clenched teeth. Each time Stinking George swallowed, John dribbled in a little more. Then, as carefully as he could, John lifted up the entrails and replaced them inside the dog, finally sewing up the long gash in the belly.

For three days the family took it in turns to sit with Stinking George, dripping milk and brandy between his teeth, talking to him and petting him to keep him quiet so that he wouldn't tear his stitches. To everyone's surprise, the wound healed and within a week Stinking George was back on his feet. By the following summer he was as fit as ever, chasing away the baboons that came to the water barrel at the back door, and doing his nightly patrols with his old friend M'dara.

It is autumn. All over the country, heavy trucks and wagons rumble along the roads, trailing swirling clouds of dust in their wake. They are laden with sacks of grain whose stout, brown bellies are full and round with next year's food. There is something pleasantly restful about the year's decline. It has none of the breathless excitement of spring, nor the thunderous pomp of summer. Rather, autumn is a time for reflection, a time to draw breath and look about, a time to consolidate the advances achieved in the summer and to make orderly preparation for the winter, a time to let one's thoughts dwell agreeably on leisurely plans for the coming spring.

The rains have left us now and each day dawns as fair as the last. Still warm and damp, the earth supports a luxuriant growth, and every tree exults in her proud regalia of leaves. Tossing their heads with indifference at the rains' departure, the cassias suddenly explode into brilliant candelabras of sulphur flowers whose spicy scent fills the evening with its swooning fragrance. Whenever the sun goes behind a cloud, however, an immediate chill is perceptible, and the dogs no longer seek out the pools of shade beneath the trees. The nights are cooler now too, and in the early mornings the air is crisp and biting with the invigorating tang of a mountain stream.

The grass alone is not deceived by the Indian summer. In the vleis and valleys it stands thick and tall, the stems still stained a soft green-sage, but now its feathered seed-heads are dusted with gold. It ripples under the wind in streaming waves of bronze and jade, the marbled colours melting and undulating in a continuous flowing movement like the current of some great river.

The soft whisper of the wind through the grass, the warm lazy days, the drowsy feeling of ripeness and fulfilment act on one like a powerful hypnotic. "Yet a little sleep, a little slumber, a little folding of the hands — so shall thy poverty come. Go to the ant, thou sluggard," I seem to hear Solomon say, "consider her ways and be wise."

The autumn at last has made me restless and fidgety, and the sense of comfortable well-being gives way to a peevish dis-satisfaction. My ducks are gone, my turkeys are gone, my jackal has gone, my guinea-fowl have gone and although the flower-beds and the vegetables are the better for their absence, my garden seems barren and empty.

"I wonder if I should get some bantams," I muse idly, while scanning the Kennel and Pets column one Sunday morning.

"For the love of heaven, NO!" says Doug.

We are still both in bed, having dismembered the newspaper, and are each lazily enjoying our favourite sections.

"Ah! Here we are!" I exclaim excitedly. "The very thing!"

Doug snorts.

"Another brace of white-backed vultures, no doubt."

"Not at all," say I reprovingly. "Something beautiful. Go on, guess!"

Doug sips his early morning cup of tea, a wary look entering his eye.

"A peacock," he declares at last in sepulchral tones.

"Yes! Right first time!"

Doug chokes and spills his tea.

"Now wait a minute," he protests, mopping himself hastily, "don't do anything rash. This wants a bit of thought."

" 'One peacock, two peahens' it says."

"Oh my God," comes a despairing groan from Doug.

" 'Ten dollars' it says. I call that jolly reasonable, don't you?"

"Since you ask, no — I call it lunacy," Doug replies with bitter emphasis. "I'd pay you the ten dollars *not* to have them! Noisy brutes, peacocks."

"They've given a telephone number here," I go on hurriedly, "shouldn't I ring them up now, before someone else beats me to it? It would be terrible to miss them!"

"You *can't* phone people at six o'clock on a Sunday morning!"
says Doug indignantly. "And besides, no one else in their right
minds would want the blasted things."
By six-fifteen I am beside myself with anxiety and impatience.
"Surely anyone with peacocks would be awake by now," I
grumble. "Anyway, it's obscene to be asleep in bed once the
sun's up."
"Well, don't blame me if they bite your head off! Here, pour me
another cup of tea, will you, before you start," says Doug.

The telephone rings and rings and rings. I am about to
replace my receiver when there is a confused clatter at the other
end of the line and a man's voice croaks "Hello".
"Good morning!" say I brightly. "I'm phoning about your
peacocks."
There are a few moments silence.
"What's that you say?" The man sounds bewildered, and his
diction is scratchy and slurred as if he's just woken up.
"Your peacocks," I reply distinctly.
"My peacocks? Did you say my peacocks?" His voice is rising,
I notice.
"Yes. The ones you're advertising in today's paper."
"But I haven't got any peacocks." The man's voice cracks with
emotion. "Listen, if this is some kind of a —" He breaks off and
has a mumbled argument with someone in the background, then:
"Hang on a minute," he says to me in the strangled tones of
someone whose mind is giving way. He holds further dis-
cussions with a third party, and at last the resumption of heavy
breathing suggests that he is back on the air.
"Look, I'm frightfully sorry," I stammer. "Perhaps they have
given the wrong number." Doug is jerking his head and rolling
his eyes in a gawd 'elp us gesture. "I do apologise for having got
you up for nothing," I conclude lamely.
"No, that's all right," the man replies, with what I consider a
remarkable show of good manners and self-control, "the
peacocks belong to my father-in-law. My wife forgot to tell me
about them, that's all. As you are the first person who has
phoned, I guess they're yours."
I thank the man warmly and replace the phone.

"How about that!" I exclaim. "They're ours!"
Doug sighs and swallows the last of his tea with the cheerful air
of Socrates draining his cup of hemlock.
"Oh well," he says resignedly, "here we go again!"

There is a story about George III and the difficulty which
his Ministers ran into while preparing him for the opening of
Parliament. At that time the poor King was recovering from one
of his bouts of insanity, but had improved so far as to be almost
himself. His Ministers brought him a draft of the King's Speech
and suggested that he rehearse it through. The King read the
speech aloud to them, but for some strange reason he said the
word 'peacock' at the end of every sentence. It was difficult to
know what to do — in every other respect His Majesty's
delivery was impeccable. At last one of the Ministers ventured
to say that 'peacock' was an excellent word to use except that,
having such mystical significance, it should not be said out loud
in front of the common people. The King duly went on to open
Parliament, pausing to whisper 'peacock' at the conclusion of
every sentence. Apparently this achieved a most stately and
dignified effect, and the King's Speech was warmly applauded
by the House!

In the days prior to the arrival of our birds, I outdid
George III — the word 'peacock' was in my mind and on my lips
continuously. I could think and talk of nothing else. For one
thing I had no pen in which to put them. The children, Doug and
I spent hours prowling round the garden discussing the suitability
of one place or another. We finally settled on the white stinkwood
tree whose graceful branches drooped down almost to the
ground, forming a natural cave within. Bearing in mind that the
peacock is indigenous to the forests of India and Burma, we
selected this shady spot and built a huge aviary round the tree,
using bamboo poles and chicken-wire. It was a curious affair
when completed, but it was very lofty and spacious with ample
branches among which the birds could roost. We called their
pen, somewhat pretentiously, the Taj Mahal.

On the Saturday morning when the peafowl were to be
delivered, both the children and I were in a state of great

excitement and anticipation. The hours dragged by and the man didn't come. At long last, shortly before lunch, when we were all exhausted and grumpy, a small wired-in vanette creaked up the drive. The three peafowl were lying down in a row, the cock in the centre with a wife on either side of him. They looked so dignified and composed that my heart went out to them at once. On being released into the Taj Mahal, all three birds immediately set to and began to preen their disordered plumage.

Rajah-Loo, the cock, was in moult and to be perfectly frank he looked thoroughly scruffy and moth-eaten. He had no train at all, and his neck and chest appeared patchy and rough. His wives, Mumtaz and Saba, were similarly tousled, which made me suspect their former owner had run into difficulties while attempting to round them up. We brought them an offering of sunflower seed and chick-weed, and then left them in peace to settle down.

That night a great dark cloud rolled over the horizon from the north, and after muttering and grumbling to itself for an hour or two, it commenced to rain. This was most unseasonal, and as far as my peafowl were concerned it could not have come at a worse time. Although we had incorporated Delilah's — or rather Josephine's kennel into one side of the Taj, the peafowl were at first suspicious of its dark maw, and wouldn't take shelter inside it.

It rained on and off for most of the day and throughout the following night. Next morning the sun broke through, but the Taj was in such deep shade that my poor birds felt none of the benefit of its rays. If the peafowl had appeared dishevelled before, now they were too pitifully wet and bedraggled for words. I was really concerned that if they didn't get warm and dry pretty soon, they might catch pneumonia. After watching them for a while and noticing that they appeared calm and unafraid, I decided to open the door of the Taj and let them out into the sunshine. Gently I undid the hasp and pushed the door back, praying that they wouldn't take off and vanish for good.

For a long time Rajah-Loo stood in the open doorway, preening and looking about. Then with stately deliberation he lifted his white feet and stalked out into the sun, followed by his two wives. I brought out a copy of *Uncle Remus* and sat down nearby with the children, to read them a story. For a while the peafowl grazed quietly on the lawn, tweaking off the grass-blades with a sideways jerk. Presently, all three birds came over and joined us, settling down contentedly to preen their feathers, fluffing them out to dry in the sunshine, and now and then tilting their heads to one side as if appreciating a particular section of the story.

In the days, weeks and years that followed, this became one of their most endearing habits. Wherever we were, whether busy in a particular part of the garden, or sitting on the verandah, the peafowl would arrive to join us. They appeared to love a story as much as the children, and would remain rooted to the spot until the tale was done.

All three birds were ridiculously tame. They soon learned that the clatter of the tea-tray was the signal for a feast, and as soon as tea arrived on the verandah they would stalk up with outstretched necks to see what was on the menu. Rajah fed from our hands within the first few days, and if one's attention wandered while holding a sandwich or piece of cake, he would bend forward politely and tweak it out of one's fingers, sharing it most courteously with Saba and Mumtaz. Indeed the thing that impressed me most about my birds was their remarkable quality of courtliness. They had a most gracious manner with one another and with us, giving a little cluck of thanks when accepting a morsel, and invariably wiping their beaks carefully on the grass when they had finished it. They never squabbled and jostled like the hens and the ducks, and were content to maintain studiously cordial relations with both the dogs and the Siamese cats.

After a few weeks Rajah-Loo began to grow a new train. His chest and neck feathers smoothed over and filled out, he sprouted fresh spikes in his coronet and his whole plumage took on a lustre and a magnificence that beggar description. 'Proud as a peacock' did at first seem an apt expression. They gave the impression of being extremely vain about their appearance, devoting many hours each day to the task of perfecting their toilette. One of their favourite preening spots was the verandah where they could admire their reflections in the french windows. After a while, however, I came to realise what a great responsibility it was, taking care of all those feathers. Well enough for a duck, say, to flick her beak over her feathers once or twice, and then call it a day. This is not modesty on the part of the duck. It is simply that her plumage is functional, like a pair of overalls, while the peacock's feathers resemble the white puttees, the kilt and sporran, red jacket and waistcoat, belted plaid and plumed bonnet of the Black Watch. It is the difference between workaday attire and Full Dress Kit. Rajah used to work over each item of his 'uniform' individually. First he would rub and polish his breast and belly with the side of his head. Next he would droop one wing and go through the pinions, layer by layer. Rajah's wings were enormous and terminated in long curved feathers of a shining apricot-bronze, each one the size of the blade of a carving knife. Above these were his 'tiger stripes', short broad feathers patterned with wavy bands of white and copper and black — a black that flashed a deep brilliant green as it caught the sun. After he had done both wings, he would twist his head round and start on his back. Just below the shoulders was a panel of small, tightly clustered feathers which we called his 'scales'. They were arranged in neat overlapping semi-circles of glittering coppery green so that his shoulders and back resembled the skin of a dragon. As Rajah moved, the 'scales' would change colour in the shifting light, now green, now gold, now a shimmering blend of the two. The scales grew larger and larger, finally blossoming into the long sweeping train with its iridescent 'eyes' of blue and green and violet.

Nor was this all! Beneath his train Rajah had two further layers of plumage! First, his 'reinforcing', a fan of stiff gold quills, each over a foot long. When the peacock elevates his tail during display, these are the feathers that do the work. Finally, like a soft cushion underneath them all, he had a thick wad of pure white fluff.

The interesting thing about all this finery was the muscular control which he could exercise over each particular section. In order to facilitate his preening, he could at will erect all his scales so that his back was ridged like a coat of mail. Then again he could lift up his train and twist it to one side, stripping each long plume from root to tip. He could even puff out the individual legs of his white breeches, one at a time, probing or poking among the feathers for the offending flea.

Next to the 'eye' plumes, the children treasured the smooth, curved feathers that came off Rajah's breast. They were of a deep glittering midnight-blue, shot with green. How a mere bird was able to support all this splendour was to me nothing short of a miracle, and all the more remarkable was the way in which Rajah-Loo could simply disappear. One would imagine that so brilliantly coloured a creature would be conspicuous anywhere, but many a time I searched the garden with mounting anxiety and concluded that he had run away or been stolen. Half an hour later I would find him and his wives lying contentedly under the shade of a low shrub or tree, enjoying a dust-bath. The instant Rajah stepped into a bush he became invisible, totally and completely camouflaged amongst the dark green leaves and black pools of shadow. Conversely, when he stalked out into the sun once more, he was transformed into a spectacle of glittering magnificence, his wings and breast and train glowing and sparkling like some rich brocade that has been embroidered with jewels.

Though less colourful than their lord, Mumtaz and Saba had a queenly elegance of their own. The basic structure of their plumage followed his, even to the train, though theirs was shorter and of a soft grey with something of the gathered fullness of a bustle. A discreet metallic green shone on their necks and shoulders, while the tip of each spike of their coronets flashed with a spark of emerald. Their faces, too, had an arrestingly dramatic quality. Their cheeks were of delicate white skin as fine and soft as kid-glove. Across it ran a broad band of black velvet feathers, angling up diagonally from the beak and tapering away to accentuate the large, lustrous eye. This dark stripe was suggestive of the extravagant make-up of a ballerina, or the kohl-stained eyelids of some seductive Arabian dancing-girl. Immediately below this black band, both Mumtaz and Saba wore a delicate dusting of lime-green eyeshadow. The whole effect was exotic, improbable and altogether lovely!

It was a delight to discover that peafowl, even more so than guinea-fowl, have a complicated repertoire of linguistic and mimetic signals. The well-known peacock's scream is only used during the mating season from August to January. It is related to the fanning of the tail, and once the bird begins to moult his train, he loses his voice. For the greater part of the year the peacock is an excessively silent bird that will only hoot out a note of warning when strangers enter the premises.

Their intimate communications are of an altogether different order. As our little trio of peafowl strolled round the garden together, they'd keep up a subdued conversation with one another. There was a soft 'chuck' that meant 'come on'; a wheezy, grating, scraping noise in the throat that said 'I've found something delicious. Come and share it with me'; and a high trill that was a signal of alarm. If one of the wives became somehow separated from the others, she would go very thin and stand up on tiptoe, blinking her eyes in a worried fashion. Presently she'd point her beak at the sky and say a surprised 'ah', such a sound as one makes when finding a lost sixpence that has rolled under the bed. If this received no answering call from the others, she'd hurry off saying 'ah' every few moments until she re-established contact.

Rajah and his wives employed a most eloquent form of sign-language. They were incredibly alert and vigilant, their heads ever twisting this way and that, cocking an eye at the heavens for hawks, or peering under a bush for snakes and meerkats. If a hawk appeared sweeping through the sky in lazy circles, the bird who spotted it would immediately puff out its neck feathers like a ruff, swaying its head back and forth in exaggerated nods to indicate the direction of the enemy. If the danger were close at hand, the bird would lay its neck parallel to the ground, a signal that meant 'run for cover!' Immediately all three of them would skim off under a bush or on to the verandah, uttering a light, purring trill of alarm.

For the first week they were with us, we shooed the peafowl back into the Taj Mahal at nights, but if left to their own devices they preferred to roost in the branches of the tall wild fig that grows behind the house. From the ground they were almost invisible, but from the window of the sitting-room upstairs we could look out on them in the evenings as they sat in the tree like dark, silent shadows. I believe they chose that place because they too could see us not ten feet away — it was another manifestation of their sociability. On waking up in the mornings they would first preen thoroughly while still in the tree. Then at about half-past six we would hear a jubilant 'ah' as each bird launched itself into the air. A moment later there would be a rushing mighty wind as the three huge birds came whooshing down over the roof to land at the run on the terrace outside the bedrooms.

I shall never forget the first time we heard Rajah-Loo scream. For six months he had never said more than a polite 'haw' to announce the arrival of, say, the butcher's bicycle.

Then one night when the moon was full, he threw back his head and let out a scream that would have woken the dead! Doug and I sat bolt upright in bed, quaking in every limb, and staring at one another with wild eyes.

"What was that?" I quavered.

It sounded as though someone was being murdered on the roof.

"It's your blasted bird," said Doug in a voice that shook. "I hope he's not intending to carry on like that all night."

"H-a-a-a-w!" screamed Rajah from the fig-tree.

"For heaven's sake!" groaned Doug.

"M-e-e-e-o-o-w!" concluded Rajah.

I could see that something would have to be done, or at this rate neither of us would get a wink of sleep. Reluctantly I dragged myself out of bed, struggled into a dressing-gown and stumbled outside. It was a breathtakingly beautiful moonlit night. As I walked under the fig-tree my foot snapped a dead twig and Rajah immediately released another blood-curdling scream.

"Shut up, you ass!" I hissed at him. "Why are you making this awful row?"

I could just make out all three birds craning their necks down to look at me.

"Now dry up, d'you hear?" I whispered fiercely.

"H-a-a-a-w!" began Rajah again.

Clicking my tongue with annoyance, I hitched up my dressing-gown and began to climb the tree. The birds watched me with lively interest. When at last I reached their level, I found a comfortable perch in a fork near-by and settled down to restore order. Every time Rajah drew breath to begin a 'Haw', I'd say 'Hsss', and he'd stop. Heaven knows how long I sat up there, shivering with cold and hissing at him through chattering teeth! Gradually the moon rolled across the sky and one by one the birds tucked their heads under their wings and went to sleep. At last, stiff and cold, I slithered down the tree and crept back to bed.

"What in hell have you been doing?" Doug mumbled sleepily. "You're ice-cold and you're covered all over with sand or something."

"It's bark," I said, snuggling my head gratefully into the pillow,

"I've been roosting in the tree with my peacock."

"You know, sometimes," Doug muttered vaguely, "I really wonder . . ."

Next time the moon was full I took care to put Rajah into the Taj Mahal for the night! He seemed less inclined to sing when on a lower perch, and confined himself to addressing a muffled 'haw' to the baker as he commenced his dawn deliveries. Since the baker did his rounds on a motor bike that made more noise than twenty peacocks, I didn't feel that Rajah-Loo could be held responsible for breaking the peace!

With the arrival of spring Rajah began to call with increasing frequency during the day, and tended to go off on his own to stand on the little outcrop of rocks where Henry's run had been, and there he used to serenade his wives. If I went to visit him there, he'd chivalrously bend forward and throw up his tail and fan out his splendid train, rattling the quills together and making them all vibrate and shiver with a purring, rustling sound like the wind thrumming in a reed-bed. He loved to show off, and would gladly put on a display for anyone who was prepared to watch — the cats, the vegetable-monger on a bicycle, a thrush — even the lawn-mower. He'd droop his wings displaying the gorgeous bronze pinions, snapping his beak and scraping the ground with his toes. He'd wheel round this way and that to give one the full benefit of both front and back views. In fact, he preferred to advance on his audience backwards, peeping under one wing to see where he was going, and then whirling around dramatically, buzzing all his magnificent feathers together, the rainbow arch of his tail almost touching the ground before him like a lyre-bird's.

Curiously enough, his wives gave the impression of being callously unmoved by his display. They would come mincing past him, looking unutterably bored by it all, while Rajah scraped and whirled and fluttered his wings in a frenzy of adoration. Mumtaz finally succumbed to him later that year, and commenced to make her nest on the very top of the compost-heap under the banana trees. The following year Saba's marriage was consummated. She was very secretive about her nesting site, surprising us all by selecting Delilah's old kennel that had been built into the Taj Mahal.

While she was sitting, Mumtaz followed a strict daily routine. At about eight o'clock each morning she would fly off her nest uttering a wild popping cry, and come winging down the garden to land outside the kitchen in a great flurry of feathers and a swirl of dust and dead grass. I had to be on hand *at once* to minister to her needs, running out with a handful of grain and a helping of grated cheese. She'd gobble it down, talking to me all the while in breathless whooping gasps between each mouthful, as if to say: "Sorry I have to rush like this, but my eggs, you know . . ." Immediately on finishing her food, she'd lope off round the corner of the house to her favourite sand-bath, and flounder about in it for a few moments, croaking urgently to herself. Next she'd dash off to find the end of the hose-pipe which ran from the borehole on to my fruit trees. Having refreshed herself with a long drink, she'd gallop away to the youngberry hedge, jumping up to pluck the ripest fruits. This was her last port of call, and from there she would commence the stealthy return to her nest on the compost-heap.

Shortly before Mumtaz began to sit, Doug had to make a quick business trip overseas, returning with several packets of herb seeds from Switzerland. I was in ecstasies, for at that time such things were quite unobtainable here. I planted the seed out in carefully prepared beds in the vegetable-garden, near the compost-heap, and watered them tenderly each day. To my delight, the seeds germinated and grew. I used to gloat over them every day, admiring their delicate little scented leaves and soft green stems. I had not been the only one who had had her eye on the young herbs, however.

One day in early October when most of the garden was hot and dry and parched, Mumtaz hatched out her three little peachicks. In the course of the morning she brought them down from the summit of the compost-heap, glittering little amber pompons speckled with flakes of jet. They came down, tripping and slithering among the big dead leaves of the erythrina, while the children and I watched them in delight. Clucking to them in soft encouragement, Mumtaz daintily led her brood in among

the herbs, scraped out a hollow in the middle of the fennel and
settled down with her babies under her wings. For three days
Mumtaz didn't move out of the herb garden. I was in despair, but
evidently she knew what her chicks needed when they were
very young. There was no other soft green growth in the whole
garden, and I hadn't the heart to chase them off. As a matter of
fact she did very little harm. From time to time they would make
sorties out into the parsley or the tarragon or the basil, but I
noticed that they were primarily attracted by the cress which
was abundant, and by the leaves of a creeping wild sorrel that
grew along the grass paths between the beds.

I should have guessed that they would enjoy my herbs, for
peafowl have the most exotic and expensive tastes. Apart from
sorrel and chickweed, they adored nasturtium flowers and
ranunculus petals. Rajah had a passion for the waxy white
flowers that dropped from the male papaw tree, and all of them
relished the shiny, damp, black seeds of the papaw itself.
Although I knew that the word 'peacock' is a corruption of the
Latin *pavo* and has nothing to do with peas, I thought it would
be interesting none the less to see if they liked them. I picked a
handful of green peas and rolled them temptingly on the ground.
The peafowl eyed the little green spheres suspiciously, first
drawing themselves up to a lofty height, and then bending their
heads down close to each pea, scrutinising it narrowly. After a
few moments' careful consideration, they stepped away from
the peas lifting their feet very high with obvious distaste and
flicking their heads sideways, a gesture of abhorrence which
they had hitherto reserved for such loathsome objects as
chongololos and cut-worms!

Grated cheese, on the other hand, was regarded as a
delicacy, and Rajah was so appreciative of it that when offered a
little, he would politely fan out his tail first and do a dance before
gently pecking it out of one's outstretched hand. All of them
adored youngberries and fruit-cake, and they were quick to
discover my white muscat and katawber grapes ripening on the
vines. They became very skilful at flying on to the supporting
pergola, and bending over to pluck the ripest grapes as they hung
among the leaves. They swallowed them whole with every

evidence of delight, and one could plainly see that they believed that we had planted the vines expressly for their benefit and enjoyment.

On the evening of their fourth day, Mumtaz took her babies to the fig-tree. She herself floated airily up into the lowest branches and then craned her neck down and called to her chicks to follow her. Between the ground and the peafowl's favourite roost there were stretches of sheer trunk that were anything from three to eight feet in height. Their accustomed perch was a good thirty-five feet above the ground.

"You're daft, Mumtaz," I told her. "You'll never get your babies up there!"

But Mumtaz knew what she was about. Without any hesitation the three little peachicks commenced to *climb* the tree, running vertically up the bark and fluttering their wings like three, big, brown moths. Up and up they went, Mumtaz springing from branch to branch ahead of them and showing her babies the easy way. The setting sun found her settled triumphantly on her accustomed perch with three little faces peering out from among the soft feathers of her belly.

I think we were all a little surprised to find that both Mumtaz and Saba made careful and attentive mothers. One refers to a person having 'a brain like a peahen', meaning they are of inferior intellect. Yet so far as I can judge, the peahen has a decidedly superior mind — she is vigilant and resourceful as a mother, good-humoured and imaginative as a companion. I loved to watch the scrupulous care with which they would demonstrate how to wipe one's beak after eating cheese, and to observe the lessons they gave their young on how to dance and fan their tails. It was enchanting to see Saba or Mumtaz with her neat grey tail flared out behind her, bowing and scraping to her babies until they imitated her, erecting their little brown feathers in a fan no bigger than a teaspoon. The whole family bowing and pirouetting together reminded me of a seventeenth-century ballroom with groups of stately courtiers dancing the minuet. Once the peachicks had mastered the art, there was no stopping them, and it was delightful to watch the little cocks attempting to impress a sparrow, fanning their tails, scraping their toes and dragging their little wings in a Lilliputian parody of their father.

Rajah was very gentle and considerate with his offspring, and had a pleasantly paternal way of bending his head down close to theirs as if listening to their childish prattle. From time to time, however, he would become bored with these domestic occupations and would stalk off on his own to find more lively entertainment. On one such occasion he was drawn away from his family by some guests, who arrived in a brand-new Mercedes Benz. Rajah, having inspected the car with a connoisseur's eye, suddenly observed that in the centre of the shining hub-cap there was another peacock. He was outraged! Dragging his wings, he made a closer inspection and located a further three rivals, one in each of the other wheels. He was squaring up to destroy them one by one when somebody saw what he was about. Thereafter when guests arrived, we draped their wheels with sacks, just to be on the safe side!

All the peafowl loved to sit and preen on the window-sills. I think they liked to glimpse their shadowy reflections in the panes of glass. These ghostly images never appeared to upset or antagonise them, but one day Rajah-Loo sprang on to the window-sill of my bedroom and was incensed to discover a new adversary confronting him from the looking-glass on the far wall of the room. This fellow had none of the diminished stature of the four he had found in the hub-caps. It was a full-length looking-glass and the bird inside it was every bit as large and magnificent as Rajah himself. Determined to get at this dangerous rival and vanquish him at any cost, Rajah devised a Cunning Stratagem. I was writing letters in my room, and the first I knew of it was a gentle hissing noise in the passage, accompanied by a slow, regular click, click. The next moment Rajah-Loo walked into the bedroom, arrogant pugnacity written in every line of his body.

"Well, Rajah-Loo," I greeted him, not guessing why he had come, "so that was your train sweeping along the floor, was it? I suppose you're after some cheese."

He had never come into the house before, but there has to be a first time for everything. I rather imagined that he was looking for company, the way the guinea-fowl had done. Gently I shooed him back down the passage and out through the kitchen door, and presented him with a piece of cheese. I returned to my letters, but in a few moments he was back again. This time he caught sight of his reflection face to face, gave a tremendous scream of rage and leaped at the looking-glass. Now all was made plain. I escorted him out and firmly shut the back door. However, he became obsessed by the peacock in my bedroom, and if the kitchen door was shut, he would come in through the dining-room, or through the french windows into the playroom, up a flight of stairs into the hall, up another flight of stairs into the dining-room and so up the passage once more. It was very difficult to keep him out. On one occasion he had joined in battle with his rival and by the time I got to him, the looking-glass was streaked with blood from his spurs. He had struck them so hard against the glass that he had broken his skin. After that my bedroom door remained shut at all times, and fortunately he never discovered the looking-glasses in the other rooms of the house.

Not long ago I came across a strange remark in John Ruskin's book *The Stones of Venice*. He said: "Remember that the most beautiful things in the world are the most useless; peacocks and lilies for instance."

At first this struck me as a most extraordinary statement from a man as well versed in the arts as Ruskin — but he is quite right, of course. One might reasonably add, of what 'use' is a swan? Of what 'use' are Michelangelo or Mozart, Shakespeare or Cézanne? Certainly the peacock is of less 'use' commercially than his clodhopping country cousin the turkey, but he is unquestionably a masterpiece, and as such he must be regarded as one of the jewels in Nature's diadem.

15

Gently Smiling Jaws

> Lepidus: *What manner o' thing is your crocodile?*
> Antony: *It is shaped, sir, like itself, and it is as*
> *broad as it has breadth; it is just so high as it*
> *is, and moves with its own organs. It lives by*
> *that which nourisheth it; and the elements once*
> *out of it, it transmigrates.*
> Lepidus: *What colour is it of?*
> Antony: *Of its own colour too.*
> Lepidus: *'Tis a strange serpent.*
> Antony: *'Tis so; and the tears of it are wet.*
>
> Antony and Cleopatra

MANY YEARS AGO when Father was a young man, he was making the journey across country from Que Que to Lupane. The road, such as it was, was very poor indeed and when towards evening he came to the drift across the Shangani River, he decided to call it a day and make camp. The crossing was likely to be tricky, and he preferred to be fresh when he undertook it. Under the trees on the river's bank it was very quiet and peaceful. Father built a small fire, cooked his dinner and was preparing to make an early night of it when an elephant came down to drink on the opposite side of the river.

For a few moments the animal stood watching him, gently fanning its ears and then, apparently reassured of Father's good intentions, it came on down to the river's edge and dipped its trunk into the river. Almost immediately there was a tremendous splashing and the elephant screamed with pain. A crocodile had taken him by the end of his trunk! It was exactly like Kipling's story of the Elephant's Child, only this tale had a very different ending. With one flick of his trunk, the elephant landed the crocodile on the bank and proceeded to stamp it as flat as a sheet of cardboard. It had not been a very large crocodile — perhaps seven or eight feet in length — but it certainly should have known better than to interfere with a jumbo!

Many years later when I was at high school, Reay Smithers, the Director of the Bulawayo Museum, offered Father two young crocs to put into our dam. I was most disappointed when Father declined, but I could understand his feelings. Only a few months previously a very great friend of ours, Ronnie Rankine, had been taken by crocs while fishing on the Zambezi. Ronnie was an altogether exceptional man, and his story bears repeating. He was one of those people who could have turned his hand to anything. In addition to being the country's leading ornithologist, he was an authority on antique silver and art. A graduate in agriculture, he was himself a most accomplished painter and photographer, a dead shot and a tireless walker. Although Ronnie was quick-tempered, impatient and inclined to be quarrelsome, these defects were offset by his originality of outlook and a very keen sense of humour. I was always a little afraid of him, but Ronnie probably did as much as any one man in Matabeleland to promote an interest in wildlife among schoolchildren, giving talks and illustrated lectures, and leading school expeditions into the wildest parts of the country.

It was unfortunate that Ronnie was on his own when the crocs got him. It was a very hot day and he had been fishing from the bank in a desultory fashion. Towards midday he must have dozed off, for the first he knew of it was a violent jerk on his right foot. Before he had time to react, he had been dragged off his camp-chair and was hauled into the river. By a remarkable stroke of luck his sheath-knife was still in his belt. Ronnie managed to get it out and fought with the croc in the river, going for its eyes until at last it let him go. He floundered back to the bank and was trying to crawl out of the water when a second croc took him by the left hand. By now he was in very poor shape with shock setting in, his right leg crushed, torn and bleeding profusely into the water. A second time he fought off the croc, but this battle was longer and more arduous. At last Ronnie succeeded in struggling to the bank, and crawled out of the water. The wave of anger that had sustained him through the second tussle now ebbed away, leaving him dizzy and nauseous. He knew that if they came for him a third time, that would be the end. He glanced down at his left hand, and saw that it was hanging on by only a few threads. He cut it off with his sheath-knife, and dragged himself to his Land-Rover. Then, using one hand and one leg he somehow managed to hold himself together and drove for twelve long miles along a narrow, bumping, twisting bush road until he reached help. Ronnie survived, but the two years that followed this traumatic experience were a nightmare of successive amputations. In the end he lost his leg completely; the arm was saved above the elbow.

Ronnie Rankine never alluded to the affair, and never grumbled about the loss of his limbs. Rather, he appeared to have the added zest for life of a man who has escaped the gallows. He had reason enough to be thankful that he was alive. It is a sobering thought that even today with all our humanitarian principles, antibiotics and sophisticated weapons, the three great killers on the Dark Continent are war, disease — and crocodiles.

It is small wonder, really, that we tend to regard the croc with revulsion, and think of him as a callous, unfeeling monster, the embodiment of evil. The ancient Egyptians, however, had a different attitude towards the reptile, regarding him as a sacred being like the ibis. In his account of Isis and Osiris, Plutarch relates that 'the Egyptians worship God symbolically in the crocodile, that being the only animal without a tongue, like the divine logos, which standeth not in need of speech'. Ancient historians relate how the people of the village of Ombos in Upper Egypt waged a furious war with the inhabitants of a neighbouring district in order to avenge the death of the particular crocodile which they used to venerate, and which the neighbours had killed.

Whether one goes to these lengths or not, there is no doubt that the crocodile is a very remarkable creature. He is not only the world's largest living reptile, but together with the turtle, he is one of the oldest forms of animal life in existence and can be traced right back to the Jurassic era. This was a period in our earth's history which was marked by a great extension of the sea and, towards its close, large areas of the land developed into freshwater marshes and swamps. One can readily imagine that under these conditions it was natural for numerous forms of amphibious life to develop and prosper. It is, I think, significant that crabs and catfish first made their appearance at this time, too, creatures which, like the crocodile, managed to keep a foot in both camps, as it were — the land and the water. The Nile

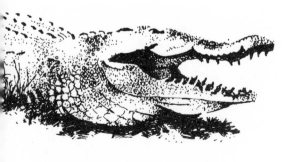

crocodile found throughout most of Africa today is substantially the same animal as his prehistoric ancestor teleosaurus, whose contemporaries included such extravagant lizards as the terrible flesh-eating tyrannosaurus, the giant atlantosaurus, the marine monster ichthyosaurus and the grotesque flying reptile, the pterodactyl. What sets the crocodile apart from these pre-historic monstrosities is the fact that where the others have died out, he has survived! Somehow or other he persisted through the cataclysmic climatic changes of the Quaternary period when most of the earth was either a desert or was locked up in a sheet of ice. Indeed, not only has he survived, the crocodile has prospered and must be considered as being one of the most successful of species. Today, crocodilians of one form or another are found in four of the world's five continents.

Why is the crocodile so successful? What is the secret of his survival? How does he adapt himself to such drastic changes of environment? Has he anything to teach us in this regard? Having just spent a year in the daily society of a crocodile, I have formulated a few tentative answers to some of these questions. As I am not a zoologist and couldn't begin to dismember a crocodile in order to study its digestive tract or its pulmonary development, I cannot pretend that mine were scientific observations. All the same, I learned many of the less obvious and more intimate aspects of the croc's daily life which may go some of the way towards an understanding of this much-misunderstood beast.

It all began in rather a curious way. One morning in early February the phone rang while I was preparing breakfast. It was Niels ·Greenfield. He sounded unusually excited.
"Is that you, Emily?" he asked. "Listen, something strange happened this morning. When Makaza opened the shade-house to water the orchids, he found a crocodile inside."
"What, inside the orchid house? A crocodile?" I was incredulous.
"Yes! He must have got in somehow during the night, and couldn't find his way out. You know the orchid house is sunk below the level of the ground, so that there is rather a high step up when you need to get out again."

"Yes, I remember . . . but a *crocodile*! Are you sure it's not a leguaan?"

The Greenfields live in the 'mink and manure' district of Borrowdale, and consequently his story had about it the same ring of unreality as that of a Detroit motor magnate claiming to have found a bison in his backyard.

"No, it's a croc all right," Niels assured me. "Not a big one, but definitely a croc."

"How simply thrilling! What are you going to do with him?" I asked.

"Well I - er -" Niels paused and cleared his throat. "I - er - wondered if you'd perhaps like to have him."

"Oh, I've *always* wanted a croc!" I replied delightedly, then added soberly, "but perhaps I'd better check with the boss first. May I come over to see him today?"

Niels said he'd be in all morning and that for the present he'd put the crocodile into a drum. Excitedly I hurried off to get the boss's approval. Doug was in the bathroom, shaving.

"Who was that on the phone?" he asked.

"Niels," I said breathlessly, "and guess what, he's offering us a baby croc!"

"Damn," said Doug, peering at his face, "I've cut myself now. What's that you said? For a moment I almost imagined you'd said he was offering us a crocodile."

"That *is* what I said. A baby croc. Isn't it exciting?" I enthused.

"I can't imagine what I have done to Niels that he should be thrusting a crocodile upon me. With friends like this," Doug went on lugubriously, "what need have I . . ."

"It's only a baby," I said soothingly.

"How big?"

"Well I'm not sure actually, but I imagine . . ."

Doug grunted sceptically and rinsed his razor.

"Jackals . . . vultures . . . crocodiles . . ." he intoned morosely, "well, I suppose it can't get any *worse* than a crocodile, can it?" he added, brightening momentarily. "But what are we going to *do* with it? I mean, we can't *keep* a crocodile indefinitely, they grow enormous, there will be an accident, one has to preserve some sense of – of – of –"

"Oh, not indefinitely," I assured him hastily. "Just until we can find a good place to let him go."

"*Is* there such a place? I would have thought the only good home for a crocodile was in a handbag factory."

"Poor wee thing!" I laughed. "I'm sure we'll manage to get him back to his river somehow."

"Fair enough," Doug agreed. "Just so long as you don't expect me to feed him, that's all."

It turned out to be quite a small croc, not more than two feet long. He was lying at the bottom of a half-drum, and looked as though he'd been carved out of oiled soapstone. He lay curved sideways like a bow, perfectly immobile, his greeny-gold eyes matching the bronze scales of his body. There was no question of his being anything but a crocodile. How he had come to be in the orchid house was anybody's guess, but we suspected that he had probably been brought back from the Zambezi valley by one of the troops. All through the bush war a steady stream of young animals found their way into the towns — baby monkeys, snakes, duikers, night apes. Many of them escaped, to wander about the suburbs until they were recaptured or had to be destroyed. It seems likely that some youngster had come across a newly hatched croc while on patrol in the valley, and had brought it home. I had heard that a newly hatched croc can snap off a man's finger. This little monster was perhaps a year old, I judged, or possibly a bit older. I bent forward to tickle his back with a stick. As the twig touched him, the croc leaped into the air like a piece of sprung steel, bending in a complete arch, and his teeth snapped shut on the stick, crunching it in half. It was so quick and sudden and unexpected that I gave an involuntary gasp of fright. Niels was laughing at me.

"You'll have to watch him," he chuckled, "or you're going to lose a couple of fingers."

Quite plainly he was not going to be too easy to handle, and I wondered how I was going to get him to my car. Makaza suggested a noose. That was how he'd caught him in the orchid house, he said. This was no doubt a practical method, but it seemed somewhat drastic. I asked Makaza if he could get me a 'limbo', an old piece of rag, and wrapping this around my hands I again approached the crocodile's back, meaning to grab him under the arms. When my hands were within a few inches of his body I pounced, gripping him firmly round the chest. He wiggled vigorously, flicking his tail and wagging his head back and forth in a most determined manner. After a moment or two, however, he gave it up and hung limply in my hands, opening his jaws in an ingratiating grin. He looked so pathetically small and helpless like that, and I relaxed my grip, feeling quite sorry that I had held him so tightly.

"How do you propose travelling with him?" Niels asked.

"I've brought a sack," I said, looking down at the little croc, "but I don't really think he'd like being put inside it. I'll just lay him on it, in the front of the car beside me."

Makaza spread the sack on the floor in front of the passenger-seat, and I gently laid the croc on top of it and quickly shut the door.

"What if he gets excited while you're driving?" Niels asked. "He might go for your feet."

"Oh well . . ." I watched the crocodile for a moment. He seemed to have turned to stone once more. "I expect he'll be all right. Thank you very much for letting me have him," I said warmly, climbing in beside him, "I'll let you know how he gets on."

My old Morris has done her first hundred thousand and is a quarter of the way round the clock for the second time. She is a grand old lady, though not in what you'd call good nick. She started up with her customary rattling roar punctuated by several loud sneezes and the stock-whip crack of a backfire, and then we jolted off, both doors banging about in their frames, the windows clattering inside the doors, the boot clanging loosely against its clip, the broken glass jingling musically inside the smashed tail-light, the clutch pedal shrieking like a banshee every time I changed gear and the inert handbrake knocking merrily against the driving seat. Through a wide hole in the floor-boards where the gear lever comes in, I could see the road whizzing by underneath, and the interior of the car was generously ventilated by an updraught that brought with it a fine rain of dust and sand and particles of dry grass. I glanced down sideways at the croc, still lying on his sack.

"How're you doing down there, crocodile?" I shouted to him over the clattering roar. I flicked my eyes back to the road. It wouldn't do to have an accident. Quite apart from the awkwardness of having to answer for the state of my jalopy, I shrank from the thought of the stern questions as to why my attention had wandered from the road.

The crocodile and I bowled along merrily, however, and he made no attempt to bite my feet or to scuttle about the car. Indeed, he barely changed his position throughout the ten-mile journey. When at last I reached home and turned off the ignition, I regarded him with a new respect and admiration.

"My word, crocodile," I said to him, "if you can stand that, you can stand anything. No wonder your ancestors survived the Gunz glaciation! You may not be pretty, but you've certainly got nerves of steel! Welcome home!"

The children decided to call him Clarence, and that afternoon we prepared a home for him. I had been puzzling over the problem of what sort of walls to construct. My inclination was to use chicken-wire so that he would have a greater feeling of spaciousness, but on several occasions I've seen a tortoise hook its stubby feet into the mesh of a fence and swarm up it like a monkey. The croc was equipped with long claws on both fore- and hind-feet, and I suspected that he might prove to be every bit as agile a climber as a tortoise. Accordingly we tore down the brick pile and built him a kind of Zimbabwe Ruins, a low oval enclosure constructed without any mortar so that, if need be, it would be a simple matter to modify its design. A pink Gladys Hepburn bougainvillaea grew in the centre of the enclosure providing ample shade, and to one side we scooped out a basin-shaped depression in the ground which we lined with black polythene and filled with water. As the polythene was somewhat slippery, the children placed several flat rocks at one end of the pond to make it easier for Clarence to get in and out.

The moment we introduced Clarence to his new home he made a bee-line for the pond, gliding into it with the liquid, flowing action of a snake. For quite some time he lay there with his eyes closed in an attitude of total relaxation, his legs dangling in the water. He seemed contented with his accommodation so we left him alone to enjoy an hour or two of much needed privacy. Fortunately, I could not resist taking a peep at him some half an hour later and was horrified to discover him clinging vertically to the brick wall, only a few centimetres from the top. He looked just like a great gecko, only where a gecko will attach himself with his suckers, Clarence used his claws, hooking them into the crevices between the bricks and hanging on for dear life. Hastily we modified the Zimbabwe structure, incorporating an overhanging lip so that he would not be able to swarm over the top.

For the rest of that day Clarence made repeated assaults on the wall, and it broke my heart to watch his valiant attempts to escape. He would prowl round and round, eyeing the curved wall narrowly. He was very shrewd at sizing up the advantage of an irregularity in our amateurish brickwork, and after gazing at one spot for a long time, he would suddenly leap upwards, hooking on to a little ledge with his claws, pulling himself up hand over hand until he reached the overhanging lip. There he would cling on until he grew tired, when he would drop back to earth and commence another circuit of the wall.

I found these attempts to escape most distressing, but steeled myself to them in the knowledge that worse would befall him if he got away. It was merciful that Clarence had chosen Niels's shade-house for a refuge, and I had nightmares imagining what might have happened to him had he been discovered by, say, a gang of mischievous boys. He could have been pelted with stones, or someone could have given him a bang with a shovel. Worse still, some hero with a .22 rifle might have shot him, and had his picture in the paper holding up his victim by the tail. Any of these eventualities might still have occurred had Clarence escaped and wandered off on his own.

"Never mind, Clarence," I told him as he lay eyeing the wall, "this won't go on for ever. I'll get you back to your river one day, that's a promise."

The first night Clarence spent flattened into the couch grass at the base of the wall, and it struck me that we had provided no place of refuge for him, no secret hole where he could escape from the world if he so desired. Accordingly, the following day Tom raked up some hay from the verge of the road and dumped a great mound of it under the bougainvillaea tree. Clarence appeared to be quite unmoved by this development, but some hours later when we visited him again, he had disappeared! For a few awful moments I concluded that he had succeeded in climbing on to the pile of hay and from there jumping over his wall, but presently Tracey found him right in the heart of his bed of dry grass. Clarence loved his heap of grass and spent many hours constructing tunnels for himself in his own private haystack. He made three or four separate entrances, some near the surface and others that plunged steeply down into the thick bed of lawn clippings that formed a mulch around the base of the tree. This haystack was Clarence's refuge, and I made it an inviolable rule that he was not to be disturbed if he had taken himself off to bed. Naturally, we had many interested visitors who came 'to see the crocodile' and many were the times they went away disappointed. It would have been easy enough to lift off the hay with a garden rake or fork and expose him in his lair, but I was most anxious for Clarence to believe that he really had somewhere that was safe and where he could escape detection. He would conceal himself so thoroughly in his grass that I revised my ideas about the advisability of walking along a river-bank, for presumably a fully grown croc would prepare an ambush in just this way.

During those first days my greatest anxiety with Clarence was over the question of his food. He refused to eat. He was very shy and timid, sinking down and lying absolutely still whenever we appeared. If we touched him he would swell his throat and huff, opening his jaws in what appeared to be a threatening gesture. On one of these occasions I dropped a few scraps of mince into his open mouth. After a few moments he closed his jaws and swallowed the meat. Later on I was able to do this again and began to congratulate myself on having found a way of getting him to take food. My optimism was premature, however, for a few hours later all the scraps of mince were lying on the bottom of Clarence's pond.

That evening as I was cutting up the cats' dinner, I decided to try Clarence with some of their oxheart. I sliced it thinly and laid it temptingly on the flat rock at the edge of his water. Clarence showed not the slightest interest. When I wiggled a piece of it in front of his nose, he huffed at me and opened his jaws, so I dropped a few pieces into his mouth. Once again he swallowed the meat, but by next morning it, too, had all been regurgitated and lay white and repulsive on the bottom of the pond.

Later that day I phoned David Blake, the crocodile authority at the Department of National Parks, to ask him how long a croc could go without food.

"Depends on how old he is," David replied, "and also on the time of year. Crocs eat less during the winter. At the crocodile farm at the Falls there is a big male who once went for six months without food. A little fellow would need to eat more frequently, of course. How big is your croc?"

I told him.

"Mm. I would give him a week, no more," David said. "If he hasn't taken food by the end of a week, I would think there is something wrong, and you ought to bring him in to me."

I thanked David Blake for his advice — the first of many helpful hints which he was to give me in the year that followed — and that afternoon the children and I put our heads together and discussed what could be done.

"What would a baby croc eat in the wilds?" Tracey asked. "He wouldn't be able to catch meat for himself, surely. He'd eat little things — shrimps, maybe, or dragon-fly larvae."

This seemed a good line of thinking, so we set out to catch grasshoppers and beetles and moths and left them all hopping and crawling about in the run. Clarence ignored them. It was all most discouraging. Tom then suggested that a young croc might like tadpoles. This also sounded reasonable, so he set off with his net and bucket to ask Joe Walker our neighbour if he could scoop up a few tadpoles from his fish-pond. Meanwhile Tracey sat down on the wall of Clarence's run to watch him. He was lying in his pond, apparently asleep. After a minute or two she flicked a big, white moth into the water beside him. Clarence opened his eyes and looked at the moth fluttering helplessly on the surface of the water. Presently he slid forward gently and snapped it up! A few minutes later he whipped his head up and caught a passing fly.

This was progress indeed! Admittedly one moth and one fly in three days could hardly be described as a square meal, but at least he was showing an interest in feeding himself. Some minutes later, when Tom arrived and tipped two dozen tadpoles into the pond, Clarence became almost animated. He submerged, opened his jaws and began to pursue the tadpoles hither and thither under the water. The children were sure that he was catching them, but the movements of his jaws were so quick that I couldn't be certain. Over the next two days, however, the tadpoles steadily disappeared and we had to ask the Walkers if we could please have some more.

Encouraged by these successes, I bought a packet of frozen kapenta, the small, silver sardine that comes from Lake Kariba. I thawed out a couple of the little fish and placed them temptingly on the flat rock at the edge of the pond. Clarence slid forward to have a closer look at them. For quite a while he lay with his snout almost touching the kapenta, then slowly and deliberately he picked one up, tossed it to the back of his throat — and swallowed! This was the largest single item of food he had taken so far, and I was delighted to find that by the following morning he had eaten two more.

From then on things improved steadily. Contrary to all my preconceived ideas about a crocodile's appetite, Clarence was a very small eater. Frequently he would refuse food altogether and go for three or four days without accepting a single fish. I began to understand how pleased the ancient Egyptians must have been when their Crocodile God accepted an offering of food. Clarence, too, always managed to convey the impression that he was bestowing a great honour on us by condescending to eat the fish we placed on his food rock. He continued to shun meat, however, and I found myself beginning to wonder if perhaps a crocodile will only turn to a flesh-and-blood meal in default of fish or other aquatic food.

All the same I continued to offer him meat once in a while, just to see whether his reactions might change as he grew more accustomed to us and his surroundings. One evening I was preparing a piece of rump steak for our dinner. A small puddle of red juice had collected in the plate under the meat. By way of an experiment, I cut off a few scraps of the rump and dabbled them in the gore to see whether this might provoke some response from my little monster. Clarence was dozing on the far bank of his pond. As I knelt down to place the meat on his food rock, he suddenly came to life, dived into the pond, shot across the water and had snapped up the steak almost before I had time to snatch my hand away. During dinner that night I told the family about this culinary triumph.

"Just imagine," I said, "I've learned that Clarence loves rump steak."

Doug looked at me.

"You're not feeding that reptile on rump steak?" he asked disbelievingly.

"Not *feeding* him as such, no," I replied hastily. "All I mean is, I persuaded him to have a little."

"*Persuaded* him." Doug pondered the significance of this. "Good God," he went on presently, "*persuaded* him. Have you not persuaded him to try a little Strasbourg pâté, some smoked salmon or a bite or two of crayfish?"

"I'll ask him," I laughed. "As a matter of fact, you may have a good idea there with the pâté. Next time we have a chicken, I'll offer Clarence the liver."

As it turned out, Doug was perfectly right — Clarence *did* enjoy a few scraps of chicken-liver, but he didn't eat more than about an ounce. Then, on Sunday, Tom suggested that we might try to catch some live fish for him, as opposed to the frozen kapenta. After breakfast we duly set off armed with rods and buckets and nets and bait. Tracey and I went to endless pains baiting a bucket with sadza and laying it on its side in the shallows to lure in the very smallest fish. In this way we managed to trap quite a few fry, just a little larger than tadpoles. Tom in the meantime got on with his rod and line and caught a number of bream tiddlers. In the course of this he landed quite a

good-sized bass — about half a pound — and after wrestling
with himself over what to do with it, he decided to present it to
Clarence 'as a friend'. Clearly, the bass would be too large for
the croc to eat, for it was almost half his size, but no doubt it
would make Clarence's life more interesting to have a companion
to share his pond.

We returned with some thirty fish of assorted sizes and
tipped them all into the water. Clarence was still asleep in his
hay, but a little later he crawled out and slithered into his pond.
Immediately he sensed that something had changed. He put on
his 'goggles' and went underwater where he began to make
passes at the fish in a decidedly determined fashion. He would
swim after them with gaping mouth, whipping his head round
sideways to clap his jaws if one tried to flick past his head. He
now looked far more sinister and predatory than I had imagined
possible, but for all that he didn't succeed in actually catching
any of them. We laughed each time he snapped at the bass
because we knew it was much too big for him.
"He's your friend, Clarence," I said. "You don't want to eat
your friend."
The fish were much alarmed, darting this way and that, and
finally sought refuge under the two flat stones at the end of the
pond.

After a bit, Clarence appeared discouraged and lost
interest. He went into his floating log routine, eyes closed, legs
dangling limply. Timidly and one by one the fish came out from
under the rocks. Presently the big bass emerged too, and made a
leisurely circuit of the pond. He paused, fanning his fins, just
behind Clarence's hind leg. Flick! Snap! With incredible speed
Clarence had whipped round sideways, and there was Mr. Bass
thrashing and flapping in the little crocodile's jaws! How had he
known the bass was there? It was impossible for him to have
seen it — his eyes were closed. Had he felt the vibrations of its
fins as it paused behind his leg? I marvelled at the little reptile's
instinct for guile, the cunning and deliberate way in which he
had given up the direct attack in favour of the ambush. The fish
was far too large for Clarence to swallow — why, it was half his
own size. All the same, there was something grimly determined

in the way Clarence now sank beneath the surface with the struggling fish clamped tightly in his jaws. He swam about a bit as if not quite sure what to do next. Tom was beside himself. Even Doug remained rooted to the spot to see what Clarence was going to do. Presently he surfaced and began to throw himself about with astonishing vigour and agility, flinging his head from side to side, almost standing up on his hind legs and twisting his whole torso back and forth in a whiplash action. All at once the fish snapped like a stick and the head end flew off into the water. Clarence champed on the piece that remained, then solemnly opened wide his jaws and down it went!

He knew well enough that the fish was too big for him, but he also knew how to solve the problem!

"You know," Doug said admiringly, "he's not the fool he looks."

In the meantime the head end of the fish was still very much alive and was trying to flee, but couldn't swim without its tail. It was all rather ghastly. Clarence pursued the bass once more, catching it without any difficulty, and resumed the rolling and flicking procedure. This time it broke at the gills and the head flew off with such force that it sailed right out of the run! Clarence ate the centre portion of the fish and then waddled off to sleep in his hay with the satisfied air of one who has dined well.

That evening Tom found the bass's head and mournfully replaced it in Clarence's pond. Clarence ate it the next day, marking the end of what might have been a beautiful friendship. Thereafter, providing for Clarence's needs became Tom's favourite occupation, and in the course of the year that followed a really close bond formed between the two of them.

Each Saturday morning Tom would set off on his bicycle with his rod, a tin of worms and the yellow kitchen bucket, returning at about noon with ten to twenty tiddlers. Clarence came to recognise the clatter of the bucket as his dinner gong. As Tom stepped over the wall of his run, Clarence would come swarming out of his grass, glide across his pond and rest his chin expectantly on the food rock. Within a short time he was taking the little fish from Tom's fingers, but this was a risky business until one learned the knack of letting go of the fish at the right moment. Sometimes Tracey and I fed him too, and each of us was bitten once or twice. It was not that Clarence was attacking us, but rather that in his excitement he'd miss the fish and fasten on to a finger instead. When this happened the danger lay in snatching one's hand away — a most natural and almost irresistible reaction. Although the bite itself produced no more than a row of little punctures, if one pulled against his teeth they cut like razor-blades, leaving instead a line of long gashes.

As a rule Clarence would take five or six fish at once, and would then turn away to go and sleep in the sun. Tom then tipped the others into the pond, and during the week Clarence would feed himself from his larder when he felt hungry. While the weather remained warm he used to fish at night, forcing his long snout under the flat rock and bumping it up and down to frighten the fish out into the open. Sometimes in their terror the little bream would leap right out of the pond. Clarence never bothered to pursue them, but concentrated on catching those that remained in the water. By the end of the week he'd have eaten them all and would be ready for Tom to go fishing again. This arrangement suited Tom very well. He is one of those dedicated fishermen, but whereas normally a bucketful of tiddlers would be considered a disappointing catch, Tom had the satisfaction of knowing that they would be greatly appreciated by his crocodile. When the big fish were not on the bite, the other lads would trudge home with heavy hearts, but as far as Tom and Clarence were concerned, the size of the fish was of no consequence. All were grist to his mill.

One morning Tom tiptoed into our bedroom, his eyes round with dismay. It was his practice to get up at dawn to see how many fish Clarence had eaten during the night. He was still in his pyjamas, and I could see at a glance that he was very upset. "What's the matter?" I whispered. Doug was still asleep. "It's Clarence," he whispered back. "He's gone." Softly I climbed out of bed, wrapped myself in a gown and accompanied Tom outside.

Although Clarence was very skilful at hiding himself in his grass, we could usually see more or less where he was. One could glimpse the end of his snout, or perhaps the claws of one of his feet, or just make out a patch of scales visible through a chink in the stems of dry grass. Certainly on this occasion there was absolutely no sign of him, but I drew comfort from the fact that the coping of his wall had not been disturbed.

"He *must* be here somewhere," I said.

"But he huffs," Tom pointed out desperately, "if we touch his grass. And I've patted it all over."

This was true enough, Clarence always huffed softly if one rustled his hay. I touched it experimentally. Nothing. I decided that the time had come to break the rule of disturbing his private quarters. We *had* to know whether or not he was missing. Gently I lifted off the whole bundle of grass. Clarence was definitely not there. I was struggling to suppress my dismay and anxiety when suddenly Tom pointed down at the foot of the bougainvillaea.

"Here he is!" he shouted joyfully. "Look, he's made a burrow!" After all those weeks, the mulch of fine lawn clippings beneath the hay had formed a dense compact mass. Clarence had tunnelled deep down into this, and what Tom had seen was the very last digit of his tail!

Clarence was 'lost' on several subsequent occasions, but we now knew to wait for the day to warm up, and then sure enough, his snout would appear at the entrance to one of his tunnels, and little by little he would ease himself out into the sunshine.

At about this time I began to make notes on Clarence's behaviour and appearance. He was so unlike any other pet I have ever kept that he was a continual source of interest and delight. The children loved showing him off to the delivery men who came to the house, and soon most of them used to stop off to look at the 'garwe' each day. My notes record that:

> Clarence excites revulsion and incredulity in all who see him. Mangani [our cook] is most disapproving of the whole venture and informs me in sepulchral tones that in Mozambique where he comes from, the crocodiles grow very big and *eat people*.

I remember those Gorongoza crocs well, and it's interesting to observe that Clarence has the same slow rolling gait of a fifteen-footer, a kind of ponderous swaying with the centre of the back held higher than the head.

All the same, he could move surprisingly fast when the mood took him, and it never ceased to astonish me how he could be absolutely immobile one moment and flashing into action the next. He had lightning reflexes, and could shoot across his pond with almost no apparent effort at all. His tail was in fact his principal organ of propulsion in the water, his feet being used purely as rudders and stabilisers. One tends to think of the crocodile's tail as being a nerveless thing that drags heavily behind him. On the contrary, Clarence's tail was a fifth limb

which he could manipulate with great skill. It was tremendously supple and mobile, and he was able to move each joint of it independently — even the very last one. Furthermore he had a very fine sense of touch in his tail and would react indignantly if one so much as stroked a scale of it with the tip of a finger.

Later on my notes record that:

> The greenish colour of his skin is only apparent when he's wet. When he's dry one can see that the skin is made up of yellow scales and black scales arranged in lovely patterns like a mosaic, with a predominance of yellow on the sides and the belly. He looks and feels horny and rough on his back, but the wide scales of his throat and belly are as soft and smooth as silk. Clarence's face is not scaly, but rather of a soft, grey leather veined with yellow

like a lovely piece of marble, with the golden jewels of his eyes set into it.

His eyes are most interesting. They stand up like knobs on the top of his head, and the pupil is a narrow, vertical slit that almost disappears altogether in bright sunlight. If he closes his eyes the whole eyeball sinks down flush with the rest of his head. Sometimes when he's dozing he'll have one eye open and the other shut, giving him a curious lopsided expression. In addition to the eyelids, he has a clear membrane which he flicks across the eye when he is going to submerge. At night his pupils enlarge enormously, giving him an intelligent, but somehow sinister appearance.

The crocodile is unique in being the only reptile with an external ear. The first time I saw this little flap of skin twitching

on the side of his head, I thought I was imagining it. The children confirmed, however, that they had also observed this phenomenon, and I subsequently learned from David Blake that the crocodile is equipped with several extra tympanic cavities in the skull, which account for its remarkable sense of hearing. Clarence's external ear was about the size of my little fingernail, and was normally held tightly against the side of his head. If he'd been under water for any length of time, he used to flicker his ears when he returned to the surface. The aperture of the ear itself was a long, narrow slit just behind his eye. He could squeeze its edges together when he went under water, and could also shut off his mouth by means of a large valve at the back of his throat. No doubt this enables the croc to swim about under water with his mouth open, without taking water into his lungs. Even his nostrils were equipped with little shutters that moved forward and sealed them off when he submerged. Together, the round knobs of his eyes and the little hump of his nostrils made up the notorious 'crocodile triangle' — the three lumps that float unobtrusively on the surface when a crocodile has you under surveillance.

One morning when Tom paid his daybreak visit to Clarence's run, he found the crocodile on the bottom of the pond. I suspect that Clarence had heard Tom's approaching footsteps, and had taken the precaution of hiding himself in case of danger. At all events, Tom decided to stay there to see for how long Clarence could hold his breath. He remained at the bottom of the pond for sixteen minutes! It is staggering to consider how far an adult croc could travel under water in that time!

Certainly a crocodile has a control over his bodily functions which, in comparison with man, is almost supernatural. Even so youthful and inexperienced a croc as Clarence was capable of physical feats of which a yogi would be proud. He seemed to be able to put himself into a kind of trance in which his whole system slowed down like that of a hibernating bear. This was particularly noticeable when he was sunbathing. When preparing for a spell of 'meditation' he would spread himself in the sun with his hind legs trailing behind him like a spaniel's, the crinkled, black soles of his webbed toes turned upwards. Presently he would take in three or four deep breaths until he was inflated like a bladder, and then all breathing would cease. Clarence would remain like that with his eyes closed, quite immobile, the only visible sign of life the continuous pulse that flickered in his throat.

Through watching him quietly hour after hour we came to discover many of his less spectacular but none the less crafty methods of catching his prey. For example he devised a labour-saving way of trapping tadpoles. Gliding into the shallow water at the edge of his pond, he pushed his head in among the shoal of tadpoles and there he lay absolutely still. Very soon a wriggling fringe of black tadpoles had gathered along the line of his jaw,

feeding from the little scraps of food between his teeth. A quick, sideways flick of his head, and the row of tadpoles had vanished!

He caught small fish in a similar way, lying dead still while a little bream swam up and began to nibble at his teeth. As the fish approached the point of his snout he made a smooth, forward movement which squeezed the fish against the side of the pond. Now it was trapped. Slowly Clarence turned his head sideways, never releasing the pressure on the fish, then — a quick, sideways snap, and the fish had gone. Once when he did this the fish became hooked up on his teeth in a transverse position so that it could not be swallowed. Clarence tried flicking it from side to side like the bass, but the fish was too small to break in half. He had another trick up his sleeve, however. With great nonchalance he brought up one of his hind-feet and scratched the fish forwards so that it lay lengthwise in his mouth, and then — down it went!

Plutarch observes that a crocodile has no tongue and so 'standeth not in need of speech'. Zoologists claim that the croc does have a tongue, but that it is fixed to the floor of its mouth. I prefer to think of a tongue as a separate organ that can be waggled about and used to assist in the manipulation of a mouthful of food. Whether he had a tongue or not, however, Clarence definitely could speak! He had quite a variety of huffs,

grunts and muffled roars, most of which appeared to indicate
annoyance. He also used to communicate with Tom by a series
of bubbling sounds which we took to indicate pleasure. He
would half-submerge his head, and then toss it upwards, at the
same time releasing bubbles of air through his teeth. He did this
quite deliberately and meaningfully whenever Tom arrived with
a fresh consignment of tiddlers.

I was surprised to find that Clarence used his hind-feet in
many various ways besides locomotion and feeding. The
crocodile's hind-feet are long and webbed with four toes, the
three major ones having long claws. (His hands, by contrast, are
not webbed and resemble those of any other lizard.) On one
occasion a number of tadpoles had gathered around the back of
his head, and I suppose they tickled. He hauled out his hind-leg,
for all the world like a dog with fleas, bent his head round and
scratched them off. He used the same method to free himself
from a floating leaf which had draped itself over his back and
was getting in his way. Even more surprising, he would use his
hind-feet to scratch himself on dry land when he was sunbathing.
A tiny black ant would climb on to his scales and begin to march
down his spine. It was astonishing that a crocodile's tough and
horny hide would be sufficiently sensitive to feel the footsteps of
an ant, but they really used to infuriate Clarence. He would first
open one eye with the irritated air of a testy old colonel who has
been disturbed in his favourite club-chair. Then as the ant
continued on its way, he would bring up a hind-leg and scrape
the insect off. If there were a whole swarm of them he would
twitch and jerk all over, finally slithering away to his pond to
wash them off completely.

The two cats were fascinated by Clarence. James, in
particular, used to spend hours sitting on the wall of Clarence's
run, staring down at him with wide eyes, his ears pricked
forward, his whiskers twitching at every move the crocodile
made. He is a big, sleepy seal-point Siamese and I suspect that
he felt a slight affinity with anything more sluggish than himself.
Dusty is the complete opposite. She is one of those small, lean,
pale-coloured Siamese cats with a narrow face and long, slender

limbs. Hunting is her all-absorbing interest in life. Look for her at any time of the day, and she will be found standing over a cricket's hole in the lawn, her ears moving continually to pick up the slightest scratch of sound, or she will be crouching in front of the rubbish-heap waiting for a mouse, or hiding behind the granite dolly-stone where the doves drink, or patting at lizards as they run up and down the trunk of the lemon tree. The first time Dusty jumped on to his wall and saw Clarence she froze, her whiskers came forward and her eyes took on a maniacal glitter. Presently she rearranged her paws and settled down to watch him.

At this stage Clarence had been with us less than a week and was still spending a considerable part of his day prowling round his wall. Dusty stared at him fixedly for some ten minutes, and then softly jumped down into his run. Immediately Clarence dropped to his belly and emitted a warning huff. For a while the two of them glared at one another, then swiftly and stealthily Dusty ran around behind the crocodile, obviously intending to take him in the rear. Clarence was every bit as quick as the cat. He wheeled round to face her, opening his jaws and uttering a harsh cough that made her draw back and blink. Then very slowly he edged himself sideways into his pond and slid under the water.

If Dusty's eyes had been round before, now they positively bulged with incredulity. Taking little tense steps forward she approached the pond, weaving her head at Clarence and sniffing suspiciously at the air. She circled the pond, but wherever she moved Clarence wheeled round to face her, watching her unwinkingly out of his golden eyes.

At last Dusty sat down and licked her front, sneering at him down her nose with a look of profound disgust, as if to say: "You may be a lizard, but I'm certainly *not* going to play with you in the water!"

Then in a show of mischievous defiance, she stretched out one long, black paw and slapped the edge of the pond in front of Clarence's nose, and bounded out of his run. Dusty never bothered to go near him again, but the dogs, on the other hand, hung around him continually.

Josephine was openly jealous of all the time we spent with

Clarence and always followed us, drooling, when we took him titbits of fish or meat. Jocelyn, the brindled cross-breed, had an idea that he might be good to chase. She had the hunting instincts of her Staffordshire mother, and used to hop into Clarence's run from time to time and 'point' at him with one forepaw raised, and look questioningly at us as if to say 'Shall I get him?' She was always most disappointed when we told her to hop out. Clarence, however, never appeared as worried by the dogs as he had been by Dusty. In the wild state he would, of course, have been subject to attacks from other crocodiles, from leguaans and from birds of prey, and I was glad to see that he had preserved some of his instincts of self-defence. They might yet be useful to him in the future.

I found it most interesting to observe the comparative responsiveness of Clarence and, say, a cat or a dog. If I go up to Josephine and say: "Hello, you good old dog!" she will smile and wag her tail and wiggle about with delight. If I say: "Bad dog," in a severe tone, she'll droop her ears and look wretched. One can elicit all kinds of responses from a cat, from playful cavorting to an angry whisking of the tail. All these responses are totally absent in the crocodile!

I sit down beside Clarence and say lovingly: "Oh Clarence, are you beautiful? Are you a lovely crocodile?"
My voice has such a tone of exaggerated blandishment that even the dogs lying near by tap their tails as if appreciating the joke. Clarence says nothing. He just lies there looking wooden.
"Clarence!" I say now in a stern and angry voice. "You're a villain! You're a horrible monster and I've a mind to give you a bang with a shovel!"
The dogs look solemn, and glance guiltily at one another. Clarence says nothing. I might as well not have spoken. I have a sudden vision of an actor's nightmare, a production of *As You Like It* before an audience of crocodiles.
"You're a washout, Clarence," I conclude laughing. "How am I to hold a conversation with you when you won't respond?"

Part of the trouble stemmed from the fact that his eyes were fixed and it was impossible to tell if he were looking at me, over my shoulder, straight in front, or into the sky. The absence of eye-movement gave him a particularly wooden expression and, added to this, his facial skin was unable to move so he couldn't smile or scowl or vary his appearance in any of the conventional ways. Then again there was the question of touch. Almost every mammal enjoys being fondled and will show its pleasure in a number of ways. Clarence hated it. He would endure being scratched on the back of the neck, but when he'd had enough he would whip round, grunting with open jaws in a hostile gesture that plainly said: "Leave me alone!" Altogether it was very difficult to get close to Clarence and to be able to regard him as a pet. I was unhappy at the lack of communication between us, feeling for his loneliness and isolation. I would have liked him to know that we were his friends, but the question had to be faced: "Did he *want* friends?"

This in turn raised all kinds of other questions. Could he care, one way or the other, whether we were friendly or not? Is a crocodile *capable* of feeling anything but anger and hunger, heat and cold? Does a crocodile have any real intelligence, as we understand it, or is he simply motivated by such powerful and deep-rooted instincts for survival that 'thought' itself is extraneous?

A dog will show fear — it whines and cringes, tucks its tail between its legs. A horse will roll its eyes, whinny and plunge. It seemed impossible that any animal could have been totally unmoved by that terrible ride in my noisy old shandrydan, yet Clarence had exhibited not one scrap of fear, not one flicker of alarm. Did he show no fear because he was endowed with godlike courage? Or was he of such a low biological order that he was genuinely incapable of experiencing such a complex emotion?

I must confess that as the weeks went by I came to suspect that a crocodile is indeed poles apart from us, and that as a mammal I could never bridge the gap. He might feed from our hands, but that did not constitute affection. True, it did indicate a degree of trust, but was this not just an extension of his desire for food? It was a discouraging thought, but nevertheless I persevered with my overtures of friendship, sitting with him whenever I had a spare moment and doing all I could to make him comfortable and respect his wishes. The children and I frequently used to have afternoon tea in his run, to familiarise him with our voices and movements. And then — at last! — one day towards the end of April, Clarence actually made a positive gesture of friendship!

It happened late one afternoon while Tom and I were struggling with his homework. He'd been given a long list of spellings, the names of various trades and professions from A to Z. We'd toiled over them, seemingly, for hours, and at last I decided that a change of scene might refresh his mind and my patience.

"Let's go and sit with Clarence," I suggested, "and continue your spellings there."

Clarence was lying close to his wall where the last rays of the afternoon sun fell on the bricks in a shaft of warm gold. I settled down on the grass between him and his pile of hay, and Tom squatted next to the pond, watching the fish. We had got as far as P, so I opened the book again and we continued: "Porter, postman, printer . . ."

Clarence turned round and faced me.

"Sailor, salesman, shepherd . . ."

Clarence aimed his chin at the sky, as if he were listening to us most attentively.

"Tailor, teacher, tobacconist . . ."

The crocodile came straight towards me, his snout still held high in the air, and I formed the distinct impression that he intended to climb on to me. He had never actually *approached* me before, and I was just a little nervous in case he was contemplating an attack. One never quite knew with him . . .

"Weaver, welder, wheelwright," I continued uneasily. Tom's concentration was wavering, I noticed, and no wonder. Clarence's jaws were an inch from my leg, and he now proceeded to open his mouth as wide as it would go, exposing his whole throat and gullet in gorgeous shades of saffron and buttercup yellow. What *did* he mean by it? Was he threatening me because I was between him and his bed of hay? Should I back off

— or stay where I was? He was definitely *saying something . . .*
"Yachtsman, yeoman, yokel," I went on in a voice that quivered
with the desire to giggle. For all the rows of teeth, there was an
element of supplication in Clarence's attitude. He reminded me
of a young bird begging for food. I decided to sit quite still and
see what he intended to do.

After some minutes he lifted one hand and placed it
tentatively on my leg. Tom's eyes were like saucers, and I dare
say mine were too. A moment afterwards Clarence pulled
himself forward so that now his head and forequarters were
resting on my lap. Then, still with his jaws wide open in an
amiable grin, he slowly hoisted himself aboard and lay down
across my knees, his throat pulsating quickly.
"Well . . . Clarence . . . !"
I was speechless.

Then and only then did I realise the significance of the open
mouth, and the impact of it struck me like a thunderbolt! It *was* a
smile! Later, of course, it seemed so natural and obvious that I
marvelled at my own blindness. We came to understand that the
open jaws of a crocodile are a symbol of two things —
submission and pleasure. During those first few days when he
had opened his jaws and let me drop mince and meat down his
throat, he had not been threatening me, as I supposed. He had
been saying: "O.K., you're the boss. Please don't hurt me."

Now at last I understood why he'd lie in the sun for hours on
end with his mouth open. It was a mark of his contentment, he
was smiling — that's all! Poor little Clarence! It had taken me so
long to understand this simple message, and I was consumed
with remorse at my own stupidity and mistrust.

Once comfortably settled on my lap, Clarence seemed
quite happy to stay there, so Tom and I began his spellings all
over again from the beginning, but somehow this time around
they were coloured with a new sense of joy and achievement.
"Actor, apprentice, attorney . . ."
Mangani, the cook, came to ask me which vegetables he should
prepare for dinner. As he caught sight of Clarence on my lap he
stopped dead with a hissing intake of breath. We discussed the
dinner arrangements, and then he hurried away, shaking his

head and wringing his hands, his lips rolled inwards over his teeth with horror. The sun was setting now, and a chill fell over the garden. Slowly Clarence eased himself off my lap and crawled into his familiar bed of hay.

This development added a new dimension to our enjoyment of Clarence's company. If he could trust us, then by the same token, we could trust him. Boldened by this knowledge we redoubled our efforts to make friends with him, and as the weeks went by, so his confidence grew. He frequently crawled on to our laps for a ten-minute doze — he also loved to lie across the insteps of Tracey's bare feet. One day Tom found that Clarence *did* like being scratched — provided he was in the water! While Tom talked to him and tickled his back, Clarence would press himself upwards, his eyes closed in apparent ecstasy. If Tom lay on the ground on his back, Clarence would settle himself on the boy's chest, the tip of his snout resting on Tom's chin in an attitude of perfect trust and mutual fellowship. Once and once only we saw him do something that appeared to be a macabre attempt at reptilian humour. Clarence had draped himself along Tom's bare legs. After a bit the ants became troublesome and Tom began to twitch and twiddle his toes. Clarence opened his eyes and looked at them. Then slowly and deliberately he crawled forward down the legs and took hold of a few toes in his jaws. He held them there for a moment, his eye on Tom as if to study his reaction. Being extremely ticklish about the feet, Tom started to laugh. Presently Clarence let go of the first lot of toes and nibbled at a few others as if to say: "Nice little morsels! I believe I might eat a couple!" Yet such was the gentleness of his bite that he didn't even break the skin!

By the end of May, winter was in the air. Now the roses were tall and straggly and running to hip. The lawns were turning brown, and each evening the night fell suddenly after a brief twilight when the horizon was rimmed in a broad band of rusty red. The nights were clear and cold, the stars crowding together, silent and watchful like the eyes of beasts in the dark. From the middle of May my warmth-loving fruits like the litchi and the custard-apple, the papaws and the granadillas, had been clothed in long sleeves of thatching grass to protect them from the frost. The avocados and the mangoes were old and ugly enough to fend for themselves, and although the banana leaves were invariably reduced by winter to tattered sheets of brown paper, the plants themselves always rose up in the spring like phoenix birds from their ashes.

I was worried about Clarence's ability to withstand our highveld winter. If he had come from the steamy environment of the Zambezi valley — as seemed likely — then he would never have experienced real cold, let alone frost.

Once again I phoned David Blake for advice. He confirmed my fears.

"The cold will kill him," he said. "You'll have to be very careful about his pond, because if the temperature of his water drops too low, he'll drown."

"And what about keeping him warm at night?" I asked. In our winters the days are blazing hot with midday temperatures up in the seventies, but at night the mercury drops down below freezing.

"Chances are he'll go into his burrow at about sundown," David said cautiously. "Incidentally, you needn't worry if he doesn't seem so hungry. But watch him if he tries to swim early in the morning when the water's cold."

As David predicted, Clarence's appetite did dwindle, which was just as well as the fish went off the bite and were difficult to catch. During the winter Tom became adept at hooking the big, brown land-crabs that lived along the stone wall of Cleveland Dam. Clarence enjoyed a crab now and then. He would take the whole creature in his jaws and bite down on it hard, cutting off the legs. These he discarded, but he crushed up and ate all the rest, even the bone-like carapace. Clarence's digestion was a continual source of amazement to me. His bowels only worked about once a fortnight, and then all he produced was a little dropping such as one would expect from a five-week-old puppy. It was stone hard and very dark in colour, so quite obviously Clarence's wastage of foodstuff was absolutely minimal. When I thought of the quantities of fish bones and other apparently indigestible things which he swallowed, I began to realise that his metabolism was on a par with the most sophisticated solvent extraction-plant. This, I feel, partially explains the crocodile's ability to withstand long periods of privation.

That winter was a severe one with heavy ground-frosts night after night. First thing each morning, I'd top up Clarence's pond with a bucket of warm water, to take the chill off it, and last thing in the evening I made sure that he had taken himself off to bed. One day he was still fishing in his pond at sundown when a large·crowd of visitors arrived. As usual, everyone wanted to see Clarence. I was busy in the kitchen, and unbeknown to me one well-meaning guest observed that Clarence was bumping his stones in order to frighten out the fish, and thought it would help him if he removed the stones from the pond. Now Clarence always used those stones as a ramp for climbing out of his water, as the polythene was inclined to be slimy and slippery. He *could* get out without the stones on a hot day, but we had frequently observed that Clarence's mobility depended upon the warmth of the day, and that as it grew colder so his ability to move declined. I was tired that night, and didn't check Clarence before going to bed. Mercifully, Dusty was being difficult that evening and wouldn't come in when she was called. Tracey went out to search for her cat, and by the light of the half moon she observed that Clarence was still in his water.

She ran back breathlessly to report this disaster, and we tumbled out of our beds to see what could be done for him. His water was freezing cold, and Clarence lay in it as stiff and still as a stone. I scooped him out gently with the garden rake and he lay quite lifelessly on the edge of his pond. I was about to run for a bucket of warm water in which to revive him when he slowly lifted his head and huffed. Then painstakingly and at a snail's pace, he dragged himself inch by inch towards his haystack. Poor Clarence, that was a narrow shave, but he seemed none the worse the following day, spending many hours lying asleep in the sun, as if to reabsorb his lost warmth!

July melted into August. Gradually the nights mellowed,

and then with its customary pounce of glee, spring was upon us! With the advent of the warmer weather Clarence underwent a dramatic change. Since February, when he first came to us, he had grown perhaps three inches in length and had put on a little girth round the base of his tail. Now all at once he developed a voracious appetite and, like any adolescent, he seemed to grow almost visibly. My notes from this period record a typical meal:

> There being no fish today, Tom offered Clarence some stewing steak. He smelled it coming, swarmed out of his pond to meet Tom half-way, snatching at the meat even before it was put down for him, drawing blood on two of Tom's fingers. I dabbed them with disinfectant and cut up more stewing steak. Clarence went crazy about it, snapping each piece up in mid-air as it was dropped, and then opening and shutting his jaws under water to wash out the bits from between his teeth.

All at once his pond was too small for him. We enlarged it and brought him a fresh heap of grass for his haystack. Now the rest of the run looked cramped and confined in comparison with the pond, so we tore down the old wall and built a new one in a much wider oval. Still Clarence continued to grow. He developed mighty shoulders, his neck thickened and his tail broadened, and when he stood up to walk he really looked as though he meant business. It was obvious to each of us that it was time something was done about getting him back to his river.

The first heavy rain of the summer prodded Clarence out of his customary lassitude. As the huge, stinging drops pelted him from the sky, he took to his water and remained submerged until it eased off. After the storm, however, he was in an excitable frame of mind, huffing to himself and prowling along his wall as he had not done for over six months.

'We *must* get him back to the Zambezi' became a refrain that I chanted mentally as each day went by. It was still school-time, however, and it would have been difficult at that stage for Doug to take leave.

In November I was chatting to Rob Gaunt, a neighbour who lived down the road. Rob was busy putting the finishing touches to a splendid cabin-cruiser that stood gleaming and beautiful in his backyard.

"What are you doing for the Christmas holidays?" I asked him.

"We're off to Kariba," he said, "to launch the boat."

"Lucky dogs," I replied enviously. Then, "You wouldn't consider taking my crocodile with you, would you? He needs to be put back into the lake."

"Sure," Rob laughed good-naturedly, "I'll take your croc. Just so long as you put him into the sack at this end!"

It was very tempting to seize this opportunity of returning Clarence to the Zambezi, but Tom was most upset when I suggested it.

"I don't want anyone else to let him go," he said obstinately, "we must do it ourselves."

I agreed. We all wanted to be with Clarence the day he returned to the wild.

      Time passed and Clarence continued to grow. In December, Lord Soames arrived to take over the administration of the country, ending seven years of civil war. These were historic times, but difficult and anxious, too, as the whole country watched tensely to see whether the delicate cease-fire would hold. We all felt the strain, and I wished desperately that Doug might be able to take a few days' leave before the children had to return to school. And Clarence in the meantime continued to grow, his appetite increasing with each passing day. Now Tom was hauling out anything from seventy-five to a hundred tiddlers in a morning's fishing, and Clarence would eat them all in a week. If there were too many fish to put them all into the pond, I used to freeze them whole, so that the supply would last a little longer. Some days Clarence was so hungry that if Tom entered his run with a packet of mince or a few frozen bream, he'd go mad, pursuing Tom round the run, snapping at the packet and chasing Tom's shoe-laces. It was funny in a way, but after witnessing one of these lively meals Doug looked somewhat grave. Later that evening he said: "You know, I'm worried about Clarence. It's high time he was taken back to his river. One of these days there's going to be an accident."

"Yes," I said. "I know."

He smoked for a while in silence, staring out into the night. "A couple of days' break would do us all good," he mused, "and we could kill two birds with one stone. We'd have to fly, of course, because I could only take off one or two days at the most, and I wouldn't want to spend them driving . . ."

I waited breathlessly, hardly daring to speak.

"Why don't you ring the Airways tomorrow," he said at length, "and see if we can fly up to Kariba next Thursday."

"And Clarence?" I breathed.

"We'll take him with us," Doug said.

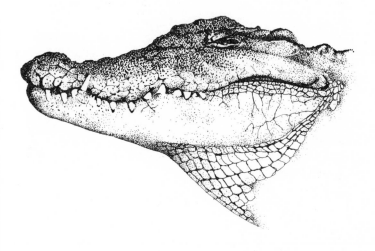

16

Crocodile Tears

> *A cruel crafty Crocodile*
> *Which in false grief hiding his harmful guile*
> *Doth weep full sore, and sheddeth tender tears.*
>
> Spenser, *Faerie Queene*

It IS ONE THING to talk glibly of taking a crocodile on holiday in an aircraft, and another matter altogether to put it into practice. I had thought vaguely that the best way of transporting Clarence would be in some kind of soft valise, or bag. Evidently Doug had been mulling over this very problem, because a few days later he asked me how I thought Clarence should travel. I told him, in a bag.

"You mean, *with* us in the cabin of the aircraft?"

"Yes, I had thought so."

"H'm. What do the Airways say about it?"

"I haven't asked them."

"You should. They might not like the idea."

"But supposing they insist that he travel in the hold as freight?" I said doubtfully.

"Then that's how he's got to travel!" Doug replied emphatically, "As freight."

Next day while Tom went fishing, Tracey and I set off to see the Airways. I approached the pleasant-faced girl who was at the reservations desk.

"Good morning," I said brightly. "We're booked to fly to

Kariba next Thursday, and I just thought I'd check if it would be all right to bring a little animal with us as hand luggage."

"Is it a little cat?" she asked sweetly. "Or a little dog?"

"Well no, as a matter of fact, it's a little crocodile," I said apologetically.

The girl goggled at me.

"A crocodile! How big is it?"

"O-o-h, about *so* big," I held my hands apart, and then judiciously brought them a little nearer together. I didn't want to alarm her.

"Oh dear," she said, looking startled. Then she laughed. "I doubt if they'll allow that. Perhaps you ought to see the people at our freight office in Manica Road."

Tracey and I trudged round to the freight office where I put all my cards on the table and cast myself on their mercy.

"He's not very big," I reassured them. "I'm sure he wouldn't give any trouble in the plane."

"How big is he?" they asked suspiciously.

"O-o-h, about *so* big," I replied, indicating a modest gap between my hands. (Tracey remarked later that as this saga proceeded, my palms came steadily closer and closer together until Clarence had shrunk to a bare eighteen inches.) The freight clerks shook their heavy heads, however, and fetched out a huge tome that catalogued the various rates for animals from all over the world. Pensively licking a finger, the girl began to flick over the pages.

"Alligator, antbear, baboon, bison," she mumbled. Flick, flick. "Camel, chameleon, chimpanzee, cougar — ah! — here we are, crocodile!" She read the regulations in silence for a moment or two, then: "Is it an alligator, an Indian crocodile or a Nile crocodile?" she asked at length.

"Er — a Nile crocodile," I replied.

"Yes, well, the Nile crocodile goes at the most expensive rate as he is the biggest," she announced.

"But he's only a baby," I protested. "He's only — only *so* big!" I gestured eloquently with my hands.

"Doesn't matter. For a Nile crocodile, you have to pay an initial flat rate and thereafter so much per additional kilo."

"But —" I began to argue.

"I'm sorry," she snapped, "these are the regulations. And it says here," she went on tartly, "that a Nile crocodile must travel in a crate constructed of wood not less than three-quarters of an inch thick, with holes at eighteen-inch intervals, each hole to measure not less than one inch in diameter, and the fastenings of the crate to be made of . . ."

"Hold on," I groaned. "Hold on. Don't bother to read any more. I'll think of some other way of getting him to Kariba."

I thanked her for her trouble, and we made our escape. Tracey was simmering with indignation.

"Silly woman!" she fumed. "She wouldn't *listen*."

"Never mind," I said soothingly. "We'll just have to go back to our original plan, and take him with us as hand luggage."

Back at home once more, I thought I'd discuss my problem with David Blake, so I telephoned National Parks.

"David," I said, "what's the best way to transport a crocodile?"

"In a bag," he replied promptly. "We always move our young crocodiles that way."

"Just as I thought," I said. "The Airways insist on putting him into a crate."

"Tell them to get lost," he replied. "That's only for adult crocs. The proper way to transport your little fellow is *in a bag*."

That evening we told Doug the whole story. He shrugged his shoulders philosophically and said: "Oh well, in a bag it is, then."

That night, however, neither of us slept very well. Doug kept coughing and kicking restlessly at the bedclothes, lighting one cigarette after another. Finally I said: "Is it Clarence that's worrying you?"

"Yes," he replied grumpily, "it is. I hate the thought of breaking the Airways regulations. We'll be searched on boarding the plane, and then where will we be? I think you had better try to borrow some kind of crate for him, and let's do this properly."

I reluctantly agreed, and next day began phoning round to enquire about a crocodile crate. Until embarking on this exercise I had never really understood the meaning of the word 'inflation', but as the morning wore on I received the impression that it might have been cheaper for us to charter our own aircraft. "This is ridiculous," I grumbled to the children, who were following these negotiations. "The very cheapest, smallest crocodile crate is going to cost us almost as much as an air ticket! We'll have to borrow a crate from someone."

As it turned out, this was easily accomplished. My friendly grocer offered to lend me a splendid crate made of steel wire. It was heavy, but of the correct size, and so well ventilated that I knew Clarence would be comfortable inside it. I telephoned the freight office and told them I'd secured a crate for my crocodile — not a wooden crate, admittedly — but better than a wooden crate because it was stronger. I was wasting my breath. Rules is rules, they said. The man I spoke to was very sympathetic, however, and suggested that I should phone National Parks to ask if I could borrow a crocodile crate from them.

"They're always exporting crocodiles by air, you know," he said. "I'm sure they'll lend you one for the week-end."

This time I rang Ron Thomson, Provincial Warden for Mashonaland South, and told him all about Clarence.

"How big is your croc?" he asked.

I told him.

"No, you don't want to put him in a crate," he said. "You want to take him in a bag."

I had the dizzy feeling you get when you've held your breath for too long.

"But Ron," I explained, desperately clutching at the last shreds of my sanity, "it's the Airways. They insist he must go in a crate."

"Oh nonsense," he said. "Just pop him in a bag and say nothing about it."

"Yes," I agreed, "and when they search us as we're boarding the plane?"

"If they search you and kick up a dust, phone me from the airport," he said.

"Ron," I replied fervently, "you're a pal!"

We were due to fly to Kariba the next day, and Doug was more uneasy than ever.

"O.K., we take him in a bag," he said truculently, pacing the bedroom as he dressed for the office, "we take him in a bag, and he goes berserk on the plane. Then where are we?"

"He won't go berserk," I said.

"How do you know? You've never taken him in a plane before."

"I've taken him in my Morris, and that's worse."

"It wasn't worse and I'll tell you why. Because in your Morris there were not a hundred hysterical tourists. What you do," Doug went on firmly, "is phone E. V. Cock, the vet, and enquire about giving Clarence a tranquillizer before we travel to-morrow."

Dr. Cock was the very man. Himself the author of a book on snakes, he and David Blake were currently involved in a joint investigation into the diseases of crocodiles. He took Clarence's case to heart.

"Travelling by air to Kariba," he said. "That's no problem. You won't need a tranquillizer. I took an even bigger croc called Charlie by air to the Victoria Falls last year."

"Really? How did you carry him?" I enquired interestedly.

"In a bag," Dr. Cock promptly replied.

I started to laugh.

"Yes, it was quite funny," he agreed, "especially when they searched me as I was about to board the plane."

"Oh Lord," I wheezed in sympathetic commiseration, "what happened?"

"Well, I said to the security officer, I said — you don't want to search this bag, there's a crocodile inside it. He said 'haw-haw' or words to that effect, opened the bag and put his hand inside."

"And then —?" I laughed.

"Well — *then*," Dr. Cock went on in a changed voice, "*then* there was quite a bit of shouting and general excitement, but fortunately the captain of the aircraft had a sense of humour, and eventually he allowed Charlie and me on board."

"Splendid!" I said. "And you're sure then, that Clarence won't need a tranquillizer for the journey?"

"Positive," Dr. Cock assured me. "You won't have a moment's trouble."

Our plane leaves at ten past seven in the morning. It is just after dawn and we are packing our bags. Doug looks drawn and haggard. The children, by contrast, are in a state of delirious excitement. I am preoccupied and muddled, trying to collect together all the necessary holiday gear and arrange for the feeding of the cats and the dogs in our absence. In addition to several tons of fishing-tackle and our clothing, we are taking with us the steel-wire crate, with the idea of putting Clarence inside it once we arrive at Kariba. The crate in the meantime is packed with the fishing box, the kettle, the frying-pan, the cool-box full of worms and a million other odds and ends. Next to our bed stands the custard-yellow valise in which Clarence is to travel.

"I don't like it," Doug keeps croaking distractedly. "It's all a ghastly mistake."

I'm not sure if he's talking about the crocodile, the week-end or his marriage.

"Don't worry, dear," I say soothingly, "I'm sure everything will be all right."

At this moment Tracey bursts into our bedroom and gasps out: "Clarence has gone! We can't find him anywhere!"

I resisted the impulse to sit down then and there and weep hysterically.

"He can't have gone far," I quavered. "Let's go and have a thorough search."

Clarence was found at last in a patch of tangled convolvulus that grew against his wall. For some reason he had not spent his last night in his customary bed of hay. By now Doug was glancing uneasily at his watch.

"Time we were off," he said. "You'd better hurry up and pack your crocodile."

While Tracey and Doug loaded the car, Tom and I took the yellow valise to Clarence's run. It was almost a year since I had actually picked Clarence up bodily, and he was a great deal larger and stronger now than he had been then. For a moment or two I stood dithering, not sure how to set about it. Time, however, was running out and there was nothing for it but to grasp the nettle. I drew on a strong pair of oven-gloves, and picked him up. He huffed but did not struggle or attempt to bite, and submitted mildly to being lowered into the valise. As I removed my hands, Tom zipped it shut, and that was that!

Clarence didn't utter a sound or make a move all the way to the airport. When we arrived there, Tom solemnly begged to be allowed to take charge of Clarence himself. This was a relief in a way, because Doug had to attend to the car, and it was all Tracey and I could do to cope with the rest of the luggage. We joined the queue at the check-in bay, and duly had our kit weighed and tagged.

"And that yellow bag?" the man asked.

"May we take that and the fishing rods as hand luggage, please?" I asked.

"Certainly."

He gave us two labels marked 'Hand Luggage' and we made our way to the departure lounge. Doug now joined us once more, smoking nervously.

"No problems?" he muttered.

"Not so far, anyway," I replied cheerfully. "Isn't Clarence being good?"

Doug grunted. We both knew that the crunch, when it came, would be at the security check before we boarded the aircraft. In a country that had been through seven years of civil war, the question of concealed weapons loomed very large. It was still customary for one's handbag and sometimes one's person to be searched on entering every shop, theatre or office-block. Naturally at the airport all these controls were more rigidly enforced than anywhere else.

A light came on over gate three and the loudspeaker announced the departure of our flight.

"*Nos morituri*," whispered Doug.

We moved forward with the small crowd of holidaymakers bound for Kariba and the Victoria Falls. Almost at once, so it seemed, I was through the metal detector (thank heaven they don't have crocodile detectors, I thought wildly), and was being addressed by the security officer.

"Any firearms, madam?"

"No," I said truthfully.

"Thank you. Next."

I couldn't believe it! He hadn't said: "Any crocodiles?"

The other two were waiting for us at the foot of the gangway. Doug was looking better already.

"Through like a dose of salts," he smiled.

We took our seats at one of the tables up in the front of the Viscount, and settled Clarence between our feet.

"Such a good boy," I said warmly, bending forward to speak to him. I opened the zip a fraction and peered in. He was lying in exactly the same position, with his head raised and his pupils very large in the darkness of the bag. I left the zip open an inch or two so that he had some fresh air. The flight took off on time, and after half an hour the air-hostess brought us some coffee. I was glad of it. Opposite me, Doug leaned back in his seat, smiled and winked. He lit a cigarette and glanced out of the window at the lazy patterns of green, blue and brown that glided by far below. He was looking more relaxed than I had seen him for months, and all at once I knew that the week-end was going to be a success.

After checking in at the Caribbea Bay Hotel, my first assignment was to make Clarence comfortable. We transferred him to the wire crate, which the children had furnished with some dry grass from the hill-slopes behind the hotel. Clarence wriggled into it gratefully and went to sleep.

Originally, when the trip to Kariba had first been suggested, I had thought vaguely that the best thing would be to slip Clarence unobtrusively into the lake in front of the hotel. Fortunately I consulted David Blake on this point. He was horrified.

"On no account should you let him go on the Kariba village side of the lake," he said. "National Parks are obliged to knock off all the crocs along that stretch of the shore. In any case it's not really a good area for him, as the coastline is steep and rocky. A croc prefers a shallow, shelving shoreline with plenty of mud and weeds. The best thing would be to take him right across the lake to the Matusadona Game Reserve. He will be protected, you see, and in addition there will be far more fish for him to catch."

We were up at dawn the following day, with francolins calling from the hill-slopes behind the hotel. The lake was slate blue and calm, and away to the south across the water we could make out the jagged, purple teeth of the Matusadona mountains. From this distance the wide apron of flat bush in front of them was hidden from sight. Our boat arrived shortly after six, and while Doug and Tom clanked off with the rods and the worms, the beer and the fishing box, Tracey and I gathered up the swimming gear, the towels and the sun-tan lotion. Between us we picked up Clarence's crate and struggled down to the jetty. As we staggered along the planks towards the waiting boat, Clarence suddenly woke up and became animated. He scuttled to the edge of the crate and stood there huffing eagerly with raised head, staring about.

"Yes, my boy," I said smiling down at him, "you're home." I think he knew.

Livingstone, the boatman, was waiting patiently to help us on board. As we lowered the crate into the boat, his expression was transformed. His jaw dropped and his eyes bulged.

"What's that?" he said in a choking voice, pointing at the crate. "It looks like a flat-dog, for sure!"

"Yes, it is a flat-dog," I laughed, "but he's only a small one and he can't get out of his box."

"Ow!" he ejaculated in a tone of disgust. "What are you going to do with him?"

"We're going to let him go in the Game Reserve," I explained. Livingstone rolled his eyes and shook his head.

"Ow! You let a flat-dog go!" he exclaimed disbelievingly. Still chuckling at the crazy ways of the 'murungus', he started the engine and headed out across the lake. Livingstone was an ace, and we always asked for him when we came fishing at Kariba. He was an excellent fisherman, and he knew the lake as well as anyone alive.

It was fairly windy out on the water, but Clarence didn't close his eyes. Instead he put on his 'goggles' and maintained an alert vigil for the full hour that it took us to cross to the far shore. "How do you think we should play this?" I shouted to Doug over the roar of the engine. "Should we fish first, and then let

Clarence go, or the other way round?"

"I think we should let him go as soon as possible," Doug shouted back, "before it gets too hot. Then we can fish at our leisure."

Already the sun had the scorching anger of a dragon's breath, and soon the approaching shoreline of the Matusadona began to dance and shimmer in a silver band of heat-haze. We passed Fothergill and Spurwing Islands, surrounded by their fringe of drowned trees. On the mainland, wavering black blobs on the shore resolved themselves into buffalo as we drew abreast of them, to melt back into shapeless ghosts when we had passed. Now we were in a part of the lake known as Hydro Bay, with the great sweep of mountains curving round it protectively to the south, and on the west the huge flat tract of the Matusadona Game Reserve, fringed with an intricate lace-work of inlets and creeks, drowned trees, reed-beds, mud-banks and floating carpets of Kariba weed.

Livingstone cut back the engine and turned the nose of the boat in towards the land. Twisting this way and that between the fossilised stumps of drowned mopane, he brought us close in to the moist, muddy shore. All at once there was a violent scuttle and a splash only a few yards away, and a yellow crocodile a little bigger than Clarence dived into the water and vanished. I shook my head.

"We'll have to try somewhere else," I said. "Crocs have a strong territorial instinct, and we don't want to poach on another fellow's fishing grounds."

All the same, it was good to know that we were in an area favoured by young crocs.

Livingstone painstakingly eased the boat out into open water once more and we proceeded to the next inlet. This was a big one, as it turned out, shaped like a 'Y', with numerous subsidiary creeks leading off it. The place was alive with birds: cormorants, herons, jacanas and wagtails. Near by on the shore a huge buffalo lay with his hindquarters in the water. He was slowly chewing the cud, while a white egret pecked the ticks out of his long floppy ears. It seemed the ideal place for Clarence, peaceful and sheltered, with a gentle beach and low mopane bush twenty feet back from the water.

Livingstone skilfully steered the boat to the land, and we jumped ashore, squelching in the soft black mud. The water's edge was patterned with the big splayed hoof-prints of buffalo, and a little further along we saw the round basins of elephant pads. Near by was a pile of fresh dung, each one the size of a cantaloup.

We carried Clarence's crate to a small narrow creek that ran into the land like a dagger. Gently I lifted him out and slipped him into the soft ooze at the water's edge.

"There you are, my darling," I said. "Good-bye, and good luck!"

Clarence hesitated for a moment like a man who sees a vision and cannot quite believe the evidence of his own eyes. Then slowly and purposefully he strode forward, waddled out into a bed of brown water-weeds some two feet from the shore, and there he lay wallowing in the warm shallow water. He closed his eyes and relaxed, dabbling gently with all four feet, as if quite overcome.

We stood in a row, staring at him.

"Well, come *on*, Clarence!" I said presently.

"Come on *where*?" demanded Tom. "Why should he come on? He's enjoying himself where he is!"

It was a just rebuke. Why indeed should he 'come on'? As usual, I had formed preconceived ideas of what he would do and how he would behave when we let him go. I had expected him to hit that water like a rocket, and immediately plunge off out of sight. Now that he wasn't doing this, I felt confused, as if something had unaccountably gone wrong.

After a bit Clarence began to take an interest in his surroundings. The water around him was alive with tiddlers, and we wondered how long it would be before he noticed them. He turned his head this way and that, and presently he paddled forward very lazily into an area of deeper water.

Now all at once, one could almost feel the excitement coursing into him like an electric current. He allowed his body to sink, leaving his famous 'crocodile triangle' floating stealthily on the surface. What made it so comical and interesting was the fact that he wasn't looking *at* us, but *away* from us. We were the safe, the familiar — and so he turned his back on us and directed his eager gaze towards the Great Unknown, peering out across the shining sheet of the lake towards the distant mountains. Now and then he'd twist his head round to glance in our direction as if to reassure himself that we were still there, while his whole demeanour was one of pop-eyed incredulity, as if he were saying: "Is *all* this really for me?"

I had always imagined that when a crocodile floated with only his eyes and snout visible, the rest of his body would lie horizontally, parallel with the surface of the water. We were now privileged to see Clarence perform this stunt close at hand and in deep water. Far from floating horizontally, he was almost 'standing' up, suspended at an angle of sixty degrees, his arms and legs spread out wide on either side. He looked for all the world like a little boy standing on tiptoe to peer into the window of a sweetshop! His whole attitude was expressive of the highest degree of curiosity and excitement.

He was *so* funny that we all burst out laughing, but unabashed, he continued his cautious scrutiny of his surroundings, slowly and gently dabbling with all four feet to maintain his balance. At last, apparently reassured, he turned his attention to his more immediate environment. He submerged and we watched interestedly as he zoomed about along the bottom, in and out of the weeds and under beds of water lilies. He surfaced close by, and turned towards Tom, flicking his head and 'bubbling' at him in an eloquent message of delight. He had found the fish!

"You know, when I think about it," Doug observed smilingly, "Clarence is one of the best pets we've ever had. He didn't bark at nights, he didn't tear the furniture, he didn't smell, he didn't make a noise and worry the neighbours, he didn't bite. I think we're mad to have got rid of him."

"Quite mad," I agreed, half sadly. "I'm going to miss him terribly."

"Me too," Tracey said promptly.

"I'll have no one to fish for, now," Tom added mournfully.

At last we left him, with many a backward glance, calling out good-bye and good luck, and I must confess that all day my thoughts lingered with my little crocodile as he began his new life. We were all a bit subdued at first, feeling a mixture of sadness and quiet satisfaction. Sadness that Clarence had gone out of our lives, and satisfaction that at last he was going to be able to lead a real life of his own.

The fishing was excellent, however, and soon a more cheerful atmosphere stole over the boat. The shores all round us were a moving pageant of wild life. We fished beside a pair of buffalo, we lunched close to a herd of kudu, we had afternoon tea amongst a school of hippo, where the sandbanks were deeply

grooved with the long skid-marks of big crocs. In the late afternoon a huge elephant bull came down to feed, not thirty yards from where we were fishing. He had some of the largest tusks I had ever seen on an elephant in this country. Generally speaking, our jumbo have rather short tusks. They say that this is because the early ivory hunters slaughtered all those with the longest tusks, and now the strain has died out. Whatever the reason, a good tusker is a rare sight, and I was pleased to see this old fellow still around. I fought off a feeling of melancholy induced by the recollection of man's destructive tendencies and glanced apprehensively across Hydro Bay towards the little creek where we had left Clarence. I wished I could have warned him against being too friendly with people.

"Take care, little fellow," I thought sadly, "and keep away from men. From now on we are not your friends, but your most dangerous enemy."

A year later we revisited the Matusadona on the off-chance that we might catch a glimpse of him. This time the lake level was exceptionally high, and huge areas of the shoreline were under water. Clarence's own little creek had flooded over into the adjoining one, making an island out of what had been a promontory. Presently I noticed that we were being watched by a young crocodile who was out in deep water, some distance from the land. He was rather bigger than Clarence had been, but the size would have been just about right for a year's growth . . . He lay floating at the surface, two golden eyes staring at us curiously. We switched off the outboard and drifted closer.

"Hello, Clarence!" I called, half hopefully. I knew it was foolish, but I wondered if he'd respond.

Slowly the young crocodile submerged and a trail of bubbles led away in the opposite direction. We'll never know, of course, if it was him or not. Clarence's life is his own now, and his true whereabouts are just another question mark added to the many mysteries of the bush.